D0819558

The Managed Account Handbook:

*How to Build Your Financial
Advisory Practice Using
Separately Managed Accounts*

Stephen D. Gresham

**CONNECTICUT
RIVER PRESS**

Published by:

Phoenix Investment Partners, Ltd.
A member of The Phoenix Companies, Inc.
56 Prospect Street
Hartford, CT 06115-0480

Copyright ©2002 Phoenix Investment Partners, Ltd. and Stephen D. Gresham. All rights reserved. No part of this publication may be reproduced or transmitted in any form or by any means, electronic or mechanical, including photocopying, recording or any information storage and retrieval system now known or to be invented, without permission in writing from The Phoenix Companies, Inc., One American Row, Hartford, CT 06102-5056 (Statutory Home Office: 10 Krey Boulevard, East Greenbush, NY 12144).

All registered and non-registered trademarks and servicemarks used herein are the property of their respective owners.

This publication is designed to provide accurate and authoritative information in regard to the subject matter covered. The publisher is not engaged in rendering legal, accounting, or other professional service. If legal advice or other expert assistance is required, the service of a competent professional person should be sought.

Editing: Steve Gresham, Arlen Oransky, Joleen Speight
Book Design: Sandy Taylor
Production: Teresa Curley
Typesetting and Printing: Connecticut River Press

First Printing: October 2002

Printed in the United States of America

ISBN: 0-9723033-0-8 (7x9 hardcover)

Library of Congress Control Number: 2002113473

For information, contact Phoenix Investment Partners at 1-800-243-4361 or www.PhoenixInvestments.com.

*To Phyllis and Glen Gresham —
many thanks for a lifetime of love,
support and guidance.*

Table of Contents

Table of Contents

Introduction

Dear Investment Colleague:

While the "separately managed account" has been around since its introduction to the marketplace in the early 1970s, this customized investment approach has enjoyed burgeoning growth in the last five years and today permeates every corner of the retail investment marketplace.

Even as we enter a third year of challenging investment markets, industry talk continues to center around managed accounts. With over $400 billion in assets already under management, experts estimate continued annual growth of 23 percent for the foreseeable future. The current growth and robust predictions for this investment vehicle are understandable. Never before has there been an investment approach that fit the requirements of so many constituents, from investors and advisors to money managers and program sponsors. As a diversified investment management firm, Phoenix Investment Partners has sought to become a leader in this arena since the mid-1990s; and in the process, we have built an exceptionally talented team. One of our leaders is Steve Gresham.

Steve Gresham is as thoughtful and insightful an observer and commentator about what works and doesn't work in the retail investment business, and more specifically, in the managed accounts business, as anyone I know. Steve's in-depth knowledge and intuitive sense come from working closely with top advisors for 20 years, listening and learning from their successes and mistakes. He is also one of the pioneers in the managed accounts business, having been an analyst, money manager, and wealth management consultant to some of the top firms in the industry.

In 2001, our firm was a client of Steve's in his highly successful consulting practice. After helping us realize our objective of achieving a leadership position in this business, Steve was persuaded by me to leave his practice to head up sales and marketing for our Private Client Group, which distributes our managed account offerings. Steve shares my philosophy that a money manager must be more than a distributor of quality products, however. It is equally important to serve as a business resource, providing tools that can help advisors develop their practice and enhance relationships with clients.

This book is one such tool. Over the past year, Steve and his team have spent hours interviewing leading fee-based advisors to gather their best practices for success. The result is an educational book that covers all aspects of managed accounts – from product basics to practice management specifics, including how to transition to a fee-based practice, develop specialized skills as a managed account advisor, and grow a thriving managed account business.

It is clear that managed accounts are here to stay and their influence will continue to spread throughout the industry. I hope *The Managed Account Handbook* helps you achieve a new level of success in this business, whether you are just getting started or seeking to grow your existing advisory practice.

John F. Sharry
President, Private Client Group
Phoenix Investment Partners, Ltd.
Member, Board of Governors, Money Management Institute
August 2002

Acknowledgements

It was supposed to be a lot easier this time. I embarked on this project with the confidence of having written another modestly successful book for financial advisors. This time, I thought I would be even better prepared, enlisting the support of my colleagues at Phoenix Investment Partners, Ltd., as well as longtime collaborators, Arlen Oransky and Sydney LeBlanc. And still, I learned along the way that any book is a big undertaking and that the support of family, friends and colleagues is an absolute requirement to achieve success.

Let me begin with my great team at Phoenix. My management team partners, Don Berryman, Ed Friderici, Vic Norton, Frank Waltman, and Gavin Whitmore, comprise the most effective and collegial executive corps I've known in over 20 years of investment industry experience. Our staff is also first rate, and too numerous to mention here, but I received special help with this project from Sharon Bray, Allie Capo, Judy Coffin, Teresa Curley, Joe Fallon, Karen Frantz, Lisa Fydenkevez, Paul Grigely, Carrie Morris, Tara Pile, Sandy Pons, Dianne Riordan, Emma Simon, Heidi Sirota, Sandie Starkowski, Sandy Taylor, Jan Wajda, and the incomparable Joleen Speight, who shepherded the project from beginning to end. Ian Bowers, Walt Zultowski, Phoenix Companies President Dona Young and Chairman Bob Fiondella provided advice and counsel along the way. The sales teams of Phoenix Investment Partners, managed by Don Berryman and Frank Waltman with Mike Igoe, Matt Hamel and Kevin O'Brien, make my job worthwhile and played a vital role in helping to identify the best managed account advisors. And I owe a special debt of gratitude to my friend, Jack Sharry, president of the Private Client Group, for his leadership and insight.

I work in the best industry of all. Great friends and associates over the years have enriched my life beyond all expectations – Hallie Baron of Schwab, Frank Campanale of Salomon Smith Barney, Mike Dieschbourg of Silver Creek SV Hedge Fund of Funds, Peter Cieszko of Citigroup Asset Management, Russ Prince of Prince & Associates, Leo Pusateri of Pusateri Consulting and Training, Chris Davis of the Money Management Institute, and Evan Cooper from *On Wall Street* magazine.

My family was behind me the entire time. Rachael and Meggie are waiting for me to write a "real book," but they still have something to tell their friends. Janie, you're the best – thank you for your encouragement in all areas of my life.

The unsung heroes of this book are Arlen Oransky, my industry partner and friend since early days on Wall Street together, whose interviews of top advisors comprise the meat of this tome, the indefatigable Sydney LeBlanc, who shouldered the multiple tasks of compiling, interviewing, and writing, and Joleen Speight, whose persistence and attention to detail made this book a reality.

And most of all, I thank the financial advisors who selflessly shared their ideas and their time so that others might learn how to better serve clients and reach greater success as financial advisors to the affluent.

Steve Gresham

Steve Gresham

New York City
August 2002

How to Use This Book

The managed accounts industry is on a roll, driven by powerful baby boomer demographics and the boomers' growing need for customized, tax-sensitive investment solutions. Financial advisors to the affluent are using managed accounts as the primary income source for their high-net-worth practices, driving demand still higher. And financial services firms increasingly seek the relative stability of asset-based fees to insulate earnings against the more volatile returns of commissions and investment banking revenue. The benefits of managed accounts extend to all of the players.

How can you best take advantage of the managed account boom? This book seeks to provide you with a personal answer. We have gathered the strategies of financial advisors who successfully adopted managed accounts into their businesses. Their best ideas are separated into topics for easier digestion. You can tackle one topic at a time – such as "Identifying the Best Clients for Managed Accounts" in Chapter 7 – and refine your strategy before taking on another aspect of the managed account world. Consider each chapter and section to be a drawer in a filing cabinet filled with the best practices of investment management consultants to which you may return many times for consultation.

Start with "The Birth and Evolution of Managed Accounts" to increase your understanding of the key factors behind the introduction of this product wave. Move into Chapter 2 for a summary of the benefits of managed accounts and their appeal to both affluent clients and successful financial advisors. Determine the fit for managed accounts in your current advisory practice and their role in your future growth. Identify your strengths as an advisor and look for ways to apply those skills to increase your managed account business. Acknowledge your shortcomings and note their potential impact on your game plan. Armed with these observations, you can then select the book sections most applicable to your situation.

By reading this book, you've taken an important step forward in the development of your practice. Ignore the skeptics who call managed accounts a fad. Managed accounts are not new and they represent a higher level of service for the investment side of your client relationships, allowing you to focus more time on the vital areas of client service and attend to the overall wealth needs of your best clients. Ignore also those people who claim you must change the way you do business. Managed accounts fit well within your natural talents as an advisor and offer you a better way to leverage those skills by becoming more consistent in your financial solutions.

The world of managed accounts is complex and each advisor has his or her own approach to the business. Take your time to find a path that is right for you, knowing that even the most accomplished practitioners had to start at the beginning. Enlist a guide for your quest – the internal and external investment consultants of Phoenix Investment Partners, Ltd., are among the industry's most experienced and knowledgeable.

Chapter 1

The Birth and Evolution of Managed Accounts

The managed account industry began amidst pension reform and has grown in response to investor's demands for a consistent process to manage their investments.

With assets of $400 billion and a five-year compound annual growth rate of 20 percent[1] the modern managed account industry is thriving. But although its current popularity is being driven by a demographic wave of affluent baby boomers, the managed account has its roots in the social turmoil of the 1960s that led to retirement plan reform.

The sixties brought a recipe of change to every facet of society, including supplying the ingredients that eventually would evolve into what we recognize today as the managed account industry. Spurring this evolution were several key legislative landmarks. Beginning with the Welfare and Pension Plan Disclosure Act of 1958 (and its subsequent amendments in 1962) that mandated disclosure requirements to curtail fiduciary abuse, these amendments were crafted to transfer accountability for the protection of plan assets from participants to the federal government. These crucial amendments were designed to thwart pension fund fraud and lackluster administration. A similar environment prevails today with the travails of WorldCom, Enron and Arthur Andersen.

[1] Money Management Institute and Financial Research Corporation, as of 12/31/01.

The year 1962 also saw the passing of the Self-Employed Individual Retirement Act, often referred to as the Keogh Act. Thanks to this legislation, self-employed small-business owners and their employees could now participate in qualified pension plans. These legislative steps were augmented by the Tax Reform Act of 1969 that spelled out the basic rules for creating and operating pension plans jointly managed by unions and employers. Five years later came the Employee Retirement Income Security Act (ERISA) of 1974. In the aftermath of the historic 1973-74 stock market plunge, ERISA was engineered to protect the benefits of participants in private pension plans. The ERISA feature that spurred development of the modern consulting industry was that plan sponsors address the issue of accountability – plan trustees had to now document the investment process and manage the assets prudently.

As a result of these regulatory directives, corporate and municipal pension plan sponsors elected to have their assets managed by professional investment managers. The downside to this decision, however, was that many of these sponsors had no idea where to find suitable management experts to do the job. Prior to ERISA, major insurance companies and bank trust departments dominated public and corporate funds, with many assets concentrated in the mutual fund arena and not being actively managed. Before ERISA's inception, state-owned and corporate pension funds could initiate investments with little or no accountability. Banks and insurance companies were the only game in town, and brokers responsible for account transactions did so at NYSE-fixed commission rates.

The first major study focusing on mutual fund performance was conducted at Harvard University in 1965 and AG Becker Corporation (forerunner of SEI Corporation) undertook a similar study three years later on institutional plan performance. The knowledge gained from these studies, particularly Becker's findings comparing performance results to benchmarks, led to the foundation of institutional consulting.

Utilizing the findings of its report, Becker approached select benefit plan sponsors and encouraged them to utilize the report's tables to gauge the performance of the banks responsible for managing their pension funds. This practice opened the door to subsequent performance and portfolio management services that, in turn, helped Becker acquire substantial institutional accounts, especially those whose trustees were uncomfortable with the intricacies of quarterly performance comparison charts.

Other firms, engaged in developing their own research criteria relating to mutual fund and pension fund performance, began contacting plan sponsors and offering their help in evaluating fresh research and management options for plan sponsors' funds. What began as a trickle became a flood as more and more firms climbed on the ERISA bandwagon. In exchange for investment policy statement guidance, asset allocation and manager selection, consulting firms negotiated to receive brokerage commissions for their recommendations. Important referral business also factored into the mix.

Niche firms emerged to capture a piece of the institutional consulting pie, widening their sphere of influence to include nonprofits as potential recipients for their advice. Soon middle markets opened up, allowing these participants to enjoy levels of management previously reserved for larger funds. The rush was on to meet the demand for institutional investment management.

The flurry of activity served as a call to action – savvy portfolio managers at banks quickly realized they should offer corporate clients more bang for the buck when it came to investment performance results. Once this realization sunk in, they soon provided consulting services of their own.

The Beginning of an Industry

If the sixties were turbulent, the decade that followed was no less volatile. The Arab oil embargo fueled the nation's economic recession, contributing to the worst bear market since the Great Depression. The Dow's decline in 1973-74, closing at 577, its lowest level in 11 years, only added to the uncertainty. By the time President Nixon resigned from office in August 1974, institutional and individual investors alike were clamoring for asset protection that could only be realized through sound investment management advice.

After the market slide of '73-'74, small- to mid-sized pension plans, wealthy individuals and family offices also sought professional advice. The early investment management consultants were poised to step in and fill the niche. On "May Day," May 1, 1975, the Big Board's fixed rates were abolished, further opening the door to the investment management consulting business. Since the NYSE no longer was able to protect the old commission structure, rates went down, pinching the margins.

As one door closed, another opened, as true competition among investment management consultants emerged. The leaders championed the competition and drove quality standards higher, spreading the impact of consulting beyond the institutional world.

Jim Lockwood of Dean Witter – and later EF Hutton – is now regarded widely as the father of consulting. He paved the way for a number of top producing brokers and advisors to capture a piece of the growing consulting industry. Other early pioneers – among them some of Lockwood's colleagues, Joe Lamatta, John Ellis, Tom Gorman and Richard "Dick" Schilffarth – added leadership to a budding niche business that would change the landscape of Wall Street.

In 1972, Dean Witter branch manager Dick Schilffarth met Jim Lockwood at a seminar hosted by the investment management division of Dean Witter, and Schilffarth liked what Lockwood had to say. After placing considerable client assets with Dean Witter's investment management services on Lockwood's recommendation, Schilffarth discovered that he enjoyed the consulting process and began to pursue the business. He later realized that smaller institutions needed management help just as much as the larger ones, and after serious discussion with Lockwood, the pair launched a new consulting product within Dean Witter called Dean Witter Plus. In March 1973, Lockwood and Schilffarth, joined by Dean Witter colleagues John Ellis and Tom Gorman, left Dean Witter and moved to EF Hutton, where they established a new consulting division and the EF Hutton Suggests program.

Lockwood and Ellis set up the Hutton consulting department to bring in corporate and government clients using investment management consulting services. It was a different way of approaching institutional sales. Instead of calling on money managers to sell investments, they called on clients to "sell" the money managers. Schilffarth developed a program for brokers who were interested in learning the consulting process, and in 1974 the first training workshop was held.

The next year the brokerage industry faced May Day, which marked the end of fixed commissions. Lockwood saw this as an opportunity to join the ranks of other fee-based professionals like CPAs and attorneys and introduced the concept of charging a fee for services in lieu of commissions. Actually, the fee was considered an asset-based commission. The fee schedule at the time was 3.0 percent on accounts up to $500,000, 2.5 percent on the next $500,000 and 2.0 percent on accounts over $1 million.

Motivated by the passing of ERISA, Lockwood's group aggressively pursued the employee benefits market, which proved to be a big success for Hutton. Following the success of Suggests, Hutton Investment Management was introduced, with account minimums of $25,000, along with Hutton Capital Management and the discretionary Hutton Portfolio Management. In 1976, the first separately managed account was introduced by Hutton and, until the mid-80s, EF Hutton was the industry's primary promoter of managed accounts. Advest, Merrill Lynch, Wheat First, Prudential and other firms soon introduced their own versions of separately managed account programs.

The Trend Spreads

Until about 1987, money managers in brokerage firm programs set their own fees and account minimums, handled their own accounting, and dealt with the clients directly. The brokerage firms introduced the managers and handled the custody and trades. In 1987, Hutton presented a new concept with Hutton Select Managers that took over the fiduciary duties of accounting, performance reporting, and client interaction. This helped lower minimums and fees and freed up the managers to do what they did best – manage the portfolios.

If technology was the engine driving the new phase of separately managed accounts, then the volatile market of 1987 provided the gas. April 1987's precipitous drop in bonds was followed in October by the historic 508 point crash in the Dow 30. Investors and brokers alike flocked to managed accounts and the stability of professional advisory firms.

Managed accounts enjoyed rapid growth as other firms saw the success of Hutton Select Managers and followed suit. Merrill Lynch, PaineWebber, Drexel Burnham and Kidder Peabody tested the waters after the tax shelter market slowed. Dean Witter joined the party in 1985 and Merrill Lynch arrived for good in 1987 with its Consults® program.

There were other strategies for fee-based accounts. Shearson Lehman offered fee-based brokerage in 1986 through "guided portfolios," where trades were run by company analysts. Two years later, Shearson acquired Hutton and marketed the Hutton Select program through brokers of both firms. Shearson brought product and technology structure to the Hutton programs, further empowering their growth. Advest and Wheat First pioneered fee-based brokerage for nondiscretionary accounts in 1989-90, and the industry was now comprehensive – any client and advisor could participate. See the historical timeline on page 7 for a snapshot of the evolution of the industry.

Where We are Today

According to the Washington, D.C.-based Money Management Institute (MMI) and

Boston consulting firm Financial Research Corporation (FRC), assets held in separately managed accounts industrywide totaled $416 billion at the close of second quarter 2002, up from $161 billion at year end 1996.[2]

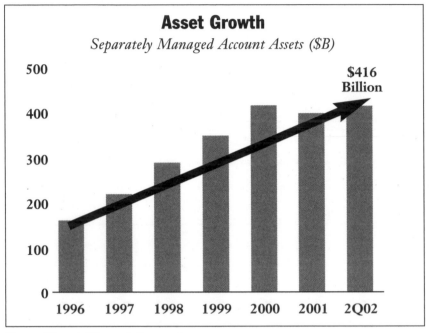

Source: Financial Research Corporation

The industry is still considered a cottage trade, according to FRC, as evidenced by the fact that over three fourths of managed accounts are held by the top five wirehouses: Salomon Smith Barney, Merrill Lynch, Morgan Stanley, PaineWebber and Prudential. Thirty-five percent of the assets are held by ten managers.[3]

You now have the basic managed accounts history lesson and know a little more about how the industry evolved. In the next chapter, we'll take a look at the benefits of managed accounts and fee income.

[2]Money Management Institute and Financial Research Corporation
[3]Financial Research Corporation as of 12/31/01

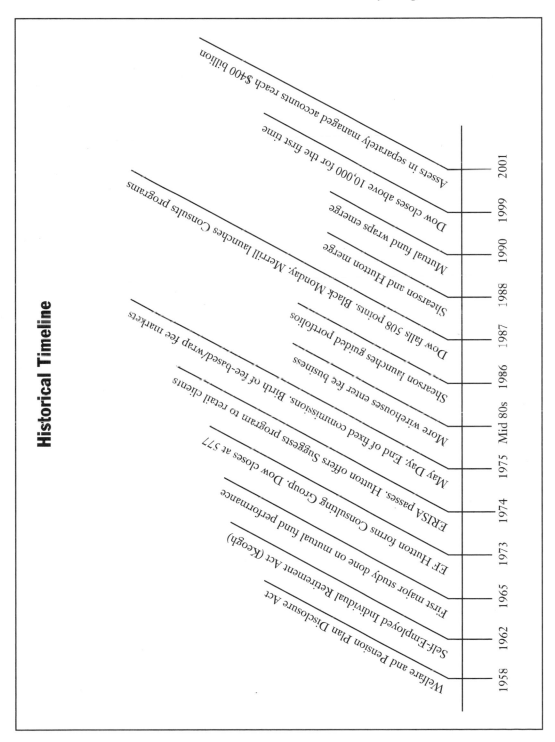

Historical Timeline

Welfare and Pension Plan Disclosure Act — 1958

Self-Employed Individual Retirement Act (Keogh) — 1962

First major study done on mutual fund performance — 1965

EF Hutton forms Consulting Group. Dow closes at 577 — 1973

ERISA passes. Hutton offers Suggests program to retail clients — 1974

May Day. End of fixed commissions. Birth of fee-based/wrap fee markets — 1975

More wirehouses enter fee business — Mid 80s

Shearson launches guided portfolios — 1986

Dow falls 508 points. Black Monday. Merrill launches Consults programs — 1987

Shearson and Hutton merge — 1988

Mutual fund wraps emerge — 1990

Dow closes above 10,000 for the first time — 1999

Assets in separately managed accounts reach $400 billion — 2001

Chapter

The Benefits of Managed Accounts and Fee Income

You can use managed accounts to build your advisory practice and create an annuity income stream leveraged by the market's growth.

The managed account industry ushered in a new era of client service and customization, yet there were obstacles to overcome. The concept of selling managed accounts wasn't well understood by brokers and branch managers, who were not immediate fans of managed accounts because they couldn't understand why the broker should forego a commission in order to get a smaller fee. Furthermore, the idea of giving away control of an account was anathema.

It was truly a short-term mindset. But keep in mind, in the mid 1980s, the industry offered 8.5 percent front-end loaded equity funds – themselves fairly new on the scene. Mutual funds were early competition to the managed account business because of the attractive loads, and even some government securities funds sported a 6.5 percent upfront commission.

Separately managed accounts became popular with consultative advisors because they offered a more significant long-term revenue stream. Both funds and separately managed accounts offered professional investment management, but managed accounts offered the potential for a growing long-term income. Farsighted advisors realized they could make more money over time selling managed account services than they could selling funds. As a reference point, the chart on pages 16 and 17 compares the features of managed accounts to mutual funds.

Overcoming Objections

The two primary objections first heard from advisors about selling managed accounts when they were introduced were:

- "You gotta be kidding! If I can't earn more than 3.0 percent on an account in a year, I shouldn't be in the business!" I heard that line from an experienced New York City broker. Advisors like him weren't calculating their return on assets and the annuity that would be accumulating.

- "I'll lose control of my best clients!" The advisors who feared this result didn't realize the advantage of leveraging their time by gathering assets and servicing clients. This would be time to do bigger and better business.

The perception that managed accounts led to reduced income was easy to counter. In 1988, I managed the consulting group at Advest Inc., a Connecticut-based regional broker-dealer. Advest did a study of our accounts to determine how much revenue per account was being generated per dollar of assets. Excluding mutual funds and annuities held away, we found an average return on assets (ROA) of about 70 basis points – a number that remains common. By comparison, a typical managed account sported a fee in excess of 2.0 percent.

Clearly, revenue improvement was possible with managed account fees. A top producer could double or triple his income if all accounts were converted to a fee basis. Firms began to preach the gospel of fees to their reps. Shearson put information about return on assets on its brokers' desktop systems so they could see not only their commission runs but also their ROA for any particular client.

Understanding the potential of fee income was critical for advisors and managers. Managed accounts offered leverage – income from assets under management plus participation in the market's growth. Now branch offices would have a new revenue dimension to look at, not simply the gross commissions of a producer. Most firms still didn't have the ROA information for their brokers, and only a few advisors were doing the business – but the word was spreading.

Commissions to Fees: Educating the Client

Many financial advisors continue to resist managed accounts. Comparisons of fees on managed accounts have been made to the fees on mutual funds. The argument is that managed account fees are too high and that clients can receive an equal benefit from mutual fund investing for a lower cost.

Yet mutual fund fees do not include transaction and other costs that are included in managed accounts. Mutual funds also net out fees before they calculate a fund's net asset value (NAV). If consulting is included, managed account clients receive valuable services on much smaller asset sizes than previously would have been possible – for about the same fee as a mutual fund. There is a role for both mutual funds and managed accounts, and many advisors employ both tools to manage a client's assets.

There is more to managed account fees. The all-inclusive managed account fee provides customized investment expertise and gives clients:

- Active account management tailored to their specific investment goals, risk tolerance and time horizon

    - Access to a personal financial advisor to develop a written statement of their investment objectives

    - Ability to exclude certain investments – for example, stock of companies that make weapons or tobacco products

- Daily portfolio monitoring as market conditions change

- Regular performance reporting and record-keeping

- Strategic tax planning

    - Flexibility to offset capital gains and losses

    - The managed account investor owns the actual security, which prevents buying into a shared, historical tax liability of a mutual fund.[1]

A joint survey[2], performed by the Washington, D.C.-based research firm VIP Forum and Chicago-based consulting firm Spectrem Group on U.S. affluent investment preference and behaviors, asked individuals about investment fees. Survey respondents said that commissions were their least favored method of compensation for financial advisors, while fees were the most favored.

Whether for fee or commission, your value is highest as a trusted advisor and is dependent on your ability to articulate your value to clients. With value established,

---

[1]Phoenix Investment Partners, Investing Essentials[SM], *Benefits of Managed Accounts*
[2]VIP/Spectrem Group 2000 Joint Study

the challenge of explaining fees to your clients then becomes moot. With one fee, your clients are getting a counselor who really knows them and has a clear understanding of what's important to them (more on fees in Chapter 3).

The Managed Account Process

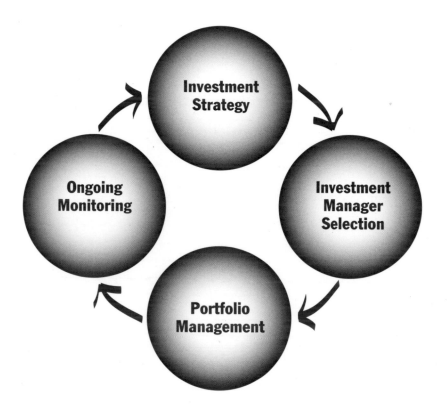

Which Programs are Best for Your Clients?

If you are contemplating a move to fee-based accounts, you have many choices. The Managed Account Sponsor Matrix on the next page offers a sampling of the programs, fees and minimums available today to your clients.

Chapter 3 Managed Account Consulting: The Right Fit for Your Practice? offers guidelines for taking inventory of your client base to determine your best prospects. Chapter 7 offers ideas about capturing additional assets and more wealth management strategies.

Managed Account Sponsor Matrix			
Firm	**Managed Account Programs**	**Minimum Investment***	**Client Fees**
American Express	• Wealth Management Services	$100,000	Fees range from 0.5%-3% and may be tiered or discounted based on the firm and each individual case.
A.G. Edwards	• Select Advisor • Private Advisory Services	$100,000	
LPL Financial	• Manager Select	$100,000	
Merrill Lynch	• Consults • SPA	$100,000 $20,000,000	
Morgan Stanley	• Access • Vision	$100,000 $2,000,000	
Prudential	• MACS • MACS CS	$100,000	
Salomon Smith Barney	• Fiduciary Services • Consulting & Evaluation Services • Investment Manager Services	$100,000	
UBS PaineWebber	• ACCESS • MAC	$100,000	

* These are standard minimums for each program, however, minimum investments may vary by manager and investment style.

How Fees are Divvied Up

The average size of a managed account is $250,000[3] and the average fee is 2.0 percent.[4] The money manager receives 30-100 basis points per year, depending on the size of the account and its investment objective. Sponsoring firms (such as Salomon Smith Barney, Merrill Lynch, and Prudential) also receive a fee covering services such as custody of the securities, trade execution, and clearing and settlement functions (allocating shares to accounts, crediting payment, etc.), as well as the costs of manager research, monitoring and reporting to the client. The remainder of the fee goes to the advisor. This part of the fee varies significantly, depending on the sponsor firm and the payout grid. See the following chart for an example.

[3]*2010: A Managed Account Odyssey. Projections on the Future of the Managed Accounts Industry.* Leonard A. Reinhart and Jay N. Whipple III, Lockwood Financial Services, Inc.
[4]Money Management Institute and Financial Research Corporation

Equity and Balanced Individually Managed Account Component Pricing

	$100,000 Account	$1 Million Household	$10 Million Household
Money Manager	50 bps	45 bps	40 bps
Sponsor	50	40	30
Custody, Clearing, Execution	30	20	10
Total Manufacturing Exp.	**130**	**105**	**80**
Advisor/Consultant	100	70	40
Total Cost to Investor	230 bps	175 bps	120 bps

Source: 2010: A Managed Account Odyssey. Projections on the Future of the Managed Accounts Industry. Leonard A. Reinhart and Jay N. Whipple, III. © 2002 Lockwood Financial Services, Inc.

Advisors and consultants who provide true consulting services have the best chance to maintain their fees because of the quality of service they provide. Selling yourself as a high-level advisor or consultant creates a higher level of value. It shows that you are truly involved in the client relationship instead of just being an order taker for a product.

Keep it Simple

"The separately managed account is one of the few financial products that clearly discloses the entire fee up front," says Leonard A. Reinhart, chairman and founder, Lockwood Financial Group. "The fee is highlighted every quarter in a visible fashion," he says. "Mutual fund expense ratios do not include execution costs and have an extremely complex share-pricing matrix. Fees are netted out of the NAV daily, so the investor does not see, or feel the pain of, the money leaving the account. The first step in understanding the pricing is to unbundle the components."[5]

This is a good way to explain pricing to your clients: Take the major components of separately managed accounts – investment management strategy (advisor), investment manager selection (sponsor firm), ongoing reporting and monitoring (sponsor firm and advisor), portfolio management (manager), and trading and

---

[5]Ibid

custody (sponsor firm) – and thoroughly explain the responsibilities and value each brings to the table. By taking the time to discuss all of these fee aspects, including your own differentiation and your process, the fee issues melt away.

Now let's consider whether managed accounts are a good fit for your business.

Managed Accounts vs. Mutual Funds

	Mutual Funds	Managed Accounts
General Features		
Access to professional money managers	Yes	Yes
Diversified portfolio	Yes	Yes
Ability to customize portfolio	No	Yes, investors can restrict specific securities from their portfolios
Manager independence from the "herd instinct"	No, if clients want to redeem shares, fund managers must sell to raise the cash to do so	Yes, money managers can buy when the herd is selling and vice versa, customizing the decision to the client's objectives
Unlimited withdrawals/redemptions	No, most funds have restrictions	Yes
Typical account minimum	$1,000	$100,000
Liquidity	Typically, next day	Three day settlement of trades
Access to asset classes	Numerous	Somewhat more limited than funds
Performance Reporting Features		
Performance reporting	Typically semi-annual some more frequent	Quarterly performance rating
Customized performance reporting	Generally no, investors must calculate their own performance, which is problematic, particularly for investors who dollar cost average	Yes, automatically sent to investors every quarter, includes performance of individual portfolios and of aggregate of multiple portfolios

Source: Money Management Institute (MMI)

Managed Accounts vs. Mutual Funds *(continued)*

	Mutual Funds	Managed Accounts
Tax-Related Features		
Separately held securities	No, investor owns one security, the fund, which in turn, owns a diversified portfolio	Yes, investor owns securities in an account managed by their money managers
Unrealized gains	Yes, average U.S. mutual fund has a 20% imbedded, unrealized capital gain[1]	No, cost basis of each security in the portfolio is established at the time of purchase
Customized to control taxes	No, most funds are managed for pre-tax returns, and investors pay a proportionate share of taxes on capital gains	Yes, investors can instruct money managers to take gains or losses as available, to manage their tax liability
Tax-efficient handling of low cost basis stocks	No, stocks cannot be held in an investors mutual fund account, so there is no opportunity to manage low cost basis stocks	Yes, the handling of low cost basis stocks can be customized to the client's situation, liquidating in concert with offsetting losses, etc.
Gain/loss distribution	Virtually all gains must be distributed, losses cannot be distributed	Realized gains and losses are reported in the year recorded
Cost-Related Features		
Expenses (excluding brokerage costs)	1.42%[1,3]	1.00%
Expenses (including brokerage costs)	1.56% average[2,3]	1.25%[3]
Volume fee discounts	No, all investors pay the same expense ratio	Yes, larger investors enjoy fee discounts
Other costs	12b-1, sales loads, redemption fees, etc.	None

[1]*Morningstar Principia Plus for Windows, February 2002* [2]*Brokerage costs estimated at 0.13% for the 10 largest funds* [3]*Costs do not include Advisor fee, which will vary   Source: Money Management Institute (MMI)*

Chapter 3

Managed Account Consulting: The Right Fit for Your Practice?

Are managed accounts a good fit for your advisory business? Here's how to evaluate the potential for success.

As a financial advisor, you can choose between two paths in building your business. One choice is serving clients by selling financial products and earning your income from sales commissions. The other option is advising clients about strategies for their wealth and earning greater control of client assets. Typically, remuneration for this second path is based on advisor fees – primarily from managed accounts.

Before you make your decision, take an introspective journey to determine whether consulting to clients and using managed accounts is really for you. I'll help you analyze your business, your clients and your goals; give you questions and checklists to use as guides; and discuss the pros and cons of the business. You'll soon have a pretty good idea whether or not you want to transition to a managed account business.

First, consider what is most important to you in the way you operate your current practice. Do you love prospecting and selling? Do you enjoy working with clients? Do you enjoy watching the market and making stock picks? Are you personally handling duties in your business that you would prefer delegating to someone else? We'll explore these issues and more in a search for the direction best matching your natural skills.

Three Benefits of Separately Managed Accounts

Working with managed accounts provides three very important benefits. If these benefits don't appeal to you, or if you don't see a fit for yourself, then managed accounts may not be the business for you. Let's review them in brief:

1. Leveraging Your Time

Separately managed accounts allow you to remove yourself from the process of managing money. You eliminate the problem of not having enough time for yourself and your business and delegate this responsibility to a professional money manager. You also eliminate the potential conflict of interest associated with transaction-based business and sit on the same side of the table as your clients.

2. Reaching Bigger Clients

Managed account consulting gives you a better opportunity to work with very large clients. Affluent clients, for example, want personalization and customization. They want to control their tax destiny. If you want to work with wealthy individuals, foundations and endowments, or small- to mid-sized institutions, then you have to upgrade your services. This is where separately managed accounts fit in perfectly – you have the time to work on more complex financial issues, not just investments.

3. Leveraging Your Income

Managed accounts allow you to add the market's returns to help boost your income. This leverage is a major advantage for those advisors who sell separately managed accounts versus those who sell only commissioned mutual funds.

Let me illustrate.

A mutual fund or securities commission is based on the initial deposit, whereas the managed account annual fee is based on the value of the portfolio every quarter. If the markets and your investment managers have positive performance, you will receive a lift in income with no additional effort. If you believe in the future of capital markets, you're creating built-in raises for yourself with managed accounts.

You can attain a far superior long-term income flow from managed accounts than you can working only with commissions.

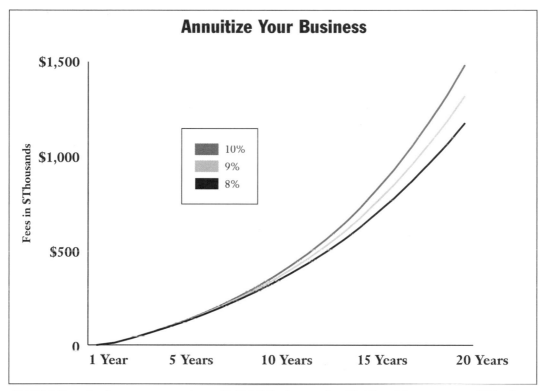

Annuitize Your Business

$1,000,000 production per year, starting at $1,000,000. Assumes fee of 2.44% with rep payout as 50% of annual fee.

Assume you open an average of two new fee-based accounts per month at $500,000 each. At the end of the first year, you will have built a business that can generate $90,000 in fees (based on $12 million of assets under management paying 75 basis points). You would have to trade an order of 500 shares of IBM about 15 times per month to earn the same amount in commission (based on a full-service commission rate of $525). The next year, the fee-based assets under management stay on the books, and you don't have to worry about trading IBM all over again!

Here's a case in point: In the late 1980s, I welcomed a top producer at a major wirehouse to a regional brokerage firm trying to promote separately managed accounts. The advisor had a large book of separately managed accounts, and at the start of his second full year with the firm, in the first week of January, I announced that he was on track to become a member of that year's Advisory Council. My phone rang off the hook with calls from other Advisory Council members demanding to know how this new guy could possibly make the Council in the first week of the year.

How did the new guy qualify? With the projected value of his managed account fees. The announcement caused quite a stir, and soon the concept of projecting annuity income from fees began attracting attention as other advisors entered the business. Those advisors and brokers who looked long-term and realized the value of advice – for themselves and their clients – were among the first to model their business for assets and fees.

Are You a Player?

As in any meritocracy, the most skilled financial consultants rise to the top. In most cases, their skill is a result of being more organized and consistent than the majority of their peers. As the managed account business has grown, certain types of individuals have gravitated toward fees. Who are these individuals and what sets them apart from the rest?

Six common qualities define the most successful consultants:

1. They love to sell.

2. They can develop substantial relationships with affluent people, whether as individual clients or as trustees of foundations, endowments and retirement plans.

3. They work closely with their clients' other advisors: CPAs, attorneys and business consultants.

4. They are not afraid of wealth or of wealthy people.

5. They understand the benefits of leveraging their value by having other professionals manage investments.

6. They can relate their added value clearly to clients and prospects.

Selling to affluent clients and having the confidence and emotional security to handle the sale (not worrying that you are going to lose control of the client) is a function of personality and temperament. Only certain types of individuals have the right stuff. Ego can also be a factor in this equation – witness the superstar tax shelter producers in the 1980s who pursued personal profits instead of client returns. Most fee-based consultants put their clients first.

Ironically, many of the brokers who were early entrants in the managed accounts arena came directly from the tax shelter business. Most of these producers had big personalities and the confidence to tackle the largest prospects. Even though selling shelters was mostly transactional, it was a complicated sale, and clients were obtained by holding seminars for wealthy professionals. These brokers were already thinking "up market" and therefore, were prepared to take on the new vision of managed accounts.

But the battle cry of the uninformed broker at the time was, Why should I give up control of my best clients?

Why indeed?

The *only* reason an advisor gives up control is to build a better business. **The individuals who realized early on that they were in the business of building a business were the advisors who grabbed managed accounts.** As they looked around for areas in which they could excel, a common denominator kept surfacing – they were all extremely good salespeople. Advisors who didn't necessarily enjoy managing money but who loved to sell and prospect could focus on doing what they did best. They could stop watching the market, stop being responsible for securities selection and finally do what they loved – selling and servicing affluent clients.

The difference between those advisors who simply sold products and those who built a business was that the advisors who wanted to run a real business didn't just sell a random list of hot products – they utilized marketing strategies. They also realized the value of leveraging their expertise and saved an enormous amount of time by turning over the management of their accounts to professional investment managers. These advisors built practices with a view toward controlling client assets, not just hitting sales targets.

With a managed account, the relationship with the client is different than it is with a mutual fund because the advisor has to sell in a consultative way. It is a more complex product – or service – and the process has to be explained. Advisors have to work with the client's CPA and attorney. Most also have to become familiar with a concept that became an extremely important part of the managed account sale – the seminar. We'll discuss this strategy in detail later in Chapter 7.

If the Shoe Fits...

If the managed account business seems to make so much sense and you're taking valuable time to read this book, you might ask yourself, "If this looks like the Holy Grail, then why aren't all brokers and advisors selling managed accounts?"

As I said, managed accounts are not for everybody. You need to take that introspective journey to discover whether this path is right for you. Consider the questions presented in the rest of this chapter and be as honest as you can with your answers. You might be surprised at the outcome.

Are Separately Managed Accounts for You?

Look at the checklist on page 27. It is designed to help you determine whether fee-based business is right for you. The left column focuses on fee business, while the right focuses on transactions. Check each statement that applies to you and determine your score at the bottom.

Did you find this exercise to be valuable and did it help clarify which type of business you are best suited for? The thing to remember is no matter whether you choose stocks and bonds or investment management, commissions or fees, you should seek your personal comfort zone. Do not attempt to be something you're not. If you're comfortable, then the next step is to set yourself apart from everyone else.

Why and How are You Different?

If you offer the same services as most other advisors, what is your differentiation? Why should clients work with you instead of some other advisor? Your differentiation is *the real value* you provide. Clients benefit from your counsel and process. One of the ways to explain your value is to say, "I'm not just selling a single security or idea. I'm proposing a serious investment process by which you can manage your money for a lifetime."

Affluent clients appreciate that you have a system, or process, that sets you apart from your competitors. Managed accounts help provide that process.

Build a Custom Stereo System

Says advisor Dan of differentiating yourself, "There are 1,000 advisors on the phones saying the same things, so you have to distinguish yourself. Use the managed account concept – it's a powerful one. Unfortunately, many of the more seasoned advisors are not focusing on managed accounts and new financial advisors are pushing products. If you understand and embrace the mechanics of the investment process, a tremendous opportunity exists to capture assets. Think about it – what will be more successful, a call to a $2 million prospect offering managed accounts or stock picks of the day? Even if you land an account and pick stocks, it's a losing proposition because many times you will be wrong. To set yourself apart from the competition, focus on a specialized area, like managed accounts, and understand that it is a customized service. It can be developed like a highly specialized stereo system, with separate select components, rather than a prepackaged unit."

Where to Start?

To begin the search for prospects, the old saw says, "Start with your book." But where? Take an inventory of your business and analyze your top clients. Use the worksheets on pages 28 through 32.

Check off the services and products you now provide to each of your clients, such as securities, mutual funds, retirement planning and estate planning. Profile at least 10 clients – better yet, 20 – and then aggregate the answers. Run the numbers on your clients' assets and see where they are invested. Look for assets that can be better managed. A perfect prospect is a client who owns a number of mutual funds and securities who now claims substantial assets. Hold on to your completed worksheets – you'll use them again in Chapter 4.

If you have accumulated large assets for a client in individual stocks, mutual funds, and municipal bonds, wouldn't you want to avail that person of the next level of personal service? Don't cheat your client, and *don't cheat yourself.* If you are truly a good marketer and salesperson, concentrate on bigger money and leveraging your time by hiring managers so you can further grow your practice.

The Managed Account Process Helps You Service Upscale Clients

Think about other ways you could approach a fee-based business. Can you upgrade your clients? Give some thought to the types of prospecting and marketing activities you enjoy that could bring bigger business your way if you focused more on those activities:

- Do you socialize among the affluent?
- Are you visible in your community?
- Are you involved in civic activities or do you volunteer for charities?
- Do you sit on any boards?
- Do you have exposure to wealth through your country club?
- Do you have good referral relationships with accountants and attorneys?
- Do you think you are equipped to work with these affluent investors by offering a broad array of financial services – not just investments? Why?

- Do you seem to naturally attract affluent clients? How?
- Are you in a position to see affluent investors on a regular basis?

If you responded affirmatively to more than half of these questions, you are poised to either begin your transition or continue building your managed account business. In the next chapter, we'll discuss the transitioning process and the importance of a business plan. We've also included some compelling statistics about transitioning we believe you'll find helpful.

Fee-Based Advisor

❏ I prefer to delegate investment responsibility.

❏ I don't feel the need to be involved in every detail or day-to-day investment decisions.

❏ I need additional time for servicing the complex needs of clients.

❏ I enjoy working with affluent individuals.

❏ I have confidence I can improve my business model.

❏ I would give up a large, short-term payout in favor of a larger income stream over time.

❏ I don't particularly enjoy researching or picking stocks.

❏ I like the comfort of using a proven process.

❏ I am comfortable explaining my added value as an advisor to prospects and clients.

❏ I obtain most of my clients through referrals.

❏ I can make a firm commitment to transitioning my business, and I have the patience required to do do.

❏ Most of my clients are affluent and require customization.

❏ I am at my best when I use a consultative approach.

❏ I typically think long term and would like to build a valuable business.

Commission-Based Product Advisor

❏ I like to be in control of all the details of my accounts.

❏ Being involved in the day-to-day investment decisions helps me focus on my clients.

❏ My clients want me to pick their stocks and manage their money and like to call me and talk about it.

❏ I'm not totally comfortable with big clients; I relate better to "Mom & Pop."

❏ I'm not sure whether I really want to change my business; I'm somewhat hesitant at this point in my career to start over.

❏ I like the thrill of a large commission check.

❏ I like studying and researching the companies behind the stocks.

❏ I do not have the patience for involved processes and prefer a faster paced business.

❏ Teaching is not my strong suit, however, I thoroughly enjoy the stock market and working with clients who do too.

❏ I obtain most of my clients by cold calling, direct mail and seminars.

❏ I like getting paid immediately for my sales.

❏ Most of my clients do not need account customization and are either stock traders or clients who need specific financial products like mutual funds or life insurance.

❏ I believe my value is in choosing the right stocks and other products for my clients.

❏ I get a lot of satisfaction from picking stock winners.

Your score: Where are your checkmarks? If you marked five or more in either column, that's probably your comfort zone.

Evaluation of Current Client Base

Who do you work for? What would your clients say you do?

Client's Name _____

Complete one sheet for each client.

Product/Services

	Check all that apply	Assets
Cash Management Account		
Securities		
Mutual Funds		
Mutual Fund Managed Accounts		
Separately Managed Accounts		
Variable Annuities		
Life Insurance		

Financial Strategies

	Check all that apply	Date Completed or of Last Review
Asset Allocation		
Retirement Planning		
College Funding		
Estate Planning		
Charitable Giving		
Disability Protection		
Asset Protection Planning		
Long-Term Care		

Source: Attract and Retain the Affluent Investor, Dearborn Trade, 2001

Top Client Analysis

What products and services do you offer? Where can you gain productivity and new assets?

Product/Services *(Check all that apply)*

Client's Name:																							Total number of clients with product/service
Cash Management Account																							
Securities																							
Mutual Funds																							
Mutual Fund Managed Account																							
Separately Managed Account																							
Variable Annuities																							
Life Insurance																							

Financial Strategies *(Check all that apply)*

Client's Name:																							Total number of clients with strategy
Asset Allocation																							
Retirement Planning																							
College Funding																							
Estate Planning																							
Charitable Giving																							
Disability Protection																							
Asset Protection Planning																							
Long-Term Care																							

Source: Attract and Retain the Affluent Investor, Dearborn Trade, 2001

Top Client Analysis

What products and services do you offer? Where can you gain productivity and new assets?

Product/Services *(Check all that apply)*

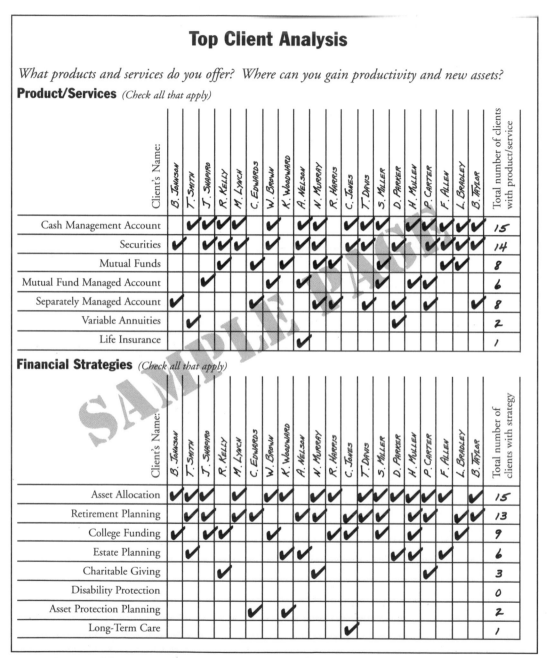

Clients' Name: B. Johnson, T. Smith, J. Shapiro, R. Kelly, M. Lynch, C. Edwards, W. Brown, K. Woodward, A. Nelson, N. Murray, R. Harris, C. Jones, T. Davis, S. Miller, D. Parker, H. Mullen, P. Carter, F. Allen, L. Bradley, B. Taylor

Product/Service	Total number of clients with product/service
Cash Management Account	15
Securities	14
Mutual Funds	8
Mutual Fund Managed Account	6
Separately Managed Account	8
Variable Annuities	2
Life Insurance	1

Financial Strategies *(Check all that apply)*

Financial Strategy	Total number of clients with strategy
Asset Allocation	15
Retirement Planning	13
College Funding	9
Estate Planning	6
Charitable Giving	3
Disability Protection	0
Asset Protection Planning	2
Long-Term Care	1

Source: Attract and Retain the Affluent Investor, Dearborn Trade, 2001

Productivity Analysis

What do you do? What would your clients say you do? Where are your new sales opportunities?

Product/Services: *(Check the number of clients you provide with these products/services)*

	0 clients	1-5 clients	6-10 clients	11-14 clients	15 or more clients
Cash Management Account					
Securities					
Mutual Funds					
Mutual Fund Managed Account					
Separately Managed Account					
Variable Annuities					
Life Insurance					

What new products/services do you want to offer?

_____
_____
_____
_____
_____
_____
_____

To whom?

_____
_____
_____

Financial Strategies: *(Check the number of clients you provide with these strategies)*

	0 clients	1-5 clients	6-10 clients	11-14 clients	15 or more clients
Asset Allocation					
Retirement Planning					
College Funding					
Estate Planning					
Charitable Giving					
Disability Protection					
Asset Protection Planning					
Long-Term Care					

What new financial services do you want to offer?

_____
_____
_____
_____

To whom?

_____
_____
_____
_____

Source: Attract and Retain the Affluent Investor, Dearborn Trade, 2001

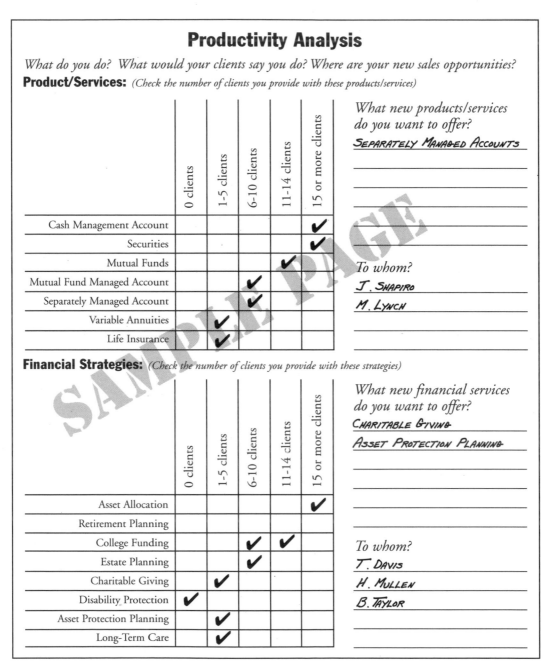

Productivity Analysis

What do you do? What would your clients say you do? Where are your new sales opportunities?

Product/Services: *(Check the number of clients you provide with these products/services)*

	0 clients	1-5 clients	6-10 clients	11-14 clients	15 or more clients
Cash Management Account					✔
Securities		.			✔
Mutual Funds				✔	
Mutual Fund Managed Account			✔		
Separately Managed Account			✔		
Variable Annuities		✔			
Life Insurance		✔			

What new products/services do you want to offer?

SEPARATELY MANAGED ACCOUNTS
_____
_____
_____

To whom?

J. SHAPIRO
M. LYNCH

Financial Strategies: *(Check the number of clients you provide with these strategies)*

	0 clients	1-5 clients	6-10 clients	11-14 clients	15 or more clients
Asset Allocation					✔
Retirement Planning					
College Funding			✔	✔	
Estate Planning			✔		
Charitable Giving		✔			
Disability Protection	✔				
Asset Protection Planning		✔			
Long-Term Care		✔			

What new financial services do you want to offer?

CHARITABLE GIVING
ASSET PROTECTION PLANNING
_____
_____

To whom?

T. DAVIS
H. MULLEN
B. TAYLOR

Source: Attract and Retain the Affluent Investor, Dearborn Trade, 2001

Chapter  4

Making the Transition to Managed Accounts

Many advisors have adopted managed accounts and transitioned to fee income. What can you learn from their experiences?

In Chapter 3, we suggested you take an introspective journey to determine whether consulting and selling managed accounts is really for you. We discussed the benefits of the process and ways to evaluate your current clients to determine whether they (and you) are the right fit for managed accounts. If you have concluded that you should be using managed accounts, you should first recognize where you are now, what business you will be leaving behind, and what business you will be taking with you.

No Changes Necessary

Beware of claims you must change your business. At this point in your career, you have achieved a certain level of success. Unless you are fairly new in the business, your practice is already defined by a certain number of clients seeking your expert advice and investment services and products. You have a quality that has drawn these clients to you. You have found your natural spot – or niche – in the business.

The question is, exactly what is that spot?

Your niche is your base – it will provide the first clue about where you should go from here. Are you still in the introspective process of discovering whether or not you are ready to do managed account business (or more of it)? Are you a rookie making the shift to managed accounts? Separately managed accounts are a challenge for new advisors because they impact short-term income. The solution is to work part-time seeking bigger accounts and meaningful assets while you build your book. You are beginning a long-term compensation formula. Be patient – most top advisors acknowledge that making the transition can be a difficult strategy for a financial consultant whether a seasoned veteran or a rookie.

Don't think of the transition to managed account business as a 180 degree move; rather determine your strengths and make them the foundation upon which you can build. Think of it as making a natural progression to the next level, and not as turning your world upside down.

If you are a veteran advisor and further along in your career, consider the types of clients you have. Since your greatest asset is your existing clientele, reflect on why they hired you. What were their financial needs? What services did/do you offer them? Where are the opportunities?

Take Inventory – and Find Your Strength

As we mentioned in the last chapter, one of the first steps in evaluating your clients is to make a complete inventory of your current practice. Pay particular attention to your top 10-20 clients because they truly define your practice. Recent research shows that high-net-worth investors seek an advisor with a good name and reputation. Twenty-seven percent – the largest percentage overall – of investors with $1 million or more net worth felt that name and reputation were the most important factors in selecting their primary advisor. The advisor's company brand and reputation lagged behind at 15 percent.[1] But how is the name and reputation of a successful advisor communicated?

By word of mouth.

Even though you may have more than 500 accounts, when you go beyond the top 20 households, it's difficult to provide a full range of services. My own research indicates that even the most successful advisors are able to provide a full solution set to only a small number of clients. Goldman Sachs generally limits their individual relationships per advisor to about 25 client families. Most good private banks, at the high end, will limit the exposure to about 25-50 relationships per private banker. In the full-service

[1]2002 Phoenix Wealth Management Survey, conducted in March 2002 by Harris Interactive[SM], © The Phoenix Companies, Inc.

brokerage business, it is not unusual for a veteran producer to have upward of 1,000 individual accounts. Although the ideal number of clients to have in one's practice is a heavily debated topic, the bottom line is that it's usually only the top 10-20 families that get your best and most complete services.

Now, refer back to the worksheets you completed in Chapter 3. If you have more clients with mutual funds than with managed accounts, it is a logical progression to offer them the more personalized solution of separately managed accounts.

If you find you are doing the majority of your work in financial and estate planning but are not capturing the assets for investment management, you are leaving money on the table. This is especially true among advisors who focus more on the life insurance needs of their clients. Accustomed to solving estate planning and business succession issues using insurance, these advisors often leave the investable assets for other advisors. You have an opportunity to complete the relationship with your clients, making the move away from protection and transition services – like insurance – and into asset management.

The most successful advisors use fee-based investment products. The AIM/Gresham survey of financial advisors conducted in 2000 found that the more successful the advisor, the larger the percentage of his or her revenues came from fees:

- Ninety percent of advisors surveyed making $300K or more (net) get some fee revenue, and fees account for at least 25 percent of revenues for more than 50 percent of those advisors.

- By comparison, only 18 percent of advisors earning $75-300K (net) receive more than 25 percent of their revenues from fees.

- Advisors predict growth in their fee business – more than half of all advisors in the survey say their business will be at least 50 percent fees in five years[2]

The tables on page 36 provide some interesting data on the shift to fee-based business.

Perception vs. Reality

Carl, a multimillion dollar advisor I once met who had an overseas private bank, said he was very frustrated with his inability to "crack the code" of selling managed accounts. Carl had very big accounts but knew that even though he may have had

Percent of Advisory Business that Is Currently Fee-Based	
None	20.3%
1 to 25%	48.6%
26-50%	18.7%
51 to 75%	3.8%
76 to 100%	8.6%

N=1097 Advisors

- Most advisors have at least some of their clients on a fee basis
- The largest proportion (the typical advisor) has between 1 and 25% of their clients on a fee basis
- Less than one in ten have 75% or more of their clients on a fee basis

Success and Percent of Advisory Business that Is Currently Fee-Based			
	Income Under $75,000	Income $75,000 to $300,000	Income $300,000 and over
None	30.1%	24.3%	10.4%
1 to 25%	55.2%	57.8%	36.1%
26-50%	0.0	4.2%	43.8%
51 to 75%	0.3%	2.1%	7.6%
76 to 100%	14.4%	11.6%	2.1%

N=1097 Advisors

- The more successful the advisor, the larger the portion of their client base that is fee-based
- Over half of very successful advisors have a quarter or more of their clients on a fee-based system, as opposed to much smaller percents of less successful advisors

Percent of Advisory Business that Will Be Fee-Based in Five Years	
None	9.2%
1 to 25%	4.1%
26-50%	17.9%
51 to 75%	39.8%
76 to 100%	29.0%

N=1097 Advisors

- Advisors predict a significant migration to fee-based arrangements with clients
- Over half of all advisors say half or more of their clients will be fee-based in five years

Source: AIM/Gresham Wealth Management Survey 2000

$5 million of an individual's money, in reality, the client probably had much more. He said his clients didn't want managed accounts. But when I went through the client inventory exercise with him, he realized he had been type-cast by his clients. We did an analysis of what services and products he provided his top clients. Most of them were buying securities and that's it. They weren't buying packaged products, consultative services, estate planning or succession planning.

Carl realized   reluctantly – that his clients perceived him as a very good stockbroker who had the pulse of the market. They liked to talk to him about stocks. But, it was very difficult for them to believe he could also discuss solutions for their serious money.

Carl was leaving assets on the table and he realized that. The clients loved trading stocks and making money that way, but they didn't want to risk the remainder of their capital. Conclusion: They didn't identify Carl as having the expertise to handle all their assets.

Dead end? Not necessarily. One course of action was for Carl to discuss with his clients the basis on which they founded their relationship – trading stocks – and tell them even though he did an excellent job at picking stocks, it was not a way to manage their serious money.

A New View of You

It's all about the client's *perception* of your expertise. You don't necessarily want to change their perception, only make them more aware of your additional areas of expertise. Once you explain to your clients that you have a specific process and strategy for managing their total wealth picture, you'll be on the path to capturing more assets.

So Carl did just this with his clients. He introduced them to his partner who worked with a more consultative process. In a similar vein, Pete and Ken are San Diego-based independent advisors who work much the same way Carl and his partner do now. Pete is the "wealth manager" doing the planning work and Ken is the portfolio manager. These types of partnerships work very well: One handles the stock picking for select clients and the other handles the managed account business using third-party managers. The clients get two expert advisors instead of one.

In many cases, advisors may think that changing the perception of how their clients see them is unnecessary. After all, why would you want to change the perception of a handful of great clients who already think you're the best? If you are providing a service and your clients are happy, why should you change your business? My answer is that, yes, the clients may be happy, but there is a competitive reality today: Clients may be happy with what you do, but why would you be satisfied with having just a portion of their wealth when one of the easiest parts to manage is the greater wealth using the investment management consulting process? That is how you can capture a greater percentage of their assets.

Your Client is Ready to Transition, Too!

Consider the following story: Gerry, an experienced advisor, transitioned a large client from mutual funds to managed accounts. Says Gerry, "The client is a married 47-year-old surgeon who has no time to spend on his finances. In 1997, he responded to a mail campaign we conducted to physicians. The mailer discussed the high-end services that our firm provides and the importance of having a professional manage your assets. We met him for lunch and we completed an extensive planning profile that included an asset allocation proposal. He also gave us a $1^1/_2$ inch pile of statements from his online brokerage account. His account was essentially full of mutual funds and was a classic study of overlapping investments. It wasn't a pretty picture.

"I had no additional contact with the client until several months later when the physician sent me a letter stating that he remembered our meeting and the valuable assistance. He wanted to visit with us again. This visit included his wife to get her on board with the process and benefits of using managed accounts. The meeting was a big success! The client has recently transferred approximately $7 million to us, mostly from a major mutual fund company. We are transitioning him slowly out of the funds because most of the account is taxable. One thing I believe gnawed on the client was the big tax check he had to write last year for the gains on his growth funds. More importantly though, the client was convinced of the advantages of using a managed account for a portfolio of this magnitude."

So, once you feel confident that you want to make the transition and you've begun to identify the right clients, this is also a good time to develop your overall business plan, including your transition goals. Don't skip over this next section; you'll understand why after you read the statistics in the following paragraphs.

Business Plans: A Must for Transitioning

In his book, *The 7 Habits of Highly Effective People*, Stephen Covey suggests to, "Begin with the end in mind."[3] He tells us to begin with the image of the end of our life as the frame of reference by which everything else is measured. In reality, this is the entire concept behind creating a business plan for yourself. Much like an architectural blueprint that is critical to building a house, a business plan provides the structure and definition needed to build your business.

It is so important to have solid numeric targets; otherwise, you can get lost in "motion" and potentially unproductive activities. Often advisors fail to use specific numbers, such as assets, clients, or income – or target their numbers incorrectly. According to my research,[4] only 20.3 percent of advisors have a current written business plan; 16.4 percent have a plan, but it is out of date; and a whopping 63.3 percent do not have a plan. The study concluded that 57.6 percent of successful advisors with incomes of $300,000 or more have a business plan. At the other end of the spectrum, 88.5 percent of those advisors whose income is less than $75,000 do not have a business plan.

Begin with Your Income in Mind

Let's say you earn $50,000 annually from your managed account business and you want to spend the next year growing your income to $150,000. Based on an industry study, the average-sized managed account is $250,000.[5] So, how many $250,000 accounts will it take to meet your annual income goal? If your goal is 10 clients at $500,000 minimum, you've reached $5 million already. Then, if you capture 20 more clients at $250,000 minimum, that's another $5 million toward your goal. It's important that your plan be "people" specific. For example, if your plan states that you need 30 new clients for separately managed accounts over the course of a year, every two weeks, on average, you will have to sign up a new account. Where will you get that client? If you look at it this way, your goal becomes easier to accomplish.

The reason I suggest you distill your income goal this way is because the managed account is a conceptual sale. Unlike the sale of a new issue or a single product offering, it's not a campaign, there's no time urgency. You need to take a sale that might extend over months or years and reduce it to daily activities. The successful advisors we know break down their business plan into people and numeric terms to more effectively stay on track to reach their goals. The following worksheet is one way to help you go through this exercise.

---

[3]*The 7 Habits of Highly Effective People*. Stephen R. Covey, Simon & Schuster, 1989.

[4]AIM/Gresham *Wealth Management Survey 2000*

[5]*2010: A Managed Account Odyssey. Projections on the Future of the Managed Accounts Industry*. Leonard A. Reinhart and Jay N. Whipple III, Lockwood Financial Services, Inc.

Income Targets Worksheet

		Sample
Incremental Income Goal:	_____	$100,000
÷ Average Fee to Advisor:	_____	1.00%
= Assets Needed:	_____	10,000,000
÷ Average Account Size:	_____	250,000
= Number of New Accounts:	_____	40
÷ Months in Selling Period:	_____	12
= New Account Target (Monthly):	_____	3 1/3

This plan requires results in a new managed account almost every week.

Goals to Call Your Own

If you currently are in the process of transition, your business plan must involve a component of how you maintain existing businesses – both for the service of clients and for the potential to add additional assets from those existing clients. The business plan takes on multiple dimensions because one half of your business plan should focus on servicing existing clients and the other half on developing new business.

When you consider your existing client base, you might think you have no numeric targets, other than to retain the business. But think about it. A great management guru once said, "You can't manage what you can't measure." Virtually every activity can be measured numerically, and a numerical measurement is an objective measurement.

One of the first things you want to do is take an inventory of clients who have additional assets elsewhere. Through improved client service, you have the potential of earning additional assets from a certain percentage of your existing client base. Make an educated guess about how much you think you could capture – 20 clients at $100,000 each? Or 15 clients who each have $500,000 with another advisor or institution? Use the worksheet on page 43 to make a list with actual client names and the numbers to give you some sense of what the financial reward might be if you provide enhanced client service to these individuals. The first section will help you to list data for your existing clients.

Prospecting New Clients

The next step is to determine the assets you will raise from new clients and to establish your goals for this area of your business plan. For example, if you determine that seminar selling works well for you, you need to decide how you are going to meet your predetermined goal of two to three new accounts each month. You might accomplish this by conducting a seminar or two each month. But what are the activities that will produce results? It's not effective to think, "I'm going to prospect more." Instead, quantify your thoughts by clarifying *who* you are going to prospect and *how often* you are going to prospect. Visualize again that you want to earn an additional $100,000 in annual fee revenue. To earn that, you then determine you need to raise, for example, $10 million in managed accounts. To do that, you need a process that generates two to three accounts a month from a pool of about 30 prospects a month. You'll need at least 10 "suspects" for every prospect. While this example is a good model to follow, you can develop your own that works for your business plan. Using the second part of the worksheet on page 43, you can quantify your goals for seminar activity and new accounts from that activity.

If you go no further than understanding the sales process for your practice and its numeric objectives, you will have taken a giant step beyond that taken by most advisors. And you will have copied the approach used by the most successful advisors who always know where their numbers are coming from. Failure to quantify your sales process ensures you'll derail at some point. The objective of quantifying the process is to help you understand the interplay between your client sourcing, qualifying and selling.

Review Your Plan

It's not necessary to review your business plan more than once a quarter. You can review a well-constructed business plan based on numeric objectives because the numbers represent a process. By way of example, every successful investment management firm has an objective process for choosing securities. Portfolio managers have to defend it and if they don't have good answers, they won't know why the process worked or why it didn't work. A successful process, regardless of what it is used for, is one you can repeat because it creates measurable results.

If you review your plan once a quarter and you see that you are not achieving your target client goals in one segment of your plan (like holding seminars), you need to take an objective look at what you've done in that area. Maybe you had two seminars a month for six months. Have you determined how many of those who attended the events actually became clients? If so, fill out your own seminar worksheet so you have an accurate picture of your goals and your achievements. You can then adjust your plan accordingly. You need to take a close look at the initial steps you took and the investment you made in obtaining your total number of seminar attendees just to make sure it's cost effective and to determine whether you want to continue holding these events.

Getting Started

The most important aspect of the entire business plan is getting started. Give serious thought to your process. Putting together the physical plan shouldn't take more than 15-30 minutes. You may not have all the data you need in the beginning, but don't get frustrated. It's better to get started and fill in the blanks with educated guesses than to not complete any of it.

Remember, your goal is to be able to measure your progress so you can manage it. Even if you estimate every data point, at least you will have a framework from which to begin. A business plan is a living, breathing document that will continue to change as conditions change. It does not stay static. The business plan is also like a spotlight. It's going to illuminate all of the elements of success, even some you may have overlooked because you weren't measuring your business. Here are four things to keep in mind:

1. Business planning is always about beginning with a numeric end in mind.

2. Measure so you can manage.

3. Try not to be consumed in activities that do not produce results. Don't confuse motion with quantifiable movement.

4. Revisit your plan and adjust your goals accordingly. Don't get discouraged; your business is a dynamic entity and one that will change over time. Be prepared to change with it.

To help you get started, take a look at the sample business plan included in Appendix A, courtesy of Joe Lukacs at International Performance Group, LLC.

Prospecting Model Worksheet

Sample

ANNUAL INCOME GOAL:	_____	_$100,000_
ANNUAL ASSET GOAL:	_____	_$10,000,000_

EXISTING CLIENTS:

B. TAYLOR	_____	_$50,000_
H. MULLEN	_____	_$100,000_
A. NELSON	_____	_$250,000_
J. SHAPIRO	_____	_$500,000_
B. JOHNSON	_____	_$50,000_
R. HARRIS	_____	_$50,000_
Total Expected From Existing Clients:	_____	_$1,000,000_

NEW CLIENTS:

		_$10,000,000_
		_-1,000,000_
Assets From New Clients:	_____	_$9,000,000_
÷ Average Account Size:	_____	_$250,000_
= Number of New Accounts:	_____	_36_
÷ Months in Selling Period:	_____	_12_
= New Account Target (Monthly):	_____	_3_
Asset Goal:	_____	_$9,000,000_
Accounts:	_____	_36_
Monthly Goal New Accounts:	_____	_3_
Formula for Closing Ratio:		
Number of Qualified Prospects per New Account:	_____	_5_
x Monthly New Account Goal:	_____	_3_
= Total Monthly Prospects per Seminar:	_____	_15_
Formula for Prospect Ratio:		
Number of Invitees per Prospect Mailing Lists:	_____	_30_
x Monthly Prospects:	_____	_15_
= Total Invitees per Month:	_____	_450_

This plan calls for making 450 seminar invitations and closing three of the 450 prospects each month.

Chapter **5**

Overcoming Transition Objections

If it ain't broke, why fix it? How to answer this question and many others from clients who could benefit from managed accounts.

Converting business from a commission basis to fees sounds like a daunting task – you'll inevitably run into roadblocks along the way. But keep in mind what I said earlier – it's simply a way to progress to the next level in your career. This chapter covers a few of the most widely recognized objections – and solutions on how to overcome them.

Underpaid in Providence

Howard runs an advisory practice in Providence, RI, built on taking solid positions in great companies; buying quality bonds; building balanced portfolios; and holding them for years. His clients are happy with his service and his solutions. Howard helps clients make decisions about their portfolios but only gets paid if a commission is generated. In many cases, his clients benefit from the advice he gives – which is not to sell at certain times, even though a sale would provide Howard a payday. He grapples with the challenge of maintaining revenue to the practice while he dispenses advice.

This is the perfect example of services rendered without compensation. It is very common among many advisors we have met who have built portfolios for clients over the years and have been underpaid for their services. The managed account, or the nondiscretionary fee-based brokerage account, is an ideal solution.

Transition Objection 1:
If It Ain't Broke, Don't Fix It!

Some advisors approach the transition by thinking of the adage, "If it ain't broke, don't fix it." However, keep in mind that client relations are extremely dynamic. Clients are bombarded by other financial services professionals, online information and financial publications. You are not working with them in a vacuum. They hear about managed account alternatives in pitches from other advisors and from stories through other affluent individuals, so you want to ensure you are in step with them.

After 2000-2001, few advisors should be complacent. But neither should you be in fear of your clients. If you believe a change is in a client's best interests, your confidence and passion will show. Many advisors who face these commission-to-fee transitions learn a great deal when they discuss their plans with the clients.

Advisor Tip

Fees for Life

Gary, a life insurance advisor, built an investment advisory business to $100 million in just three years. Even though his clients perceived his actual expertise in charitable giving and family foundations, they didn't appreciate that Gary was also an expert in investment management. His remedy was to show his clients the process of the investment policy statement and of the investment managers. He told his clients this was an area he developed in addition to his insurance background.

Says Gary, "When I switched from commissions to fees, it took two years to make up the lost income, but now that the transition is behind me, my business is better than ever. We add about 10-12 new clients a year and lose a few, largely as a result of death. My goal is to serve just 20 clients, with $5-10 million in investable assets each."

When the general brokerage business declined in 2001, as much as 25-30 percent from the previous year, results from individual brokers who offered managed accounts and consulting services were down far less and a great many were actually up. These advisors and brokers insulated their practices against situations that could have been much worse.

Gerry experiences few objections to transitioning clients to managed accounts. The most common one relates to fees, he says, but is easy to explain. Says Gerry, "Once clients understand that the total fees can be similar to mutual funds, they generally are sold. If you take the performance and fees out of managed accounts and focus on the process, it becomes much easier for clients to understand the concept. Stay away from the alphas and betas! Our fee for a $1 million account is about 150 basis points, which is similar to an equity mutual fund, so they can relate to that."

Some of you may still be thinking, Why change? The reality is that over the years you have built a practice that has tremendous value. If your firm permits, you can sell a portion of your practice or your book or share it with another advisor on a payout basis. Being able to profit from the winding down of your personal involvement by anointing a successor and creating your own succession plan is a tremendous benefit. If your business makes a transition to separately managed accounts with professional investment management firms, you maintain a strong financial stake in what you've built over the years but reduce your daily involvement.

If you are *still* not convinced and do not feel this is the right business for you, then it's far more beneficial to realize that now. Don't try to pretend to be something you're not. If you do, you might create something half-heartedly. You'll be unhappy, and your clients might not understand because you won't be giving them your total commitment.

Transition Objection 2: My Income Will Suffer!

This is a very real concern for many advisors. Income can suffer in the short term for many, but there are ways to buffer the problem – transitioning gradually, weeding out the smaller clients and focusing on capturing additional assets from your larger clients. For some advisors who already have an established business, though, the best way is to go cold turkey.

Like many other successful advisors, Ron wanted to make the transition because he was eager to provide a unified story. His cold turkey approach was to tell his new story to all of his clients all at once. He told them he believed that a fee basis led to a better approach to managing money and he hoped they would feel that way, too. As a result of his communication with his clients about his conviction of managed accounts, he was able to transition nearly all of his accounts. Take a look at the table on the next page.

My research found that 37.6 percent of advisors with incomes of $300,000 and over who made the change cold-turkey found that approach extremely helpful to their businesses.[1] They went cold turkey because they wanted to provide a singular focus. By showing their level of commitment, these advisors led most of their clients to the new process.

What type of producer actually goes cold-turkey?

[1] AIM/Gresham *Wealth Management Survey 2000*

Typically, they are the larger advisors who realize that to take the next logical step up, they need to take a step or two back. For the most part, they did suffer a temporary loss of income, and they could financially afford to do this more easily than could the newer advisor. Advisor Ron says making the transition cold-turkey was tough for him for about a year. Then he realized more assets from current clients who saw the merits of the more comprehensive strategy.

Success and Importance of Fee-Based Strategy: Switching Over to Fee-based All at Once		
Income Under $75,000	**Income $75,000 $300,000**	**Income $300,000 and over**
Extremely Helpful — 35.6%	52.6%	37.6%
Somewhat Helpful — 0.6%	6.0%	2.4%
Not Helpful At All — 63.8%	41.4%	60.0%

N=1097 Advisors

Source: AIM/Gresham Wealth Management Survey 2000

Cutting Loose

George, an advisor in the Midwest, made the transition to managed accounts and narrowed his focus to a smaller number of families. He eventually converted all of his accounts and stripped his book down from 600 accounts to just over 100. He was rewarded with 30 percent more assets and 25 percent more income within nine months of making his transition.

Says George, "After my assistant and I began to sort through my book of clients, I realized that many individuals were not really clients; they were buyers. It soon became clear to us that we'd collected a lot of accounts over the years, but relatively few of them had developed into relationships. This was troubling because we wanted to be advisors to our affluent clients, not just brokers peddling stocks to anyone who called."[2]

To determine which kinds of clients to concentrate on, it's important to understand

---

[2]*Attract and Retain the Affluent Investor.* Stephen D. Gresham and Evan Cooper, Dearborn Trade, 2001.

that the process is not simply one of "weeding out" your current book of clients. Work on the process of profiling the type of client you want and work toward obtaining more clients like that. It's really a growth strategy designed to attract more clients to a higher level of service.

Remember, it's all about focus and perception. We talked about the client's perceptions of you and your area of expertise. If you want to make serious steps forward in your practice, you may have to take a step back like Ron.

For the most part, the legitimate needs of your clients provide the most successful transition. Advisors Mort and Roger had clients buying mutual funds and stocks and bonds but did not have comprehensive investment policy statements or the plan needed to accompany the investments as they grew. Mort and Roger were originally bull market brokers, having been in the business since the early '80s. As their clients grew, they developed an affinity for managed accounts because their clients needed higher level investment management. By being in tune with those developing client preferences, and by implementing more advanced planning tools, Mort and Roger both flourished.

Almost every day I hear stories from advisors about how they are losing clients to management firms and private banks. In many cases, it's clear that the clients thought they had outgrown their advisors. By continuing to educate your clients about your process (e.g., investment policy statements, manager selection and monitoring), you will stay in touch with their perceptions – good and bad – and have the ability to refine your services.

The key point to remember is that you are building off existing strengths. Your affluent prospect or client understands that you have a dynamic and serious process involved in your practice now. Think again about the demographics of your clientele. Do you have business-owner clients? Do you handle their individual securities business, but not their company pension account?

Without an investment management process, those clients do not see you as a logical candidate to take over the management of their pension plans. They like working with you, discussing stock trades and the market and so on. They just don't want your trading skills applied to their pension funds. As trainer Leo Pusateri says in his book, *Mirror Mirror On The Wall*,[3] "What do you think your clients would say if you asked them what it is you do?"

---

[3] *Mirror Mirror On The Wall Am I The Most Valued Of Them All?* Leo J. Pusateri, Financial Entrepreneur Publishing, 2001.

You might be very surprised to hear their answers.

Use Your Professional Strengths, Your Community, Your Hobbies to Transition

In Chapter 3, we discussed a number of ways to reach the affluent. You might want to take a moment to think about trying these new avenues to reach this target market. Del is well known for circulating among the charitable boards in this community, just as is Gary in Toledo, OH, among the family foundations. By contrast, Del's colleague, Jim, is very well known on the golf course at a prestigious country club in his community and is also a club champion. This distinction gave him access to virtually all affluent investors in that arena and helped him prospect for new business. For Jim, transitioning to the managed account process was the perfect solution for his lifestyle, as well as for his clients, even though he previously had a very successful trading business.

Teaching Clients

Do you like to use client education as part of your business? Jock and Richard in Toronto have an educational process for each client that is planned up to two years in advance. The pair map out a progression of topics they believe are important to the development of a successful investor. At each quarterly meeting, the regular review of results is augmented by discussion of a new topic – such as estate planning or asset allocation. The team's goal is to continue to lead their clients by challenging their knowledge level.

If you are good at running public seminars and educational events, you can make an easy transition. Investment managers who are supportive of your efforts will make themselves available as guest speakers at your seminars, as well as financial supporters of the seminars. By exposing your clients to investment management "experts," you gain a new level of credibility with the affluent and gain a meaningful prospecting opportunity, too (more about seminars is presented in Chapter 7 and allying with wholesalers in Chapter 8).

Transition Objection 3: Clients Question the Change

It should be easy to determine whether clients should transition or not: Smaller clients either do or do not have enough money to realize the benefits of managed accounts. Larger acccounts will or will not value the benefits of customization or more diversification among managers. Many of them will have an incentive to give you additional assets because they will clearly see the advantages.

You might broach the subject of transitioning to a larger client with a total of $500,000 to invest; "We like to give our clients exposure to various asset classes. To do that, we typically manage money by placing $100,000 of a clients' assets with a large cap core manager and allocate the rest among other asset classes." But, with a smaller client who may have only $50,000 to invest, "To get that kind of diversification for you, I have to use individual mutual fund portfolios. As your assets grow and you're able to add money, we can take a closer look at separately managed accounts to better tailor your solution with more control over your taxes." Always give your clients an idea of where you're going next so they can realize the transition is real – and logical.

More often than not, clients will not ask why you haven't told them about managed accounts before. But they might say something like, "I was perfectly comfortable working with you the way we have been for years. Why change it?" State your reasons with conviction, and most clients will understand the benefits – just as Ron's clients did. Advisors who have difficulty moving clients to managed accounts and fees typically don't really believe in the benefits of the move, and that lack of conviction comes across in their discussions with clients. They just throw it out there as one idea among many. Clients detect the lack of commitment and believe their advisor was not truly invested in the concept.

Too Much of a Good Thing

Erik also is firmly committed to the value of managed accounts and likes to educate his clients. Says Erik, "When migrating clients to managed accounts, we tell them that this is how real money is managed. Institutions do it this way. We take them through the process and explain the discipline and philosophy behind the concept. One question we ask when we get resistance is, what is your sell discipline? This is particularly relevant to the investor who likes to be in control. Of course, most investors don't have a sell discipline, which is one reason they do so poorly. As a compromise to the control issue, we suggest those clients keep a small piece that they can manage with us on a small scale in addition to the externally managed account. This can be used in special situations with certain clients."

A Guide to Transitioning Unsuitable Clients: Don't Do It

A word of caution here. One big pitfall lurks when you make the transition to managed accounts. Be prepared that some of your clients are not going to be appropriate for the transition. This is the most difficult aspect of the change. This is when you will first confront the fact that you simply can't work with everyone.

If you want to enjoy the type of benefits that accrued to Roger, Mort, Ron and other successful advisors who made the transition, all of whom are earning more today with greater assets than they ever thought possible, it's necessary to experience that moment of truth when you realize that some clients just don't fit the mold.

It is uniformly true that individuals who bit the bullet and let go of smaller clients – along with the clients who insisted on being self directed – are the advisors who have made the most successful transitions.

Advisor Tip

Harry transitioned a number of clients from mutual fund or individual stock portfolios with heavy concentrations in a few names to managed account portfolios. After they understood the advantages, those clients quickly recognized the tremendous level of risk associated with holding just a few positions in a large portfolio. Says Harry, "We conducted a tax sensitivity analysis with various portfolio managers over a 36-month period to assist in the conversion process and systematically transitioned these concentrated positions to the "model" portfolio which is more broadly diversified. Clients are generally happy with the change in their portfolio's risk profile."

So, What *Do* You Do? A Time for Clarity

Remember, it's not just what *you* think you do, it's what your *best clients* think you do. You are defined by your clients. And you are defined by the process you use. Affluent clients provide the best referrals and they will bring additional affluent clients to you. This is almost exclusively the way most advisors obtain new business. Think about Carl – most of his clients said he was a risk-taking stockbroker. Some who had serious money to invest and would have been attracted to the managed account process said he would not have been their choice. Yet, he found a way to make the transition and it helped changed his clients' perception of him. Use the Cocktail Party Test and Unique Value Proposition worksheets on pages 59 and 60 to formulate a clear definition for the value you provide.

All successful transitions are simply the logical next step in growth. I can't say this enough. Advisors may feel as though they have undergone substantial change, but it's been much more of a cleansing – or a clarity of focus – than anything else. Some advisors may say their transition was a massive effort, that it was terrible. If you stop and think about it, all you need to do is extend to the next level, which you already are doing quite well.

The Client Garden: Time to Weed

It's safe to say that most veteran advisors have long-term clients who suit their temperament and fit well with the services they provide. But, due to the sales nature of the business, some advisors may have accumulated a few clients who don't fit. Some advisors and brokers never say "no" to a prospect and consequently, have clients on the books who don't match their desired profile. For example, they may be clients who are potential referral sources or those with few assets who are friends of good clients. They may be clients who might come into more money at some point. These clients are all difficult to part with, but many of them just don't materialize into solid, long-term business.

As we said earlier, since it is so critical that your name and reputation drive the word-of-mouth sale, it continues to be the most important element in determining the type of investors who hire the high-end financial advisor. Therefore, it is critical that your practice be limited to the kind of people you want to duplicate. They are the ones with whom you will distinguish yourself, and who will ultimately lead to more referrals.

The exclusivity of your services will draw a certain type of client. These individuals are willing to pay a higher percentage of their income to avail themselves of special and custom services.

Most firms are promoting fee-based business, managed accounts and consulting. One firm in particular has created a specific program to discourage smaller accounts. Every firm has weighed in, in some way, with a wealth management focus. The financial advisory firms of the future are focused on these key areas, and as an advisor today, you will benefit tremendously from the trend toward an upscale clientele.

Many sales managers have come from a transaction background and have not fully embraced these initiatives. So, if you are planning to make the transition and want to focus on wealth management, you can benefit strongly by getting a buy in for your efforts from your local sales manager. Let's take another look at George's practice. George's managing director was very supportive every step of the way, encouraging him about the progress he was making. That made it so much easier for George, knowing he could depend on the support and encouragement of management.

In the financial services industry since 1980, George began his career trading futures in the Chicago pits. About 10 years later, a friend who worked for a wirehouse told George about the firm's new emphasis on financial planning and consulting. The idea appealed to George because he was ready to transition out of the futures and stock business and into a more value-added area of counseling for his clients. He soon joined his friend and became a broker.

George liked the approach of financial planning and in the early '90s, began providing clients 60- to 80-page plans for $175. Soon after, he developed an aggressive prospecting campaign and spent a great deal of time networking with centers of influence, namely CPAs and attorneys. Says George, "By the mid-90s, I was doing more business and – theoretically – lots of planning. But the reality was that I was out chasing new business rather than implementing what I said I would do in the financial plans we had developed."

George was spending more time selling than he was advising and was not comfortable in that mode. "I finished '97 with $422,000 in production," says George, "and $48 million in assets. I had 630 accounts and I had done 211 comprehensive financial plans." Quickly he began to realize that more was not better. He had reached a plateau, was overwhelmed, exhausted, and worried he was not delivering to his clients what he had promised.

After careful evaluation of his business, he determined that he could effectively service 100 clients. But he wasn't clear whether he could make a living serving such a small number of individuals. Long hours of calculating and analyzing led George to realize he was, in fact, operating two separate – and very different – businesses: a brokerage business and an advisory business. It then became clear that the brokerage side was interfering with his responsibilities as a valued advisor. George's assistant helped him confirm that phone calls from small brokerage clients outnumbered calls from larger advisory clients by an overwhelming ratio of 17:1.

Armed with this information, George and his assistant created criteria, or screens, that he used to rank his clients. He developed 11 key screens that helped him cull and manage his current book of clients.

1. *Account by Production Report*
   This screen is a report of each account by production for the first eight months of the calendar year.

2. *Value of Assets Report*
   This is a report of each account evaluated by the value of assets.

3. *List of Priority Clients*
   A rundown of clients holding assets of at least $250,000 at the firm or

contributing $5,000 in production for the year (George had 40).

4. *Likeability of Clients*
A more subjective, but important, criteria was whether or not George liked his clients and vice versa.

5. *Investment Approach Acceptance*
This screen helped George determine which clients believed in his managed money approach.

6. *Financial Qualifications*
A crucial element in establishing which clients had significant assets to implement George's suggestions and/or plans.

7. *Premier Client Capability*
Clients who were likely to use more of the firm's services.

8. *Hard-Dollar Profitability*
This screen includes all expenses incurred while traveling or entertaining certain clients.

9. *Soft-Dollar Profitability*
These are the time costs incurred and should be added to the hard-dollar costs.

10. *Price-Value Test*
A crucial element for George, and any advisor, who needs to screen out clients who insist on negotiating fees or receiving discounts.

11. *Future Growth Opportunities*
Another very important screen to determine which clients might assist the advisor in capturing more assets. George discovered referrals, family business opportunities and other ways to increase business.

Although George had developed a remarkable way to cull clients, capture assets, and increase time for himself, he admits he was baffled. Says George, "It took us four months to get to those 11 screens, and when we finally analyzed which clients made it through all of them, we ended up with just 33 clients. At first, we thought it was impossible: How could 631 accounts yield just 33 good clients (who represented about 100 accounts)? How could we base a business on 33 clients?"

George crunched some numbers to see what would happen to his annual income if he worked with those 33 clients alone. The outcome was startling. George said that if he gave up all the remaining clients, he would lose only nine percent of his production. He decided to rework his business plan.

His new plan included "creating, implementing and monitoring life plans," as he began to describe it. According to George, too often financial planning is a one-time event that is soon forgotten. His "life plan" is a process that allows George to be involved with the client on a continuing basis. It gives George the opportunity to follow the client along the wealth life-cycle process and change the financial plan as the client evolves.

But George soon discovered that filtering clients through the entire 11 screens was too time consuming, so he devised a custom three-part strategy that allowed him to assess clients in about 30 minutes. Here are the parameters George eventually chose:

1. It is imperative to like the client and that the client like me.

2. We must agree on the business and investment philosophy.

3. The client must have the financial solidity to implement the investment plan.

Once George crafted his three-step "weeding" process, he then wondered how his remaining 33 clients would react to his change of business. Says George, "I met all 33 clients for two- and three-hour conversations and explained my new plan. I said I was making a huge commitment to this new way of doing business and asked them to help me fill another 45 slots, which would bring my total client list to 78. If they didn't help me, I explained, I'd be right back scrambling to get clients and not being able to give them [current clients] the attention they deserved. Happily, they went along with me."

How Is George Doing Now?

George contacts his best clients at least 12 times per year and meets with each an average of four times. His clients receive biannual portfolio reviews. He sees each client for one full day every year. He includes breakfast-through-dinner sessions, not just an afternoon of golf. "I want to spend time at their place of employment, at home, and over meals getting to know them better and truly understanding what is important in their lives," says George.

Within the first few months of his day-long meetings, George captured three new multi-million dollar clients all by way of referral.

As a result of his new business model, George was also able to develop a client management system that allows him the necessary time to devote to his clients without being rushed or overwhelmed as he was in the old days. He has regularly scheduled phone appointments and in-person meetings, and each client has a time slot each month "for the rest of their lives," says George.

Most of his clients are not interested in the stock market or any other particular investment. Taxes, estate planning, life insurance, business advice, and other issues are most important to them, he says. George oversees average client assets of $1.6 million and a return on assets of about one percent.

His advice to other advisors who want to change their business model? "To pick their own business objective and live it passionately; they have to believe and act on the belief that more is not better, and they have to change their outlook," says George. "What I've done is a lifestyle change; it's not a diet."

How You Can Benefit from George's Experience

Are you wondering what might happen to your own business if you followed a path similar to George's? Answer the following questions, which are fashioned after his original 11-step screening process,[4] and make a list of your pros and cons.

- How much revenue does each of your accounts generate?

- How many assets per account?

- Which accounts do you or your firm consider "premier" based on revenue generation, assets or other important criteria?

- Do you like your clients? Do your clients like you? It's important to include feedback from your sales assistant, partner, team members, and any others in your office.

- Are your clients in sync with your investment style and process?

- How wealthy are your clients? Rank each one according to their asset size (or what you think it might be, as well as an amount you might possibly capture).

- How many clients buy more than one service from you?

- Do you have clients who are expensive to maintain, e.g., hard dollars?

- Are some of your clients demanding of your time, draining you of energy, e.g.,

---

[4]*Attract and Retain the Affluent Investor*. Stephen D. Gresham and Evan Cooper, Dearborn Trade, 2001.

soft dollars?

- How many of your clients ask for discounts or want to negotiate fees?

- Do your clients have good referral sources; do they represent networking possibilities for you?

By answering these questions honestly and listing all of the pros and cons of maintaining your current client base, you might find – as George did – that by culling your client base, instead of losing revenue, you gain time to devote to your larger clients as well as capture more assets. In the long run, you ultimately increase your revenue and the quality of your clientele. Use the "What Makes A Great Client?" worksheets on pages 61 and 62 to help you with this process.

Support and Guidance Are Key

To all of the sales and branch managers reading this book, please recognize that your support is perhaps the most critical factor in the success of many of your advisors. Much like a prolonged exercise and weight loss program in response to doctor's orders, it's better if you have a personal trainer coaching and supporting you than it is to go it alone.

What Do You Do?
The Cocktail Party Test

What do you say when someone asks you, in a cocktail party setting, "What do you do?"

(Give a one sentence answer) _____

_____

_____

_____

_____

Sample 1: "I'm a financial advisor."

Better: *"I help wealthy families create, implement and monitor life plans."*

Sample 2: "I manage money for affluent clients."

Better: *"Our team helps affluent business owners preserve their wealth through business succession and estate planning."*

Source: Attract and Retain the Affluent Investor, Dearborn Trade, 2001

Defining What You Do
Unique Value Proposition Worksheet

Background: What have you done that would impress an affluent client?
College degree? Industry tenure? Professional designation? Expertise?

_____

_____

_____

Sample 1: *"I have 20 years experience as a financial advisor."*
Sample 2: *"I am a Certified Investment Management Consultant."*
Sample 3: *"I have an MBA from Harvard."*

Firm/Team Structure: Prove the depth of your capability — show what you can do to serve
the client better than another advisor.

_____

_____

_____

Sample 1: *"My group includes a full time estate planning specialist."*
Sample 2: *"Our team maintains a limited clientele — preserving a ratio
of one professional for every twenty client families."*

Client Focus: Who are your clients? Can you prove your knowledge and expertise
with a specific group?

_____

_____

_____

Sample 1: *"I have counseled more than 100 retirees from your company."*
Sample 2: *"We focus on the sale and succession needs of small business
owners like you."*

Service/Product Focus: What do your clients buy from you? What would they say you sell?
What is your product or service expertise?

_____

_____

_____

Sample 1: *"I manage my clients' wealth using professional investment managers."*
Sample 2: *"I am an expert in charitable giving and family foundations."*

Source: Attract and Retain the Affluent Investor, Dearborn Trade, 2001

What Makes A Great Client?

Client's Name _____

Complete one sheet for each client.

Product/Services

	Check all that apply	Data
Gross revenue/account		
Assets/account		
Do you like them?		
Do they like you?		
Philosophically in line		
Can they execute?		
"Total wealth" prospect?		
Profitability – hard dollar		
Profitability – soft dollar		
Growth potential		

Source: Attract and Retain the Affluent Investor, Dearborn Trade, 2001

What Makes A Great Client?

My ideal client has the following characteristics...

Revenues: _____
_____
_____
_____

Assets: _____
_____
_____
_____

**Growth
Potential:** _____
_____
_____
_____

Referrals: _____
_____
_____
_____

Compatibility: _____
_____
_____
_____

Source: *Attract and Retain the Affluent Investor, Dearborn Trade, 2001*

Chapter **6**

Developing Your Managed Account Skills

Part 1: Selling the Benefits of Managed Accounts

The seven primary benefits of managed accounts and how to qualify prospects and clients.

Many years ago, a big life insurance company created a memorable commercial slogan to help brand its services: "Too busy making money to manage it?" This question resounded loudly throughout the financial services industry and many of us began asking the same question of our clients.

The answer we often hear from affluent business owners is that they can make better investment returns for themselves managing their own businesses. Why, they ask, would they trade the relative certainty – or the comfort zone – of making money in their business for the "speculation" of the stock market?

Good question.

Keep in mind that investors have different levels of interest in managing their wealth. They may wish to be more involved in the investment side but have no interest in the estate planning area, for example. Some prefer a hands-on approach, which is not particularly compatible with the managed account solution, while others enjoy a fully discretionary relationship with their advisor.

Time, control and expertise all play big roles in a business person's life. You may have clients who could probably invest on their own, but prefer to turn the job over to a professional so they can do other things with their time.

Let's explore the various benefits of selling managed accounts, beginning with an important element we all can use more of: Time.

First Benefit: Time Savings

Business people and private-practice professionals who are too busy to manage their money are great candidates for managed accounts. Typically, they are too busy running their businesses to worry about second-guessing their money manager. Remember, the managed account, for the most part, is a fully invested position with someone with whom neither you nor the client will have day-to-day contact. That kind of arm's-length relationship simply will not be attractive to some investors.

The Busier the Better

Time issues invoke control issues as well, as they tend to go hand in hand with the busy client. According to veteran consultant Erik, when he and his team migrate clients to managed accounts, they take the educational approach if clients seem hesitant. Sometimes clients want to be in control because they don't understand the process and how it works to their benefit. Once educated on the specifics, they reach a comfort level and give the advisor room to work.

Second Benefit: Access to Expertise

It is theoretically possible for clients who have time and control issues to still be considered candidates for a managed account, but only if they freely admit that their expertise is not investments. Recent markets have been terribly humbling for

Advisor Tip

Ted, an advisor in the Midwest, believes the busier the prospect, the better the prospect. Says Ted, "The business person needs to focus on his or her own company and let us manage the finances. The client must have the mentality of, 'I have other things to do and can't focus on managing my assets.'"

If clients have plenty of time to oversee their investments, to call you and discuss them, and are actively involved and interested in the market, then the time issue of managed accounts is not a benefit to them. They enjoy the process, they like the game. And they're not good prospects – move on.

many people, who may now be convinced of the value provided by professionals. When managed accounts were popularized in 1987 as a product and process for the affluent market, one of the main reasons they were so quickly embraced was because they were introduced in the aftermath of the market crash of that year to an audience looking for help.

The double whammy of the '87 stock and bond market crashes sent investors running from their own bull market success – they had enjoyed rising prices since 1982. Now investors were seeking professional management because they were convinced they did not possess the expertise necessary to manage their assets. The years 2000 and 2001 provided the same experience for many baby boomers who now dominate the affluent marketplace. According to the 2002 Phoenix Wealth Management Survey, approximately 46 percent of baby boomers became affluent in the preceding five years and more than 80 percent became affluent during the 1990s bull market. See the chart below.

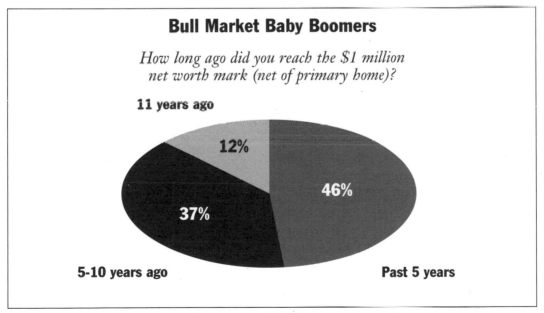

Bull Market Baby Boomers

How long ago did you reach the $1 million net worth mark (net of primary home)?

11 years ago — 12%

5-10 years ago — 37%

Past 5 years — 46%

Source: Phoenix Wealth Management Survey 2002. © The Phoenix Companies, Inc.

Personal experience with poor performance is the most significant factor in teaching many investors they don't have the expertise necessary to manage their own assets. It's the less-than-stellar performance of their account and their inability to take action that usually hits home. See the charts on the next page.

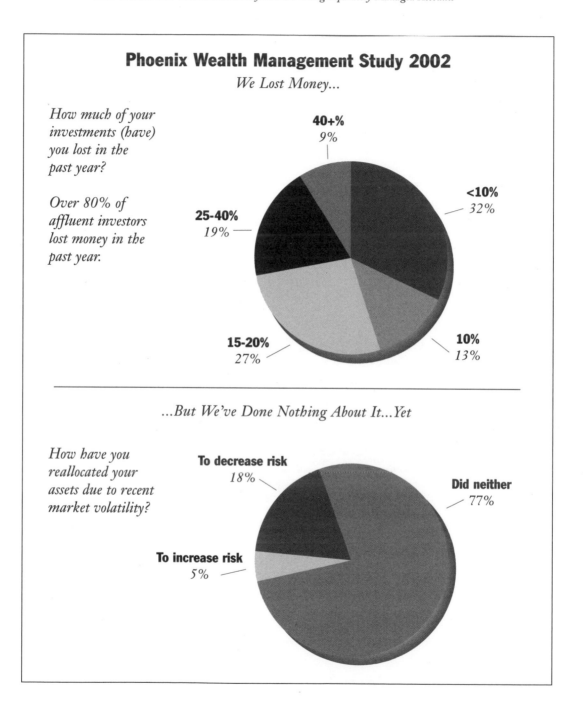

Phoenix Wealth Management Study 2002

We Lost Money...

How much of your investments (have) you lost in the past year?

Over 80% of affluent investors lost money in the past year.

40+% 9%

<10% 32%

25-40% 19%

15-20% 27%

10% 13%

...But We've Done Nothing About It...Yet

How have you reallocated your assets due to recent market volatility?

To decrease risk 18%

Did neither 77%

To increase risk 5%

Missing Clients

Another consultant we know states that among his reasons why managed accounts are best for him and his clients are time and expertise benefits. If Mike needs to reach his clients with an investment recommendation, they may be too busy to discuss it. In other words, says Mike, "I may not be able to reach my client!" With a discretionary managed account, he doesn't have to wait a day or more for a discussion and possibly miss a window of opportunity. "I don't want to be limited to my own firm's research, either. There is a tremendous amount of expertise available within an outside manager's firm, and to have that availability is a big advantage." Mike also points out two other very powerful considerations when discussing the viability of managed accounts with prospects and clients. "No one rebalances their accounts for stock splits and, in some instances, won't even do so for changes in risk tolerance. Plus you need a sell discipline and most investors don't have one."

Third Benefit: Consistency of a Process

The introspective process of the investment policy statement, the action plan of multiple manager solutions, and the ongoing monitoring and rebalancing of the portfolio – that process is superior to what individual clients can do on their own. If they don't have the time, they can't do a good job selecting stocks and deciding when they should be sold.

A key benefit of an investment process is that it avoids impulse decisions that, ultimately, can hurt performance.

One big challenge you may have is dealing with the fact that the success of the markets is limited to a small number of days in the lifetime of the market. From January 1, 1982 through March 30, 2002, there were 7,287 days. The average annual return was 11.7 percent. Without the 50 best days, the average annual return drops to 2.4 percent, which is less than the historical average return of t-bills (i.e. cash rate). See the chart on the next page.

These are the things you should explain to your clients and show how they relate to the value of a process. If you told your clients that if they had missed the market's 50 best days, they would have been just as well off in cash, you'd scare the heck out of them.

Let's think about what we are asking of the affluent investor in the example above. Since we do not know when the 50 best days are going to occur, we are asking them to have the patience and the confidence to stay fully invested over a 20-year period of time where the gains are sporadic and unknown. Essentially, we are telling them that to beat cash, they must stay in the market to catch a random collection of 50 days. On its face, this is an intellectually offensive statement to make to anyone with any degree of intelligence! The only way to convince clients to hang in there for the long term is to educate them about the benefits of staying in place and to have confidence in the process.

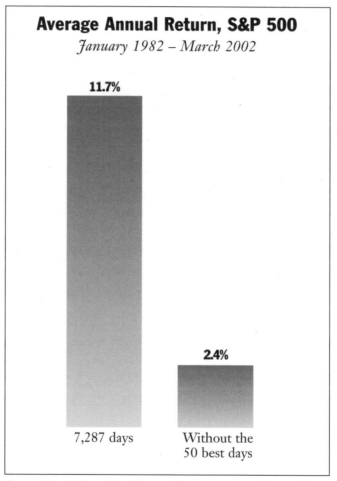

Average Annual Return, S&P 500
January 1982 – March 2002

11.7%

2.4%

7,287 days

Without the
50 best days

Source: Zweig Consulting. Past performance is not indicative of
future results.

Understand the Importance of the Process

The primary value added by a managed account is the disciplined decision-making investment process. Some of your clients may already understand that. Reaching others with that message is crucial. Chuck, an advisor who runs a large practice in the Southeast, agrees. "Investors generally can't get that discipline themselves, and they can't get it from mutual funds." He discusses the advantages of transitioning to this type of program in a letter to clients outlining the tax advantages and customization. If new clients focus too much on the fees and what the performance numbers look like, he believes they are embarking on a disastrous two-dimensional decision. "The process is the key to success. That is why managed accounts work," says Chuck.

Fourth Benefit: Finding the Right Manager

Another key benefit of the managed accounts process is the "unearthing" of managers that a prospect or client might not discover on their own. How do you find a manager? Do your clients believe they can use Morningstar's star ratings to determine who the best fund managers are? Remember, Morningstar does not call you when a manager slips in rank. The main issue is not just the initial due diligence of manager selection, but also the ongoing supervision and review.

For example, if your large cap manager drifts away from his or her style, do you take that opportunity to choose another large cap manager? While the client's account is very important to the manager, that manager has thousands of similar client accounts. If you want to keep your clients' best interests at the forefront, then you are going to watch this manager closely by monitoring the management and style. It is important for your clients to know that you are focused on protecting their investments and are taking proactive steps.

Sometimes a client might tell you he or she doesn't recognize the name(s) of a particular manager you've selected. That can be a positive benefit. The lack of household names on the manager roster is a reinforcement of the process. How? Explain to the client that your firm has discovered this manager and this particular manager doesn't manage mutual funds, so

Advisor Tip

No More Mumbo Jumbo
Says advisor Dan in New York about the process, "We cut through the mumbo jumbo and explain to our clients in plain English how the managed account process works. There is a right way and a wrong way to do managed account presentations. The right way is to position yourself, the advisor, as the cornerstone. Once you explain the process, you describe how your tools differ from others. Just because your client might have an advisor across the street at a competitor firm who uses the same manager doesn't mean that client will end up with the same results. We explain that important tax issues also can impact overall return. This type of investigative, focused interaction sets us apart with clients and gives us a tremendous edge as a firm."

they are not a big name your client might hear every day. However, the manager does advise some of the largest pension funds for major institutions.

You might use the following rationale: "What fits within your comfort level? The brand name of a mutual fund company you've read about in *Money* magazine? Or the name of a manager gleaned from the due-diligence team of a consulting firm that has billions of dollars already placed with that manager who has also been selected to run, for example, the pension fund for the state of Connecticut?"

An Unknown Manager

This question of not recognizing the manager invites comparison and education and is a very powerful selling tool.

But before you decide which manager is best for the client, you need a game plan. For example, when you build a house the first thing you need is a blueprint. You don't start hiring subcontractors right and left. If you allow these specialists in before you determine who you need, what you need, and when you need them, you're headed for disaster. Someone needs to create the blueprint and manage the process: the architect. You are the architect working with the homeowner (investor) and the subcontractors (money managers). You don't want the roofers building the kitchen or the electricians putting in the plumbing. Even if they could do it, it's not their area of expertise.

Once you've found the appropriate manager(s), talk to your client about the manager's style, time horizon, potential downside, proven principles, and how you're developing an integrated solution for your client's money management needs with this manager. Discuss the importance of not being too hasty in judging the manager on too short a time frame. Some top advisors say that the client should focus on a 10-year time horizon. And certainly most would say a client should plan to invest for at least three to five years, which would effectively take into account a market cycle (more on manager evaluation follows later in this chapter).

Fifth Benefit: No Conflict of Interest

If this is defined as how you can increase your financial gain by better serving your client, then certainly the fee-based concept eliminates this concern. The best way to increase your income over the long term is to help your client increase the value of his or her account. You both benefit.

But beware of another hidden conflict. With their fortunes tied together by the fees, an aggressive advisor and investor might select a single manager with the highest returns, not only for the potential benefit of the client, but also for the potential benefit of the advisor. This, unfortunately, unites the aggressive investor and aggressive advisor in a perilously concentrated run toward a bigger performance number that compromises the entire process. Don't be a victim. Maintain control of the process.

Conflict of interest can be more than an advisor putting personal financial gain ahead of a client's interests. It can also mean subjective decision making. Show your prospect or client how working with managed accounts eliminates conflicts of interest in the decision making process by highlighting the multiple levels of decision making. I like to call this the "Hierarchy of Expertise," which is shown graphically on the next page.

At the individual securities selection level, a professional advisor employs analysts and portfolio managers. Above them is the consulting group of the sponsoring advisor firm, e.g., Salomon Smith Barney, Morgan Stanley – another layer of professional analysts who select and provide the ongoing due diligence of the asset management firm. Then there's the expertise of the financial advisor who helps with the client's financial goals and objectives and makes the manager match. This is one powerful way to eliminate the conflict of interest that typically occurs from too much reliance on one person or on one firm's research.

Who might typically benefit from this Hierarchy of Expertise? Perhaps the clients in the following example: A married couple was being interviewed on a popular morning television talk show. The husband was smiling, happy to be on national TV. His wife looked much less enthusiastic about her appearance on the show. Sitting next to her was a financial advisor. This couple had the devastating experience of losing 70 percent of the value of their 40l(k) plan. The TV host asked the financial advisor, "They thought they were properly diversified. How could this have happened to them?" The financial advisor replied, "This is really a case of too much of a good thing. Our analysis of the six funds they own shows that 80 percent of the holdings overlapped in one sector, which was, of course, technology."

Working with a consultant or advisor on a managed account gives clients a higher level of analysis and monitoring of the investments and can avoid potentially disastrous situations. Steve, a prominent consultant on the East Coast, manages about $1.2 billion for 350 households. He explains to clients that by using external managers, he avoids conflict – although he works for an investment banking firm, his

Hierarchy of Expertise

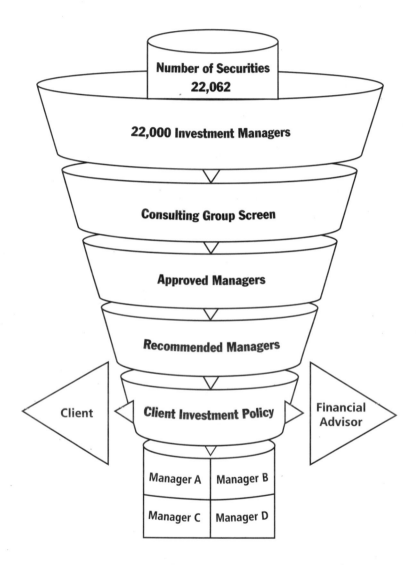

managers do not. Buy and sell decisions are based on external research, not internal. Objectivity is a key selling point and is met with a receptive ear by clients he has transitioned and by prospective ones. He simply tells clients that he relies on outside expertise – and there is plenty of it – to pick stocks and build a portfolio. The story works!

Sixth Benefit: Customization

Does your client buy off-the-rack or tailor-made clothing? One of the great benefits of the managed account process is the ability to tailor, within reason, a portfolio to the needs of your client. That customization process begins with the investment policy statement (specific needs and objectives). While it is true that the individual managers may not do anything much different for your client than they would for any other client, it is important to know which manager (or combination of managers) will create the correct mix for each of your clients.

Customization comes in a second form. This is the ability to eliminate from consideration (again, within reason and

Advisor Tip

World Series Advisor

Dan in New York uses his own custom analogy for the Hierarchy of Expertise. Says Dan, "A good discussion of the advisor as the cornerstone in the client/advisor/manager relationship centers around the structure of the New York Yankees. Here's what I say: "You, Mr. Client, are George Steinbrenner. You hire me, Joe Torre, your advisor. I don't play the game (manage the money), but I have Bernie Williams and Derek Jeter to do so. With you, Mr. Client, I can bench people, hire new people, and, ultimately, fire them. As New Yorkers, prospects like this comparison, even if it is a simplified way of explaining the process and its benefits."

without compromising the manager's mandate for managing clients at the brokerage firm) certain stocks your client might find uncomfortable to own. For example, if your client worked for IBM for 20 years, he might want that stock eliminated from the portfolio, since he already owns a considerable amount. If your client is concerned about the environment, she might want to eliminate some securities or managers that would not screen out companies that might be considered by some people to be unfriendly to the environment, like automobile manufacturers or paper companies. If your client is a pacifist, she might not want stocks or managers who invested heavily in defense, for example. If your client has specific religious beliefs, he might want to avoid companies in the gaming business. Social exclusions over the years have also involved tobacco and alcohol stocks.

A third form of customization is in the area of taxation. If your client has a taxable account, you can help him or her harvest tax losses and shelter gains in some other area. You may also be able to protect your client from wash sales. According to a study done by Prince & Associates, most high-net-worth individuals are "very" or "extremely" interested in tax management services like managing their tax liabilities to minimize current income. In addition to tax mitigation, asset protection was the second highest concern of high net worth individuals.[1]

Mike is among the many consultants who believe the tax-advantaged benefits of managed accounts can be the real value added for clients. "We control the tax ramifications and capital gains. With mutual funds, the account is not in your control. Think back to 1987 when valuable stocks were sold in fund portfolios to meet redemptions by panicking shareholders. We didn't know what they were selling. With managed money, we do."

And, Mike warns that with funds, a client's redeployment options can be limited. In other words, he says, you can't control your gains in funds, take your losses and have a truly effective personalized strategy. "Mutual funds are really a starter investment strategy. The sophisticated investor not only needs managed accounts but should also consider five to 10 percent of the portfolio in hedge funds. This type of mix will become more common in the next few years as investors and advisors become better educated about alternative asset classes."

Seventh Benefit: Prestige

Handled correctly, timely information from you and the manager(s) helps educate your clients and affords them the prestige of knowing their account is being handled by an institutional-caliber professional. You can expose your clients to an array of writings, audiotapes, market commentaries, live web site events, and meetings with the officers and portfolio managers from the management company.

Says Phoenix Investment Partners' private client group president, Jack Sharry, "Managed accounts carry a certain cachet in so many ways, and that includes higher level communication between the money manager and advisor – and, in turn, the advisor with their client. At Phoenix, in addition to visits, phone conversations and written communications, our investment consultants (wholesalers) engage in interactive dialogue with advisors through our Web site, www.phoenixinvestments.com. Using PartnersLink[SM], an Internet-based communications tool, our investment consultants in the field and those who support advisors over the phone can make presentations or share information in "real time" with advisors – or advisors and their clients if desired. We also offer a number of business development tools for advisors, both online and in hard copy. One of the more popular is *Complementary Investment Analysis*[SM], which enables the wholesalers and advisors to collaborate and create customized managed account presentations. And now, through PartnersLink[SM], we can provide this service

---

[1]*Private Asset Management online*, Institutional Investor Publications, August 2000

interactively. Of course, while technology advances are remarkable, the Web will never replace the personal contact that is essential to developing and maintaining solid, lasting relationships between wholesalers and advisors, and advisors and clients."

Qualifying Clients and Prospects for Managed Accounts

Take the time to think some more about your client base. In Chapter 3 you identified your top 10 to 20 accounts. You also considered various ways to reach more affluent, upscale clients. Now, consider which of the clients or prospects you've identified are best suited for the transition to managed accounts. Jot down names as they apply to the following points:

- Which of your clients do you believe understand the benefits of a process?

- Which of your clients make snap decisions?

- Which of your clients are prone to emotional decisions?

- Which of your clients have a sell discipline?

- Which of your clients have difficulty making a decision or take too long to decide?

- Of your clients who are in business, who have their own business plans?

- Who among your clients would disrupt the process?

- Which of your clients are goal oriented?

In addition to answering these questions, complete the "Benefits of Managed Accounts Prospect Worksheet" on page 76 to identify prospective clients who are well-suited for managed accounts.

The clients and prospects who possess the positive attributes of understanding the process, having a sell discipline, who have their own business plans and are goal oriented are logical choices for managed accounts.

Let's Get Started

Once you've effectively discussed the benefits of managed accounts with the appropriate clients, it's time to get started. The information-gathering stage is next, and we'll discuss this important step in the following section.

Benefits of Managed Accounts
Prospect Worksheet

Consider the key benefits of managed accounts and list names of clients and prospects that might be attracted to these benefits and why.

BENEFITS	NAMES	NOTES - WHY?
1. Time Savings Prospects value their time for other aspects of life		
2. Access to Expertise Prospects know they are not investment experts and need help		
3. Consistency of Process Prospects that may have many investments but no strategy		
4. Finding the Right Manager Prospects who seek the comfort of manager selection & tracking		
5. No Conflicts of Interest Business owners and prospects who value a relationship based on mutual incentives		
6. Customization Prospects seeking a personal approach and a higher level of service		
7. Prestige List clients that would be impressed by having the same investment manager as pension funds and large corporations		

Part II: Information Gathering and the IPS Questionnaire

The Investment Policy Statement is the foundation for your managed account solutions – and an excellent opportunity to build rapport with your clients.

There is no more valuable tool in the client communication process than the investment policy questionnaire. Obtaining complete information and creating a good investment policy statement (IPS) helps drive the investment solution. A much overlooked sales tool, the IPS is the foundation of client communication, and when used correctly, the process of information gathering allows the bonding between you and your prospects to begin.

The information-gathering phase is the first place you begin to distinguish yourself from other advisors. You may already be skilled at getting your prospect to feel comfortable with you in the initial information-gathering stage. Now let's focus on further refining your skills so you become more successful in your approach.

Yellow Pads Will Do

To obtain the information you need from a client, it is not necessary to work through a complex financial planning questionnaire. Many of the best advisors I know work with simple yellow pads in the beginning. My belief is that all of the support documents and questionnaires that traditionally are used in this initial information-gathering stage can be minimized. Keep them as support tools to pull out of your toolbox when you need them.

It's important to keep this first meeting as "human" as possible for as long as possible. Sometimes, questionnaires and hefty documents are construed as crutches – evidence that you are not comfortable with the process. If your prospects are experienced investors, they've been around this getting to-know-each-other track before. As consultant Leo Pusateri often says,

"Business is first a meeting of the hearts, then it becomes a meeting of the minds."[1]

While some prospects and clients are delighted to come forward and discuss personal information, others are more discreet and perhaps less forthcoming about confidential information. Before trying to learn more about the prospect, think about ways in which you can make him or her comfortable with the process.

Working with Clients - Information Gathering

The setting in which you and your prospect first meet is critical. If the individual is comfortable in the environment, it's usually easier for him or her to talk openly. A Boston advisor I know couldn't get his prospects to open up in face-to-face meetings. He said he had better luck gathering information over the phone.

Welcome to My World

But if you stepped into his office, you would understand why people were not comfortable. The advisor's office was stacked with dozens of notebooks holding client statements. When the prospective clients looked around the room and saw huge books titled A, B, and C all the way down to Z, they felt intimidated by the sheer number of clients competing for his time. Another reason: The office itself was a mess and there was activity everywhere. His staff and other advisors were running around – it was an open forum. Think about that: Would you want to sit down with your banker in a big lobby with no walls or doors and discuss personal information while applying for a home mortgage you needed? The most successful private banks provide confidential discussion areas for their best clients.

What could you do to help make your prospects and clients feel more at ease? Always ask prospective clients where they would feel most comfortable talking with you. Make sure your environment doesn't work against you. Consider the following:

Your Environment Checklist

• Where do you meet with prospective clients?

• Since the one-on-one meeting is the best possible scenario, where do you think your prospects and clients would feel most comfortable?

• Is your office quiet?

---

[1]*Mirror Mirror On The Wall Am I The Most Valued Of Them All?* Leo J. Pusateri, Financial Entrepreneur Publishing, 2001.

- Is your office private?

- Do you have evidence of client records and books lying around?

- Is your computer screen away from your line of sight?

- Do you listen only to your prospect or client, not take phone calls or allow yourself to be pulled away by other distractions?

- Try sitting where your prospects sit during a meeting with you. What do you see and what does it say about you?

Your prospects are forming an impression of you. Remember that. That's why you want to keep the focus on them. Think about how your office reflects you and your personality, work habits and values. You don't want an excessive amount of decoration or luxury that would distract your prospects. If you were a client, how would you react? Be objective. Have a good friend, spouse or manager view your office and solicit their opinions about what it says about you.

Positioning

Our industry battles the perception held by many investors that advisors will accept anyone as a client. That's simply not true. The most successful advisors start out by determining (with the client) whether they are a good fit for each other. And that begins with the initial interview. What is your goal for an initial interview? It's not so important that you get your points across – you can do that later, after you establish a bond with the prospect. Expect to talk about yourself and do a lot of explaining about your background. Keep in mind that you need to spend a significant chunk of time with your prospect during that initial interview just establishing that bond and getting to know him or her better. Chuck tells us he always spends at least two hours with a prospect in the first meeting.

Profiling Marathon

Keats agrees with Chuck about spending as much time as you need to get to know your prospect. Says Keats, "The process of uncovering if the client will, in fact,

Banking On Success

David in the Ft. Lauderdale area sent his decorator to several private banks and asked her to duplicate that "feel" for his office in a wirehouse branch. The result is an effective blend of rich furnishings and high technology that represents confidence and achievement. Family photos are mixed with interesting trinkets – all inviting a view of the advisor that makes prospective clients feel he has already shared something personal about himself.

delegate really begins at the profiling stage in the first meeting. This should be the longest meeting you have. Many advisors take 40 minutes profiling and two hours offering solutions. We do the reverse – two hours of profiling, several days working through scenarios and proposal development, and then we have a brief meeting to present solutions and alternatives to the client. The concept is to get beyond the data gathering to the core attitudes. Can this person delegate philosophically? Ask the client, 'Do you like this idea/concept?' Find out how he or she delegates in his or her own business. Ask, 'Is there is a dollar amount that will allow you to maintain your lifestyle? What help do your children need to reach their goals? Here is your life as it is today. What do you want it to look like in 30 years?' Those are the kinds of questions that need to be asked. Get the big picture first, dig in to the details, and talk about who will manage the money later. A logical, disciplined approach to uncovering core values in the client generates trust – only then will he or she delegate. This is not an easy process, but it works.

Remember, some prospects hire you as a result of a bad experience with someone else – such as that of the 2000-2001 markets. Whether they've admitted that upfront or not, it is one of the most important subjects to get out in the open as soon as possible. I suggest a very simple dialogue, something like this: "Mr. Montgomery, we've been through a terribly difficult market over the past two years. What have you been doing during that time? How have you fared?"

After the double-down of 2000-2001, many investors were not angry; they were in despair. One of the first things they needed to do is just talk about the experience. No matter the situation, your prospects must be able to speak openly about their investing past. It is the first step on the road to recovery. In many cases, this candor is the first opportunity to differentiate yourself from other advisors. These types of conversations are not dependent upon questionnaires or financial planning documents, as we mentioned. Try to connect personally with your prospects and keep track of what your prospects are uncomfortable revealing in the way of personal or financial information. Take notes. What are their primary concerns – and fears?

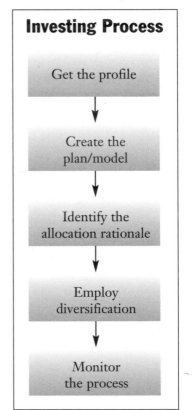

Investing Process

Get the profile

↓

Create the plan/model

↓

Identify the allocation rationale

↓

Employ diversification

↓

Monitor the process

Sharing is Bonding

One of the traits shared by many affluent investors is they have an extraordinary ability to judge people. Whether they've been in sales, created products or built a team, the affluent really know how to size people up. Chemistry develops fast and you can achieve rapport – or not. I'll bet you landed your best clients because of the "click" between you – not because you had the best presentation book. Remember Leo Pusateri's words: "Business is first a meeting of the hearts, then a meeting of the minds." Rapport is the first phase of the relationship.

Interviewing Prospects

Affluent clients are almost always referrals, and your first meeting with a referral is the most important. Within the broad category of "referrals" are major differences. Consider how an initial information-gathering session might unfold:

1. **The Fan**. A prospect comes to your office and already has a good sense of who you are and what you do. This is the ideal referral – he or she's come to you and considers you the expert.

2. **The Skeptic**. A prospect visits you and asks what you do and how you do it. This is the "show me, prove-to-me" type of individual who needs more information right away. This person is less likely to be a good prospect because, many times, he or she is too critical. You should treat these individuals with care, though, because they could be the "walking wounded." Perhaps they were beaten up in the recent bad markets and feel so uncomfortable that they just don't know whom to trust.

3. **The Evaluator**. This type of prospect is comfortable with a little more give-and-take with you, more conversation and more two-way sharing of information. This person is honestly searching for a new advisor.

Reality Checking

Ted, a well-known advisor in his town, says, "Most of our clients are very sophisticated and place a tremendous amount of trust in our guidance. When bringing a new client on board, one of the questions we always like to ask is, 'If you give me $1 million and it quickly becomes $750,000, what will you do? Will it affect your lifestyle? How will you feel?' The purpose of this is to really qualify client sensitivity to market variance and make sure we have the right relationship. It also injects reality into the process."

During this phase of the interview, it's likely you'll take mental notes of how this prospect is similar or dissimilar to those clients already on your books. Beware of those who are too unlike the individuals with whom you currently work. How many different kinds of personalities, temperaments and egos can you effectively serve? Ross Levin of Accredited Investors in Minnesota says, "One difficult client can take more of your time than 10 good ones. That's why you also need to be proactive in determining whether the prospect is a good fit for you as well. A bad client relationship will only deteriorate and cause you grief later on."

Uncovering your client's goals is crucial. Ask your prospect what her investment goals are and discuss, specifically, a dollar amount that would make her feel secure financially. According to the Phoenix Wealth Management Survey 2002, approximately 58 percent of the survey respondents said they would feel wealthy only if they had $5 million or more. Three-fourths of them said they'd need to have $3 million. And ultimately, what is your clients' most important financial goal? Maintaining their standard of living in retirement. According to a study by Spectrem Group, over 80 percent of high-net-worth individuals said "assuring a comfortable retirement" was their most important financial goal.[2] Quality of life is expensive.

Robert W. Fiondella, chairman and chief executive officer of The Phoenix Companies, Inc., says changing demographics and the aging of the U.S. population will drive demand for innovative service in the wealth management arena. Fiondella, the chair of the American Council of Life Insurer's (ACLI) CEO Retirement Security Steering Committee, has spent the past decade developing solutions to address pressures affluent and aging Baby Boomers face in accumulating enough wealth to maintain their lifestyles.

"These investors know the future of Social Security is less than certain and that their retirements may last 30 years or longer," Fiondella says. "Add that dynamic to the coming transfer of wealth between generations – where projections show between $40 and $136 trillion will change hands over the next 50 years – and it's clear they need advice and counsel. Developing the right plan for distributing income is key," Fiondella says.

To help you determine the type of services and products your prospects and clients need, take a look at the Wealth Management Picture.

Review all of the areas and discuss with your prospects and clients the ones of greatest

---

[2] 2000 Affluent Market Research Program, Spectrem Group

concern to them right now. Talk about how you plan to deliver solutions to those issues. During the interview process, you'll soon discover the state of their financial health, using this chart as a blueprint for building a financial solution.

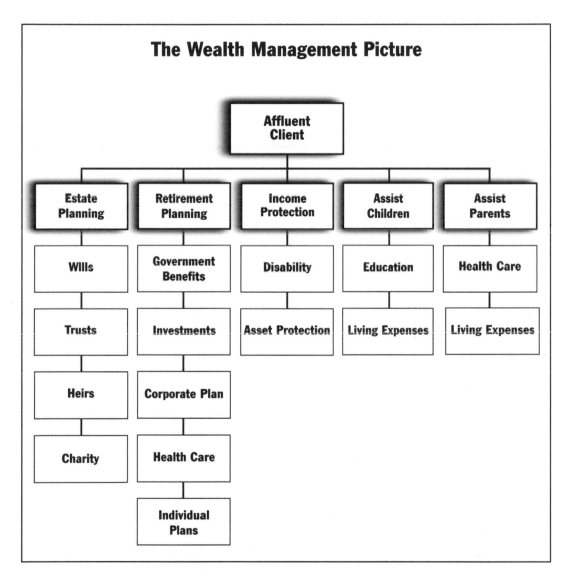

The Wealth Management Picture

- Affluent Client
  - Estate Planning
    - Wills
    - Trusts
    - Heirs
    - Charity
  - Retirement Planning
    - Government Benefits
    - Investments
    - Corporate Plan
    - Health Care
    - Individual Plans
  - Income Protection
    - Disability
    - Asset Protection
  - Assist Children
    - Education
    - Living Expenses
  - Assist Parents
    - Health Care
    - Living Expenses

Estate Planning Questions

- Do you have a will? When was it last updated?

- What's the primary goal of your estate plan? Avoiding taxes? Providing for your family? Charitable giving?

- Do you have a living will?

- Do you have a durable power of attorney in the event you can't be reached or can't make decisions?

- Who are the principal beneficiaries of your estate?

- Do you have guardians for your children? Trustees for the estate?

- Do you own life insurance? What kind? How much? Who are the beneficiaries?

- Do you own life insurance directly or is it in a trust?

- Do you have enough life insurance? Why do you think so?

- Do you have a business? What is the business worth? Are your key employees adequately provided for? Would you consider adding executive benefits to their packages?

- What kind of succession plan do you have for your business?

- How would you fund the succession plan?

- Do you have any kind of buy/sell agreement for your business with partners or potential successors? Is it up to date? Is it adequate?

Retirement Planning Questions

- What is your retirement package worth?

- How much of your net worth is tied up in retirement assets?

- Who are the designated beneficiaries of your retirement package?

- Did you know that you could "stretch" the tax-deferral benefits of your IRA over a number of generations?

- Did you know that you could "convert" some of your excess retirement funds to an income tax-free asset?

- Do you think your current asset allocation matches your investment needs? When did you last look it over? When did you last make changes?

- What is your plan for retirement? When? Where? What do you hope to do?

- What kind of retirement plans do you have? What are the assets? How are they invested? Are you confident you have enough resources set aside for retirement income? How much do you think you'll need?

- Do you control the asset allocation and investment decisions for your retirement assets? Who helps you? Do you need more help? What kind of help would be the most beneficial? Are you on track to reach your investment goals for retirement?

- Do you own long-term care insurance? Do you think you need it?

- Do you know when you're eligible to draw money from your retirement plans? From which account would you first draw income? Last? Do you own any annuities?

- What does your employer or your company contribute to your retirement plan? Are you vested?

- Have you calculated your expected income from Social Security? How about your benefits from Medicare?

Income Protection Questions

- How will your family survive if your income is cut off by an untimely death?

- How would a disability affect your income? Do you have disability insurance of any kind? How much? When do the benefits begin after a disability? What is the maximum monthly check and how long would you be eligible?

- Do you own personal liability coverage? Are you confident you have adequate coverage for yourself, your family, your business? Have you ever been sued?

- Does your business have adequate protection against lawsuits for sexual harassment, product liability, workman's compensation claims?

Assisting Children Questions

- Do you have children? How many? Ages? Names? Plans for more? Are any of the children from other marriages?

- What are the schooling plans for the kids? How much will it cost? How have you provided financially for those needs?

- Do your children participate in saving or investing? Do they have accounts of their own? Roth IRAs? UGMA accounts? 529 plans?

- What about living expenses for the kids? If your kids are grown, do you provide any financial assistance? How? Do you expect that support to grow/stay the same/decline?

- Do you have any grandchildren? How are you assisting them today? In the future?

- Do your children have "special needs" because of a physical or mental reason? Did you know that without adequate planning, they could lose all of their federal and state assistance?

Assisting Parents Questions

- Are your parents living? Grandparents? Ages? How is the health of each? Where do they live? Any medical history to be concerned about? What kind? Are you providing any care?

- How will your parents provide for their expenses in retirement? How about medical care? Do they own long-term care insurance?

- Are you providing care for any older relatives or friends? How long have you been doing so?

- Are there any other relatives or friends for whom you might one day be responsible? When? In what way(s)? How will you manage those responsibilities?

- Do your parents have a will? Have they completed their estate plan?

- How will their estate plan impact your plan?

Ask to See the Big Picture

To do the best possible job for your prospective client, it's important to uncover where additional assets are held. Ask whether he or she has other advisors. Explain that you need to know so you don't duplicate their work. This is a tricky topic and may require a bit more skill in questioning, but the issue is becoming increasingly common among top advisors. In the Phoenix Wealth Management Survey 2002 of high-net-worth investors, 81 percent of those that were interested in having a primary advisor said they would be very comfortable sharing personal financial information with their advisor.

One of the reasons some financial advisors fail to understand their clients is because they are afraid to ask the toughest questions up front. For example, how much money do you *really* make? What is your entire financial situation? Where do you keep all of your assets? One thing that advisor Mike likes to do in the initial questioning process is to get "yes" answers three or four times to relatively straightforward questions and then to inject a hard one, such as a person's real income level. This is not an attempt to trick anyone, but to set the right mood for getting accurate information that is extremely valuable. And asking in a direct, professional manner increases the chance you'll get a truthful response.

Aggregation – It's the Future

Another area to confront is the dynamic between account information aggregation and the client's need to keep some information private and away from certain advisors. Schwab has done considerable focus work over the years about the attitude

> **Advisor Tip**
>
> **Binding With Clients**
> John, an advisor in Louisville, gives his clients a three-ring binder with various sections devoted to different wealth management topics, such as estate planning. He then asks to review it periodically. When he does, he often discovers additional statements and the names of other advisors. Rather than be offended by the disclosure, John congratulates the client for addressing the issue. He then might ask for more information about the other advisor's solution.

investors have of their advisors. Investors in one focus group were asked whether they had all of their assets with their Schwab advisors. They laughed. They couldn't contemplate putting all of their eggs in one basket. But, in fact, they could benefit enormously from aggregating the information to make it easy for them to make overall decisions. Distinguish between your clients' needs for convenience versus their concerns about confidentiality.

Jon, a successful advisor, created an excellent method of uncovering his clients' assets. He is a big advocate of the comprehensive client reporting process (consolidated statements) and believes that this is the only way to gauge what a client really has under the hood and what to do with it. In fact, in 1985, when Jon was with a major wirehouse, he was creating consolidated statements himself on computer. "A lot of people didn't even know how to use a computer in 1985. I'd ask my clients for copies of the statements for their 'away' accounts so I knew what they had. No one was doing this. Put all of the holdings on one page, value it, put their name on it, send a personalized letter and guess what? You've got a way to capture more assets!" Today, some advisors still don't make it easy. They don't even ask what the client has with another firm! "How can you possibly expect to implement an asset allocation plan when you don't know who has the money?" says Jon, who looks at himself as a quasi-owner of his clients' assets. He prides himself that he has 86 percent of his clients' known liquid assets.

Says veteran advisor Gary about uncovering assets, "The first part of this process involves capturing as much information about the client as possible. We need to know exactly what he or she has with another advisor. If the client brings us $5 million and the overall portfolio is worth $20 million, we need to know all of the other holdings and who has them, otherwise, we won't accept the account. We want to complement what the other managers are doing."

Financial planner Lewis in Georgia agrees with Gary. If he discovers that a client has assets elsewhere, he will ask for copies of their statements from the other firms. For example: He has a $1.5 million client and knows that the client has over $1 million with another advisor. He asked to see what was in the other portfolio – not to replace the other firm, but to develop a balanced style with the other portfolio. The client had copies of the statements sent to him.

The most successful advisors simply will not move forward with a prospect or client until they have all of the necessary information from the individual. That posture sends a message to clients that the advisors are not willing to risk exposing themselves in the form of giving bad or incomplete advice. The not-so-subtle message to the investor is, "If you are willing to work with an advisor who won't ask these same questions, you're not working with a professional."

Top advisors use the following tactics to help get more information from clients and prospects:

1. "To do our best job, we need to see your total financial picture. Please provide us with copies of your other account statements."

2. "If we were to buy a stock for you that had recently been sold by another of your advisors, did you know you would still be liable for the tax consequences under the wash sale?"

3. "We give you advice based on our knowledge that these are all the assets you have exposed to equities. If you have more, then we are committing financial malpractice."

All Financial Journeys Begin with the Information Road Map

The information-gathering process actually becomes the formal declaration of account guidelines. Once you understand the overall needs and concerns of the investor, you lock down the parameters used to select managers. Prematurely recommending the managed account is one of the pitfalls of selling to affluent investors. **It's good to remember that the managed account is only a funding strategy**. If you haven't first determined the client's wealth issues, then you won't have a clear idea of how – and in which vehicles – his or her wealth should be invested.

Part III: Presenting the Solution and the Process

The managed account solution is the first step in a process that will evolve to match both the dynamic markets and the changing needs of your clients.

When you have successfully obtained the signature on a new managed account document, you quickly realize this is just the beginning of a long-term relationship with your client. It's not the end of the sale, it's the beginning. Your client is looking to you for guidance and supervision, as well as for the protection and growth of his or her assets. Most importantly, the client has a goal for those assets and you need to understand that goal.

Styles – In Fashion and Out

Reaching those important goals requires a plan and a process. It's important to promote the concept of investment process and to maintain a disciplined investment approach throughout the relationship. Avoid the pitfalls faced by advisors who did not heed their own mandates for process. In particular, recognize the benefits of owning a variety of styles and market capitalizations. "Historically, no one has been able to predict when growth and value go in and out of favor," says Ed Friderici, vice president of marketing at Phoenix Investment Partners. "Nevertheless, one can predict that growth and value will always trade leadership," he says. "Look at the graph on the next page. In 1999, we saw growth outperform value by over 25 percent. In 2000, we witnessed a whipsaw effect with value outperforming growth by almost 30 percent – the largest disparity ever. The lesson here? Diversification never goes out of style."

The leadership change in style can also be a signal to rebalance your client's portfolio. On the next page, I've highlighted several types of rebalancing options to consider. The successful advisor creates a disciplined investment process in an environment where performance-chasing investors have been undisciplined.

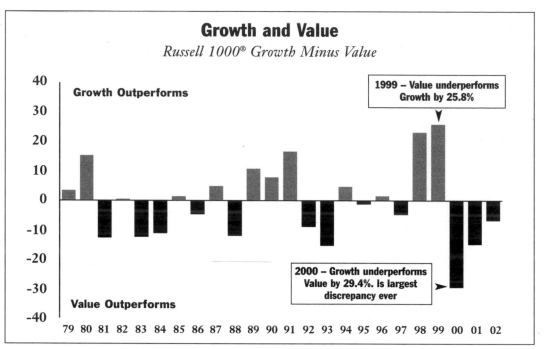

Growth and Value
Russell 1000® Growth Minus Value

Growth Outperforms

1999 – Value underperforms Growth by 25.8%

2000 – Growth underperforms Value by 29.4%. Is largest discrepancy ever

Value Outperforms

79 80 81 82 83 84 85 86 87 88 89 90 91 92 93 94 95 96 97 98 99 00 01 02

Source: Frank Russell Co. 1/1/79-3/31/02. Past performance is not indicative of future results.

Types of Rebalancing

Periodic	monthly, quarterly or annually
Threshold	percentage-based move from target, such as +10%
Range	adjusted back to limits of range rather than target allocation
Volatility-based	range based on expected volatility, *i.e. small caps might have wider range than large caps*
Active	as needed based on market conditions

As we've discussed in earlier chapters, allowing the client to invest in only one manager also can represent potential "financial malpractice." Many clients, through no fault of their own, end up with a single manager, believing this is the right strategy. Advisors who allow this to happen could be asking for trouble. Market leadership changes all the time. See the *Elements of Diversification* chart on pages 96 and 97.

Says veteran advisor Steve of the use of multiple managers, "Engaging a minimum of two managers is crucial – you must have more than one investment style so you don't get backed into a corner. If a client does not have at least $100,000 to invest with each of two managers, I'll use mutual funds as a temporary alternative."

One of the most compelling tools I've ever seen to help educate investors – and their advisors – about the dangers of a single market segment is the *Elements of Diversification* chart that you just looked at on page 96. This graph clearly illustrates the changing market leadership among asset classes and styles. In addition, the chart's reverse side (page 97) depicts the changing leadership of market sectors and is a great visual to help your clients understand the value of multiple managers in their portfolios.

A successful investment solution is a complete solution. It's quite possible your client might have several other relationships with other brokerage firms and other asset managers, leading the client to believe that he is fully diversified. However, if you don't have that information, you can't be sure. It's unacceptable for you to take the risk that your client fully understands the need for diversification. If you haven't created your own multi-manager solutions, now is the time to do so. Liz Christian, senior vice president, investment consultant for Phoenix's Private Client Group, uses a value-added tool to help advisors with manager diversification. The *Complementary Investment Analysis*^{SM} (CIA) was developed by Phoenix to model multi-manager solutions. Says Liz, "Many of the advisors we work with already have a very good understanding of the correlation among managers in their firm's consulting program. Nevertheless, we see situations where an advisor either has too few managers – that would not provide proper diversification – or they are overweighted in a certain area of the market – like growth. I usually walk them through how important proper diversification is by showing them our *Elements of Diversification* chart, which illustrates just how fast leadership changes year after year.

"I usually offer two versions of a manager proposal (CIA): one that includes managers they currently are working with, and the other that includes a more diversified model. I make sure to ask the advisor about the client's risk tolerance before suggesting any managers. Providing two proposals allows the advisor to see both versions back to back with the results over a defined period of time. It usually is very clear that the more diversified portfolio is better able to sustain the volatility of the marketplace over time."

Liz continues, "Multi-manager modeling helps the advisor demonstrate to new clients how under- or over-diversified or under- or over-weighted in certain sectors of the markets they might be. The CIA process has been a very effective way to remind the advisors and the clients how important it is to remain properly diversified, not only in sectors of the market, but also in value and growth." Take a look at sample pages from a *Complementary Investment Analysis* on pages 98 and 99.

Industry data indicates that over 30 percent of all accounts offered by managed account sponsor firms have only one manager. One wirehouse sponsor reports that more than 50 percent of its clients in its managed account program have only one advisor. That is simply not a good idea. Here's a good way to explain the risk to your client: "You may believe you're diversified, but you're not. We need to make sure you recognize the problems you may have from being too concentrated with a single manager." Educate clients about leadership changes in the market.

Product Neutral

It's important to use the flexibility of creating multiple manager solutions, not just out of separately managed accounts, but also combined with mutual funds. The first priority of a good consultant is the integrity of the investment process.

You don't have to discriminate among separately managed accounts, mutual fund managed accounts, and mutual fund marketplaces because as long as you obtain the investment solution for your client, the products are irrelevant. John McCormack, senior vice president, investment consultant for Phoenix Investment Partners, recommends using separately managed accounts in conjunction with mutual funds if it makes sense for the client. "Managed money comes in many different flavors," he says. "For many, the definition of professional management is mutual funds. For the high net worth, it's separately managed accounts. In some instances, the best customization is both. Let's say a client has $300,000 to invest. He or she might consider $100,000 in a large cap growth managed account, $100,000 in a large cap value managed account and the rest allocated among four or five funds with other styles to ensure diversification. It's not all or none and it's not either or – an effective solution can really be a blend of products."

Don't be in a rush to become an annuitized fee-based advisor. Your most important responsibility is to the underlying investment integrity of your solutions.

Opportunity to Educate

One of the real challenges for advisors today is grandiose client expectations. As I write in mid-2002, we have been blistered by the 2000-2001 double down. But despite that shakeout, most affluent investors got started in the heady bull market that began in August 1982. Affluent investor demographics show that 94 percent acquired their wealth during the bull.[1] The market was propelled by increasingly great expectations as investors rushed the market seeking their share of the heady gains. That is perhaps the greatest challenge you face as an advisor – knowing that investors' expectations are still quite high. Talk to your clients about the fact that emotions can cost them money and discipline can help them make money.

Unable to Act

According to a study conducted in October 2001 by Opinion Research Corporation, 80 percent of affluent investors (with investable assets of over $100,000) surveyed soon after the events of September 11, 2001, forecasted an average annual return of 13.5 percent in the financial markets over the next ten years. Another survey of high-net-worth investors (with a net worth of $1 million or more) reported that they felt "the worst was over" for the economy in the next five years.[2] Over three-quarters of these high-net-worth investors were maintaining their existing investment portfolio despite the market volatility – 77 percent in September 2001 versus 65 percent in June 2001. Five percent of the respondents in both June and September planned to reallocate for increased risk – to take advantage of lower prices. Among the remaining respondents, those in September were less likely to reallocate their investments for decreased risk – 18 percent in September versus 30 percent in June. Conclusion: Most investors were paralyzed and didn't know what to do. So they did nothing and missed the bounce off the bottom when the markets turned up.

The bursting tech bubble and the 2000-2001 disaster of large cap growth stocks have taught clients a valuable lesson about risk – a lesson needed to make clients focus and seek a process. Be aware, however, that many investors are still basically optimistic that a lot of the gains will continue, albeit in reduced form. To get investors back into action, you need to educate them about the opportunity and then show them the process by which you will exploit the opportunity. Education is the first step. Educating investors is itself a process of establishing realistic expectations. Not a simple task!

Reality Bites

One successful advisor and branch manager we know in Fort Lauderdale, Florida,

---

[1] 2002 Phoenix Wealth Management Survey, conducted in March 2002 by Harris Interactive℠, ©The Phoenix Companies, Inc.

[2] Ibid

takes the annual returns of an individual manager, shows them to clients, and says, "Let's talk about what happened in the market in 1981." He shows them every single year of the individual manager's track record. He shows them when the manager was down, and up, even in the quarters. Instead of talking to the clients in terms of percentage drops, he talks in terms of dollars. "Your clients may say they can handle a drop of 10 percent," he says, "but how would they feel about a drop of $50,000, for example?" And, when discussing the amount of the investment, don't talk about a hypothetical $500,000 – use the actual account balance they place with the managers so everything is discussed in real terms. You might say to your clients, "Here's your account value, based on what would have happened had we hired Manager X in 1981. At that time your account would have been worth $500,000. Six months later, the market had fallen eight percent and your account would have declined to $460,000. How would you have felt? Let's talk about what would have happened if you had been with only that one manager in 2000 or 2001." Show the pain as well as the gain. That 12 percent annualized five-year return looks good on paper, but the actual experience was more bumpy.

This modeling strategy makes the scenario real. It's a good idea to portray the scenario using the actual dollar amount the client wants to invest. Use this approach to fully illustrate the benefits of a multi-manager process. Model the returns of complementary managers to show what might have happened to illustrate the benefits of diversification.

Reality Check

With realistic client expectations now more firmly in place, it is appropriate to ask your client whether he or she should reconsider the answers to your investment questionnaire. The questionnaire, which gathers the details needed for the investment policy statement, should not be a one-time document. Regular review of the questionnaire and investment policy statement is no different than going to the dentist for a six-month checkup. You still have all the same teeth, and you may not need any new dental work, but it's still wise to schedule periodic checkups.

After you and your client complete the questionnaire and formulate the investment policy statement, you should discuss several managers you feel are compatible with the client's goals. You've chosen three. Your client might counter, "You've just given me the names of three professional money managers. I don't know any of them, and I've never heard of them." Here is another opportunity to discuss your process of evaluating and choosing managers from the expanding universe of professionals managing money today.

We know a successful advisor who used the Tech Wreck in 2000-2001 and the events of September 11, 2001, to trigger discussions among all of his managed account clients. "It's appropriate in this market environment for us to look at your original questionnaire and investment policy statement," he told his clients, "and let's talk about potential changes we might make and explore the possibility of getting you into the market in a more aggressive posture to take advantage of the drops." He told his clients that while the original questionnaire helped form the blueprint for an investment solution, that solution requires occasional "maintenance." That maintenance process can include rebalancing the portfolio – or no action at all. But suggesting a review will reinforce your relationship with clients.

Regardless of whether you actively rebalance your accounts, market dips and bounces provide opportunities to reinforce your value as a consultant (see chart below).

Past performance is not indicative of future results.

By providing a course of action – or inaction, if appropriate – you remind clients that you are watching the markets, as are the chosen managers. The extra layer of supervision provided by you and your firm is comforting to your clients.

Let's now broaden our view of the client relationship and examine the all-important review process.

Investing Essentials™

Elements of Diversification

Market leadership changes dramatically from year to year — and predicting the next winning style is impossible. That's why a strategy that includes a variety of investment styles and asset classes makes sense for most portfolios. Diversification increases the likelihood that you'll capture the best the market has to offer while lowering overall portfolio volatility. **Your best bet? Diversification.**

BEST ◄————————► WORST

	1987	1988	1989	1990	1991	1992	1993	1994	1995	1996	1997	1998	1999	2000	2001	2002*
BEST	Int'l 24.6	Int'l 28.3	Large-Cap Growth 35.9	Fixed Income 9.0	Small-Cap 46.1	Small-Cap 18.4	Int'l 32.6	Int'l 7.8	Large-Cap Value 38.4	Large-Cap Growth 23.1	Large-Cap Value 33.2	Large-Cap Growth 38.7	Large-Cap Growth 33.2	Fixed Income 11.6	Fixed Income 8.4	Fixed Income 3.8
	Large-Cap Growth 5.3	Small-Cap 24.9	S&P 500 31.7	Large-Cap Growth -0.3	Mid-Cap 41.5	Mid-Cap 16.3	Small-Cap 18.9	Large-Cap Growth 2.7	S&P 500 37.5	S&P 500 23.0	S&P 500 33.4	S&P 500 28.6	Int'l 27.3	Mid-Cap 8.2	Small-Cap 2.5	Int'l -1.3
	S&P 500 5.3	Large-Cap Value 23.2	Mid-Cap 26.3	S&P 500 -3.1	Large-Cap Growth 41.2	Large-Cap Value 13.8	Large-Cap Value 18.1	S&P 500 1.3	Large-Cap Growth 37.2	Large-Cap Value 21.6	Large-Cap Growth 30.5	Int'l 20.0	Small-Cap 21.3	Large-Cap Value 7.0	Large-Cap Value -5.6	Small-Cap -4.7
	Fixed Income 2.8	Mid-Cap 19.8	Large-Cap Value 25.2	Large-Cap Value -8.1	S&P 500 30.5	S&P 500 7.6	Mid-Cap 14.3	Small-Cap -1.8	Mid-Cap 34.5	Mid-Cap 19.0	Mid-Cap 29.0	Large-Cap Value 15.6	S&P 500 21.1	Small-Cap -3.0	Mid-Cap -5.6	Large-Cap Value -4.8
	Large-Cap Value 0.5	S&P 500 16.6	Small-Cap 16.2	Mid-Cap -11.5	Large-Cap Value 24.6	Fixed Income 7.4	S&P 500 10.1	Large-Cap Value -2.0	Small-Cap 28.4	Small-Cap 16.5	Small-Cap 22.4	Mid-Cap 10.1	Mid-Cap 18.2	S&P 500 -9.2	S&P 500 -11.9	Mid-Cap -5.7
	Mid-Cap 0.2	Large-Cap Growth 11.3	Fixed Income 14.5	Small-Cap -19.5	Fixed Income 16.0	Large-Cap Growth 5.0	Fixed Income 9.8	Mid-Cap -2.1	Fixed Income 18.5	Int'l 6.1	Fixed Income 9.7	Fixed Income 8.7	Large-Cap Value 7.4	Int'l -14.0	Large-Cap Growth -20.4	S&P 500 -13.4
WORST	Small-Cap -8.8	Fixed Income 7.9	Int'l 10.5	Int'l -23.5	Int'l 12.1	Int'l -12.2	Large-Cap Growth 2.9	Fixed Income -2.9	Int'l 11.2	Fixed Income 3.6	Int'l 1.8	Small-Cap -2.6	Fixed Income -0.8	Large-Cap Growth -22.4	Int'l -21.2	Large-Cap Growth -20.8

* Year-to-date figures as of June 30, 2002.

The above table is presented for informational purposes only and is not meant to represent the performance of any Phoenix product. Past performance is not indicative of future results.

International is represented by the MSCI EAFE® (Morgan Stanley, Capital International Europe, Australasia, Far East) Index: An arithmetic, market value-weighted average of the performance of over 900 securities listed on the stock exchanges of several developed markets around the world.

Fixed Income is represented by the Lehman Brothers Aggregate Bond Index: Measures broad bond market performance.

Small-Cap is represented by the Russell 2000® Index: Consists of the smallest 2000 companies in the Russell 3000® Index, representing approximately 11% of the Russell 3000 total market capitalization.

International investing involves added risks such as currency fluctuation, less public disclosure, as well as economic and political risks. Equity securities tend to be most volatile, while fixed-income securities offer a fixed rate of return.

Mid-Cap is represented by the Russell Midcap® Index: Consists of the smallest 800 securities in the Russell 1000® Index, as ranked by total market capitalization, representing approximately 35% of the Russell 1000® Index total market capitalization.

Large-Cap Growth is represented by the Russell 1000® Growth Index: Contains those securities in the Russell 1000® Index with a greater-than-average growth orientation.

Large-Cap Value is represented by the Russell 1000® Value Index: Contains those securities in the Russell 1000® Index with a less-than-average growth orientation.

S&P 500 is a capitalization-weighted benchmark that tracks broad-based changes in the U.S. stock market. The index consists of 500 stocks chosen for market size, liquidity and industry group representation.

Performance of all cited indices is calculated on a total-return basis with dividends reinvested, as reported by Frank Russell Company. Indices are unmanaged and not available for direct investment.

PHOENIX INVESTMENT PARTNERS
Committed to Investor Success℠

1-800-243-4361

www.PhoenixInvestments.com

Sector Leadership *Also* Changes Dramatically From Year to Year

- Every market sector, from technology to health care, has its time in the spotlight, but no one sector can claim the spotlight all the time.

- That's why diversification is key. Balancing your investments across a broad number of sectors can help cushion against big swings in one group or another.

- Phoenix Investment Partners' investment managers invest across a variety of sectors for true diversification.

BEST ← → WORST

1995	1996	1997	1998	1999	2000	2001	2002*
Health Care 54.5%	Information Technology 43.3%	Financials 45.4%	Information Technology 77.6%	Information Technology 78.4%	Utilities 51.7%	Consumer Discretionary 2.0%	Materials 8.7%
Financials 49.6%	Financials 31.9%	Health Care 41.7%	Telecomm. Services 49.3%	Consumer Discretionary 24.1%	Health Care 35.5%	Materials 1.0%	Consumer Staples 5.7%
Information Technology 38.8%	Consumer Staples 23.2%	Telecomm Services 37.1%	Health Care 42.3%	Materials 23.0%	Financials 23.4%	Industrials -7.0%	Energy 4.2%
Telecomm. Services 37.3%	Industrials 22.7%	Consumer Discretionary 32.3%	Consumer Discretionary 39.6%	Industrials 19.9%	Consumer Staples 14.5%	Consumer Staples -8.3%	Financials -4.2%
Consumer Staples 36.2%	Energy 21.7%	Consumer Staples 30.5%	Consumer Staples 13.9%	Telecomm. Services 17.4%	Energy 13.2%	Financials -10.5%	Consumer Discretionary -9.8%
Industrials 35.9%	Health Care 18.8%	Information Technology 28.1%	Utilities 10.0%	Energy 16.3%	Industrials 4.5%	Energy -12.3%	Utilities -14.2%
Energy 26.0%	Materials 13.4%	Industrials 25.3%	Financials 9.6%	Financials 2.3%	Materials -17.7%	Health Care -12.9%	Industrials -15.4%
Utilities 25.2%	Consumer Discretionary 10.5%	Energy 22.6%	Industrials 9.3%	Health Care -11.5%	Consumer Discretionary -20.7%	Telecomm. Services -13.7%	Health Care -16.7%
Consumer Discretionary 18.2%	Utilities 0.2%	Utilities 18.6%	Energy -2.0%	Utilities -12.8%	Telecomm. Services -39.7%	Information Technology -26.0%	Information Technology -31.5%
Materials 17.3%	Telecomm. Services -2.2%	Materials 6.3%	Materials -8.0%	Consumer Staples -16.6%	Information Technology -41.0%	Utilities -32.5%	Telecomm. Services -34.7%

Source: Phoenix/Zweig Advisers LLC. FactSet.
*Year-to-date figures as of June 30, 2002.

The above table is presented for informational purposes only and is not meant to represent the performance of any Phoenix product. These sectors are not available for direct investment. Past performance is not indicative of future results.

Distributed by Phoenix Equity Planning Corporation, member NASD and subsidiary of Phoenix Investment Partners, Ltd.

PHOENIX INVESTMENT PARTNERS
A member of The Phoenix Companies, Inc.

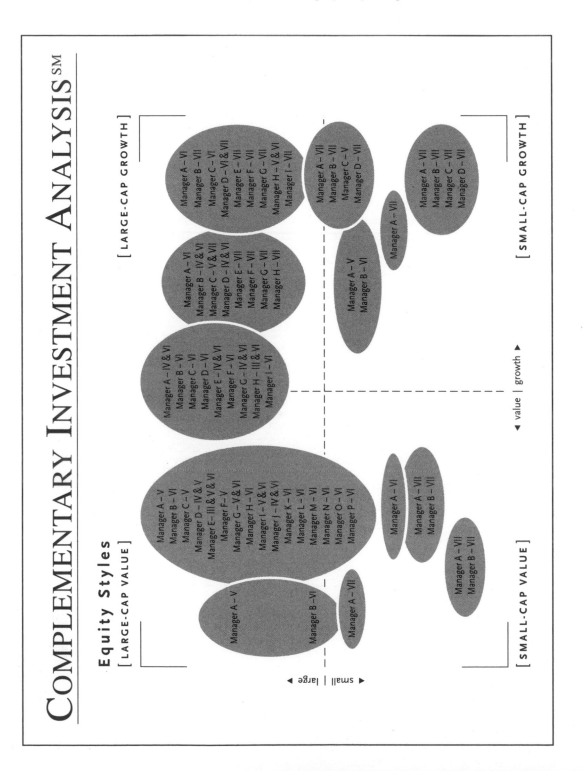

COMPLEMENTARY INVESTMENT ANALYSIS℠

Equity Styles

[LARGE-CAP VALUE]

[LARGE-CAP GROWTH]

[SMALL-CAP GROWTH]

[SMALL-CAP VALUE]

◄ value | growth ►

◄ small | large ►

Manager A – V
Manager B – VI
Manager C – V
Manager D – IV & V
Manager E – III & V & VI
Manager F – V
Manager G – V & VI
Manager H – VI
Manager I – V & VI
Manager J – IV & VI
Manager K – VI
Manager L – VI
Manager M – VI
Manager N – VI
Manager O – VI
Manager P – VI

Manager A – V

Manager B – VI

Manager A – VII

Manager A – IV & VI
Manager B – VI
Manager C – VI
Manager D – VI
Manager E – IV & VI
Manager F – VI
Manager G – IV & VI
Manager H – III & VI
Manager I – VI

Manager A – VI
Manager B – IV & VI
Manager C – V & VII
Manager D – IV & VI
Manager E – VII
Manager F – VII
Manager G – VII
Manager H – VII

Manager A – VI
Manager B – VII
Manager C – VI
Manager D – VI & VII
Manager E – VII
Manager F – VII
Manager G – VII
Manager H – V & VI
Manager I – VII

Manager A – V
Manager B – VI

Manager A – VII

Manager A – VII
Manager B – VII
Manager C – V
Manager D – VII

Manager A – VII
Manager B – VII
Manager C – VII
Manager D – VII

Manager A – VI

Manager A – VII
Manager B – VII

Manager A – VII
Manager B – VII

COMPLEMENTARY INVESTMENT ANALYSIS℠

Investment Management Composite
Cash Flow and Market Value Growth
January 1, 1988 through March 31, 2002

Year Initial Investment	Manager A Large-Cap Value $100,000 20%	Manager B Small-Cap Value $100,000 20%	Manager C Large-Cap Core $100,000 20%	Manager D Large-Cap Growth $100,000 20%	Manager E Small-Cap Growth $100,000 20%	Ending Value $500,000 100%
1988	23.2%	29.5%	19.0%	11.3%	16.9%	$583,740
1989	25.2	12.4	36.2	35.9	24.5	721,183
1990	-8.1	-21.8	-3.6	9.5	-12.2	651,748
1991	24.6	41.7	31.0	40.0	-55.0	879,352
1992	13.8	29.1	8.5	8.8	5.8	970,919
1993	18.1	23.8	6.1	11.9	12.1	1,084,206
1994	-2.0	-1.5	2.7	2.5	-1.3	1,059,254
1995	38.3	26.8	33.0	30.8	33.5	1,371,060
1996	27.9	27.4	27.8	17.0	15.1	1,649,667
1997	35.9	35.3	33.7	33.5	23.8	2,138,421
1998	18.8	-14.7	35.6	31.5	19.1	2,473,680
1999	8.3	-7.1	30.2	40.6	19.4	2,868,096
2000	31.1	16.1	-6.5	-12.8	13.4	3,044,831
2001	-6.1	24.4	-14.4	-14.5	-11.8	2,852,467
2002	3.2	10.3	-1.6	-1.4	1.5	2,906,605

The chart is for illustrative purposes only and does not represent the performance of any single investment. Past performance is not indicative of future results.

Part IV: Client Review Meetings

Effective client communications demand much more than a quarterly performance report. Here's the formula for a better review meeting.

The ongoing review of a managed account is a critical process unto itself. To keep your clients on the course you have planned together, you must reinforce the plan. Regular meetings with your clients provide the venue for reviewing the account, but you should take special care not to make the account and its performance the sole focus of the meeting. Allowing the account to be the meeting's focus risks developing short-term expectations that undermine the entire managed account relationship and its long-term benefits. Experienced managed account consultants have learned to review their clients' accounts as part of review meetings that address "big picture" wealth issues, such as retirement and estate planning.

That's an important fact to remember in providing managed account solutions – the managed account is only a funding strategy for a specific financial need. It's the strategy for how to invest or accumulate the investment and is not by itself, the destination. You want to revisit the total wealth management picture regularly to discuss the implications of why the client is investing her money, and determine whether there is a need to change the plan. The wealth management need is first, the investment ramifications of that need are secondary.

Don't Lead with the Numbers

Too many advisors have trapped themselves in a cycle of short-term expectations by starting off the managed account relationship with a first meeting based on the quarterly performance review. These well-meaning folks get themselves in trouble by unconsciously subordinating their judgment to that of their clients. "Here's your quarterly managed account review," they say, "What do you think of it?" Instead of discussing the goal of the investments – the estate plan, the retirement plan, the charitable gift – these advisors allow the managed account report to stand alone.

Consider the situation. First, if you deliver a hard copy of the review, it is typically six to eight weeks after the end of the quarter. Think about how that compares to the other data your clients receive about other accounts they may have. Any client with online capability can review his or her account almost immediately. Waiting six weeks for a back-dated report is a misfit in a technological world. For the affluent investor, this is the modern-day version of the Pony Express!

The average client has a time horizon of longer than 20 years. Why should they worry about one quarter? But unless you educate clients and keep the review in perspective, your clients will use it as your "report card." Many advisors have so many clients, they use the report as a communication vehicle and the excuse for a meeting. Your role is bigger than a quarterly performance report.

Act Like an Institution

Individual clients would benefit from knowing how bigger investors handle their managed accounts. For example, private banks conduct in depth portfolio reviews for their affluent clients, but these reviews usually take place only once a year. Why? Because the markets don't change that often, and the bank wants to set appropriate client expectations about that lack of change. Consider institutions like state and corporate pension funds. These plans have strict investment policy guidelines that direct their investment managers to specific allocations. When market activity drives the allocations out of balance – from a target of 60 percent equity to, say, 65 percent, the managers know they need to

Advisor Tip

Happy Birthday

Consider putting the quarterly investment management account report in its proper context. It should never be the focus of the meeting. It is merely a support document. Consider the posture taken by wirehouse advisor Chuck, who reminds his clients about meetings in a memorable way. Says Chuck, "Our meetings are conducted with clients right after their birthdays. This customizes the meeting and keeps the focus on the client. We tell them, 'Your birthday is the time you take stock of your life.' Handling meetings this way allows us to focus on long-term planning issues."

reduce the equity exposure to the client's investment policy of 60 percent. No meetings – and often no calls – are held to discuss the move. It's automatic. The review meetings held with the plan's trustees might revisit the strategy, but these meetings do not typically involve the minutiae of rebalancing the account to the investment policy guidelines. It is quite common, however, for the investment managers to offer insight and even recommendations for a change in asset allocation based on a firm's view of the markets during the annual review meeting.

Earlier I noted that 77 percent of high-net-worth investors in a survey had not rebalanced their portfolios in the aftermath of 2001's rocky markets. By contrast, only 9 percent of institutional investors had not rebalanced during the same period. I recommend you follow the practice of many top advisors and eliminate the quarterly managed account meeting. In its place, create a true client review session that focuses on the client's overall wealth needs. Remember, a good review meeting can be a tremendous opportunity to capture more assets. Let's look at a format to achieve both goals.

The Business Review Meeting

As a financial advisor to affluent clients, you are a successful business person serving other successful people. Consider the implications of that relationship and how you should conduct all aspects of your business. David in South Florida has decorated his office like the office in a local private bank. He also maintains a high profile for his team through his active involvement in the March of Dimes. He is a local business leader and believes that a consistently professional setting, combined with a genuine interest in community affairs, is attractive to his clientele. His success confirms the strategy.

Review meetings with clients also reflect your approach to business – and say a lot about you. Ask yourself the following questions:

- Do you have a meeting agenda?
- Do you have suggestions for your clients that you've planned in advance – or do you develop ideas off the cuff during the meeting?
- What is the goal of the meeting?
- What do your clients expect from a meeting?
- Do they need to prepare?
- Where do you meet?
- Do you take calls during the meeting?

These are not simple issues. Let's explore them all.

First of all, remember that most affluent individuals are busy business owners or professionals. They work with you in part because they have neither the time nor the interest in managing their financial affairs. That places you and your team in a position of providing service. And as a service provider, you must respect your clients' time. Time is often part of the "profit" from working with you, allowing your clients more time to spend on their business, with their families and with their other (fun) interests. They appreciate efficiency and effectiveness. A good rule of thumb for meetings with your affluent clients is to guide the meeting toward answering the question, "What problem did we solve today that will improve my client's life?"

Remember to consider the entire process and, as Stephen Covey suggests, begin with the end in mind. The most effective organizations maximize the value of their directors by creating agendas to help guide the meetings. Why not approach your client meetings in the same fashion? Most affluent clients have a similar experience – perhaps with their own board of directors, as well as with some type of charitable organization. They are familiar with the rules of the road used in these meetings, such as *Robert's Rules of Order*. I'll expand on that format shortly, but for now, imagine the professionalism conveyed by creating a written agenda for your client meetings.

A written agenda accomplishes a great deal with very few words. A colleague of mine once said, "He who arrives with an agenda controls the meeting." And that control means not only ensuring your ability to take charge at the outset, but also to guide the conversation toward important issues and lessen the chances of getting sidetracked into areas like discussing the market's recent performance. Several top advisors we know, such as a very successful wirehouse advisor in Montreal, prepare written agendas and fax them to the clients in advance of the meetings. The advisor says that in this way, he is able to draw the client into the meeting process. He reports greater success in preparing the client both mentally and emotionally for the meeting, as well as soliciting from the client any additional topics or issues he wishes to discuss. "Because we don't meet in-depth more than a few times each year, the clients require some preparation for us to get the maximum value from our meeting."

Your Turf or Mine?

The location of your meeting is extremely important. As we said earlier, your office should project the image of the professional that you are. However, you should also consider visiting your clients at their offices. They may be pleasantly surprised at the suggestion and will appreciate you taking the time to meet at their convenience. Two Boston-area advisors I know operate as a team. They report that meeting on the clients' turf removes potential distractions of their office and allows clients to relax. The pair recently took off a day from the office and visited one of their largest clients at his horse farm in New Hampshire. Not only did they enjoy the time out in the country, they allowed their client to show them his passion – a dimension of the client they did not know but now contributes to their understanding of his goals. Both parties now feel more in sync.

A Matter of Time

How long should your client review meetings be? Several factors contribute to the length, such as the number of topics to be discussed – which you can determine roughly with the agenda – as well as the complexity of topics. Beware of trying to accomplish too much in a single client meeting. Advisors I observe often underestimate how much time to devote to a particular topic. Leave yourself room to discuss an unforeseen issue with the clients. You might learn something new about them. You'll find that three 90-minute meetings annually are perfect for some clients with whom you have frequent conversations. Others might need a half-day to get through some sticky issues. One successful advisor says he gets right down to business and needs only 15 minutes, while George in Indianapolis enjoys spending a full day with each of his top 35-40 client families at least once each year. The time frame I hear most often for review meetings is about 90 minutes per session about four times each year – top clients only.

Look Out the Window Before Giving the Forecast

Just like the weatherman that checks outside before going on the air, always get a reality check prior to your client review meetings. What is the most important goal of the meeting? What is new with this client? What do you need to know? Consider possible family issues, career or business concerns, community affairs – anything that might affect your client's state of mind. Financial issues are secondary if a client's business is in trouble or a child is doing poorly in school. It is also important to review all pertinent financial information about your client prior to the meeting. Combining this with your perspective on your client's real life issues will help you to have a more informed discussion with your client – and to prepare an appropriate agenda for your meeting.

Plan the Meeting

Now it's time to draw up an agenda. Most organizations conduct their meetings according to the guidelines offered in the venerable *Robert's Rules of Order* – the blueprint for successful meetings. Robert's Rules provide a step-by-step approach to conducting a meeting and keeping it on track. Many of your clients are business people and are used to this structure from charitable group director meetings or their own company meetings. See the simple graphic on the next page depicting the key components of the meeting.

Let's apply that structure to a client review meeting, reviewing each step and the benefits to your meeting plan.

Minutes of the Last Meeting

What better way to get the meeting started than to review your last meeting? Your notes of the last meeting will help both you and your client recall what was said and establishes a jumping off point for the current meeting. There are other benefits, such as using the minutes as a not-so-subtle reminder of the services you provide. That's important. Many times your busy clients don't remember what you

> **Robert's Rules of Order**
>
> - **Minutes of the last meeting**
> - **Old Business**
> - **New Business**
> - **Set priorities**
> - **Develop action steps**
> - **Set date for next meeting**
> - **Adjourn**

have done for them, and they need to be reminded of your value. The minutes will also reveal any specific actions the client may have agreed to take at the last meeting, giving you a chance to ask whether the client has taken that action. The minutes can also establish the tempo and tone of the meeting – businesslike and efficient. And the minutes establish your command of the meeting.

Old Business

Are there any open topics or concerns not addressed since the last meeting? What actions were taken since the last meeting? You reinforce your value and your leadership role in this part of the meeting, since you are reviewing activities conducted on behalf of the client. You may also tip the balance of power in your favor – especially if the client has neglected to complete an assignment from the last meeting and you executed your duties.

"Committee" Reports

Companies and charitable boards typically task a group of directors to focus on a particular topic of concern to the whole group. These committees then report back to the larger board. Use the investment managers you've hired for the client in the same way. Use their managed account portfolio review as part of the "committee report." This is the first time an account statement should be used in the meeting. The minutes and your review of old business establish the flow of the meeting and prevent a premature plunge into the details of the performance report or account statement. Give yourself a chance to take charge and to let the client become acclimated to the meeting process.

By remanding the portfolio review to the role of a committee report, you also reinforce your objectivity. You and the client hired the investment managers in order to execute an overall plan. You should not be defensive if the manager has not performed the role he or she was hired to perform. Don't fall victim to the tendency to take blame for a bad performing manager – or credit for an exceptional performance. This is perhaps the most important point in a client review meeting. It reinforces to your client the nature of the investment management process and your role in it as an advisor. You and the client together deal with whatever has happened. Review the facts, make observations, and make recommendations to the client for action. How do you both feel about the manager and what the firm has done since you last met? Is everything on track?

Other "committee" reports include any product that your client owns. Look over variable insurance policies, mutual funds, variable annuities – anything that requires periodic review. How are these products performing relative to the role they were supposed to play? It is very important that you review all of this information prior to meeting with the client. You don't want any surprises during your "reports," or you will lose the objective role of advisor.

New Business

What new financial issues is your client concerned about? What new issues should you present to the client? Remember that wealth management is a journey, not a single event. As your client's advisor, you should be aware of what financial issues your client should tackle next. This portion of the meeting is the ideal time to alert your client to those issues and to bring his or her attention to the risks of not taking care of those issues immediately. This is the time to capture new assets.

The best tool for this phase of the client meeting is Phoenix's Wealth Management Picture which we introduced in Part II of this chapter. Consider the questions that correspond to each box (on the next page). What issues have arisen in the client's life since you last met? Does the client have concerns about any of the specific areas illustrated by the diagram? You should also think about situations you have seen in your practice and in the industry that might impact the client. For example, if you read an article about long-term care costs, you might bring that topic up to the client. Real-world examples are even better. If one of your other clients had an experience involving one of these topics, that by itself can be a compelling topic to discuss with this client – assuming confidentiality, of course. Real-world examples also convey a sense of urgency that may spur your client to action. This part of the meeting is your

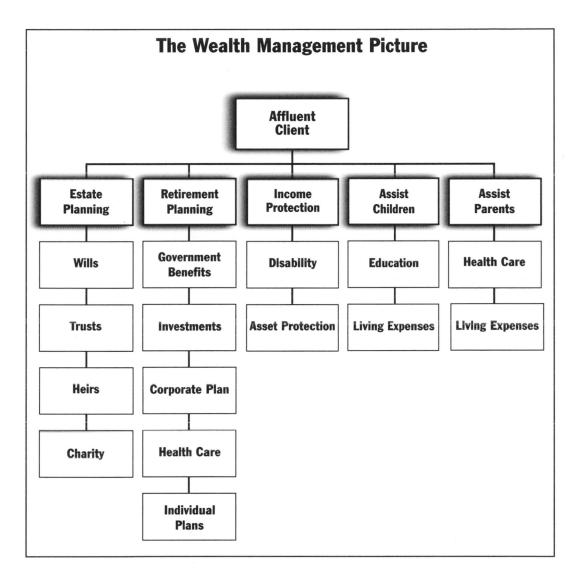

The Wealth Management Picture

opportunity to stretch the client's view of his or her financial situation to include the issues of life and family. After all, those issues are the most important of all.

Another helpful tool for you to use with your clients is the Future Shock worksheet on page 113. This exercise can help you to help your clients see their future and to make key financial decisions to realize their goals. Getting clients to share their hopes and fears about the future can cement enduring client relationships.[1]

---

[1]*Attract and Retain the Affluent Investor*. Stephen D. Gresham and Evan Cooper, Dearborn Trade, 2001.

Setting Priorities

You have now covered old business and any new business that arose between meetings. Now is the time to choose from among these business items any issues that require action subsequent to this meeting. What are the most important issues to tackle right away? In what sequence should they be addressed? Confirm the issues' significance with your client and set a timeline/deadline for their completion. Determine who will address which items.

Action Steps

Resist the temptation to take action during the meeting. Some issues are simple, such as discussing alternative investment ideas for a retirement plan. But other topics are more complex and should be handled after the meeting to ensure careful consideration. Some decisions, such as firing an investment manager, should be handled with care so as not to make a hasty decision and to avoid giving the client the impression that such an action can be determined quickly during your meeting. Do not hesitate to tell your client about any topic, "I'll research that and come back to you with additional information – including my recommendation."

Next Meeting Date

It's also important to formally set a date of your next meeting. Set the date before your client leaves the meeting and mark it on each of your calendars. As the date of the next meeting approaches, you might consider sending two hand-written reminder notices of the meeting date to your client, one to her home and one to the office. A dental practice I know does exactly that and asks its clientele – mostly busy executives – to fill out the addresses on both reminder cards so that someone at each address will notice!

Vote to Adjourn

Here's a point that even the most experienced advisors sometimes overlook: Be sure you hear everything your client has to say before ending the meeting. He might be on the verge of offering you another account when you look at your watch and mention you have another appointment in five minutes. You just lost that opportunity to capture additional assets. Don't rush, and always ask your client mid-way through the meeting if he is comfortable with the allotted time you are spending.

As you adjourn the meeting, remember to ask whether your client has anything more to add to the discussion, determine whether all the issues were covered, and thank your client for her time and ongoing business. Review any action items that arose, the date you'll next meet and express your gratitude for any additional accounts or funds provided to you during the meeting. You cannot thank clients too often for doing business with you.

Parting Thoughts

Some advisors I've met send the clients a review of the meeting. In the same spirit as providing the written agenda in advance of the meeting, these advisors want the clients to remember what they discussed at the review meeting. Action steps are highlighted, as is the date of the next meeting. Consider this follow up step.

More Detail on Portfolio Reviews

Despite these caveats, the portfolio review is an important part of the client review meeting and warrants special attention here. The ongoing review can give your clients insight into how their managers invest. Key members of investment management firms have meetings with clients so they will understand their views on the market, stock selections, and details about their style and philosophy. For example, managers at Roger Engemann & Associates (REA) present a story about a company to better illustrate the firm's process. During the client meeting, the portfolio manager gives an overview of the company, its history, management team, product or service, its market, competition, and the success it has had. She also reports on the firm's track record of earnings growth, as well as REA's earnings and growth estimate and the elements that will drive that growth over a five-year period. Included also is an analysis of how the company fits into the clients' portfolios, what the specific weightings should be and the rationale.

Finally, REA records the valuation of the stock and compares P/E ratios to other competitors. This type of information can be shared with your clients during conference calls or at seminar presentations.

Don't underestimate the value of the human connection in this process. When evaluating money managers, a key point is to work with someone articulate and who will be available to your clients. You don't want your clients calling you asking, "How is my account doing?" If your client is calling you with such questions, it may indicate you need to do better servicing. A little bit of preemptive sharing from you and the managers goes a long way.

Ongoing reviews and follow-up calls about portfolio performance should be conducted by you, not by an assistant, unless, of course, you have a team set up to do this in a way that diversifies the job responsibilities. Some advisors we know, like Geoff in Vancouver, have at least two team members in on every meeting so there is always a backup if the clients need to speak to someone about the managers.

Is the Honeymoon Over?

So, now you've gotten a few quarterly reviews under your belt, you've had several meaningful discussions with clients about the management style of their selected firms. What happens next? Inevitably, after a few quarters, one manager will probably be doing better than the others. How unusual would it be for the new investor/new client to say, "Manager X is doing so much better than Managers Y and Z, why don't we move all the money to Manager X?" This is the first test of your process. And this is where your explanation of multi-managers fits in nicely.

According to advisor Ted, not everything works out in the short term. Says Ted, "One couple invested $2 million with us – both were physicians, she worked part-time and cared for their young son. We explained the benefits of managed accounts and invested $800,000 of the $2 million in a managed account program with a growth manager. Last year that account was down 34 percent! How did we handle this? We re-sold the process of managed accounts, not the performance. We explained the downturn in the markets and the importance of using multiple investment professionals with different investment styles. We explained the failure of market timers and the flexibility of changing managers if the style of the manager drifted. They elected to stay the course."

How to Explain the Multi-Manager Concept to Your Prospects and Clients

To explain the changing roles of different sectors, styles and asset classes, there is no

Advisor Tip

Shifty Business

Paul has a favorite success story about a 20-year client who is a retired surgeon. He has approximately $2.5 million in his IRA and pension and profit-sharing plan. He also has $1 million in property and supports himself with $15,000 per month from his IRA. Says Paul, "Both he and his wife came to a dinner meeting, and he was convinced of the advantages of using multiple managers after my explanation – in this case three for $100,000 each. He knows that his portfolio needs a shift to provide more income. The game plan by year-end is to export more money to the managers just assigned, add two more managers and re-set the fixed income allocation."

better tool than the *Elements of Diversification* chart shown earlier in this chapter. Tell your client that market leadership varies and that you created a multi-manager solution for her because it's difficult to know exactly which manager is going to outperform whom. No one ever really knows when the party is going to be over. Rather than wait until the music stops and the client has to grab for the best performing asset class, you can tell your client that it's best to participate with managers who are complementary to each other. Reference the *Elements of Diversification* chart, re-cap your initial meeting with your client, and say, "Now we see one manager doing better than the others, as we expected. It's not an accident; that's the way it is supposed to happen. We are never certain which of the managers will perform the best, but one will always be in the lead. This manager is leading – for now. He will be replaced by another in due course. We never know who or when."

If you look at the *Elements of Diversification* chart again, odds are you'll see that the best performing manager does not often repeat the following year. Given this, you don't want to encourage your client to begin second-guessing the manager's performance. Give them information, but also give them guidance and perspective. Clients need to know they may be expecting too much performance too soon. Your job is to coach and educate your clients about how long it can take for the process to reap results, the order in which this typically occurs, and more about your process for making changes.

For example, let your client know that you don't necessarily fire a manager because they underperformed for a quarter or two. But you must have a good answer for any condition under which you would fire one. The consulting department at your firm should have criteria that outline what they look for in the selection of a manager. Review that criteria for your client when he gets a little nervous. **Remember, education is most effective in the moment**. Present supporting material like the *Complementary Investment Analysis* SM with its historical modeling to provide perspective.

Don't Be Bullied

Some inexperienced advisors allow their clients to bully them into putting all of their money with one manager. In fear of losing the client, they acquiesce. They wind up losing the client later when the portfolio falls out of favor. Remember, you don't need a bad client so much that you would be willing to commit financial malpractice during the process. You may wind up losing the respect of the client, and you will have done them a disservice.

The review process is easily outlined to clients and prospective clients as evidence of your added value. Affluent investors seek and crave expertise. Seek every opportunity to prove yours.

Future Shock Worksheet

	Current Year	Plus 5 Years	Plus 5 Years	Plus 5 Years	Plus 5 Years	Plus 5 Years	Plus 5 Years	Plus 5 Years
Year								
Client's Age								
Spouse's Age								
Child's Age								
Child's Age								
Parent's Age								
Parent's Age								
Parent's Age								
Parent's Age								
Business Partner's Age								

Future Shock Sample

	2002	2006	2011	2016	2021	2026	2031
Spouse	36	40	45	50	55	60	65
Spouse	36	40	45	50	55	60	65
Kid 1	3	7	12	17	22	27	32
Kid 2	1	5	10	15	20	25	30
Mom	61	65	70	75	80	85	90

Source: Attract and Retain the Affluent Investor, Dearborn Trade, 2001.

Part V: Manager Evaluation, Selection and Monitoring

There is both science and art to the process of manager evaluation. In this chapter you'll find the most valuable measures of manager performance and how to apply them.

Evaluating, selecting, and monitoring managers involves sound judgment and significant due diligence. The search is complicated and technical as risk patterns, return history and turnover rates need to be analyzed to best match a client's performance, tax and long-term financial plans. Most consulting firms do the research on managers and, when approved, include them on an internal list to help you decide which managers might be best suited for your clients.

Many advisors and high-end consultants prefer to do their own manager search and selection, but even if you don't, it still is important to understand the process so you can relate it to your clients when explaining why you offer certain managers. Even if you do not conduct the due diligence yourself, it's crucial you know the steps to take.

Donald B. Trone, president of the Pittsburgh-based Foundation for Fiduciary Studies and co-author of *Procedural Prudence* and *The Management of Investment Decisions*, emphasizes that advisors need tools and information to assess their manager choices. Don says that it's important to know the details of the manager evaluation criteria, even if you are choosing them from a preferred list. "Objective and quantifiable criteria should be used to choose and monitor managers," he says.

Here are five critical questions Don suggests you ask any manager you are considering for your clients:

1. **Ask for retail and institutional performance figures**. If a manager shows you returns for his or her retail managed accounts, ask for the performance numbers for his or her institutional separately managed accounts. If the numbers are different, ask why.

2. **Find out, specifically, which portfolio manager will handle your accounts**. For any track record you're shown, ask who created the record. Is it the same person or team that will be handling your clients' accounts? In many cases, one team handles retail clients, while another handles institutional.

3. **What are the trading procedures?** Will your clients' trades be included with those of the manager's institutional clients?

4. **When will your clients be fully invested?** Find out how long it will take for the money manager to fully invest your clients' funds into the market. Determine whether this strategy meets your clients' expectations.

5. **What particular tax-advantaged strategies are used?** Many managers say they offer tax-sensitive trading strategies; you need to ask for specifics. Tax-advantaged strategies may include the following: purchase of low-dividend-paying stocks, year-end harvesting of losses, low turnover, and selling first of highest-basis shares. Remember of course that the best after-tax returns can begin with the best pre-tax returns!

Before you begin your search, use your clients' investment policy statements as guides to find the money managers to implement the strategy you have in mind for them. Don says that many times, advisors doing their own searches put too much emphasis on manager selection and not on the overall investment structure.

For example, industry studies indicate that a prime component of a portfolio's return is strategic asset allocation, which determines the percentages to be invested in each broad asset class. Begin your manager search with the total picture in mind.

Let's now review how a few industry analysts evaluate and choose managers for their approved lists. You'll see a number of similarities in the due-diligence process and have a better understanding of the intensive work the analysts perform.

An Inside Look at Manager Selection

The evaluation process involves a lot more than just reviewing and comparing performance records – and Don Trone drives home that point. The due-diligence teams at major brokerages agree with him and tell us that success is in the detail work. Says a leading analyst of his firm's due diligence procedures, "First, we use industry databases to evaluate managers. For separately managed accounts we look at the manager's track record – for large cap growth or large cap value, we prefer five years performance. For small cap or other specialty, we'll look at fewer than five years, but the managers must have great numbers.

"Next, we have a preliminary meeting with the managers. Our key investment officers assess the managers' investment processes. We talk one-on-one with the portfolio managers, the management team, the research people. We have a concise, but thorough, list of questions.

"When we monitor the managers, the same individuals who handle the upfront analysis also do the monitoring – this creates consistency in our process. We employ performance attribution analysis to gauge how the managers are doing and look for a match between what we expected and what actually transpired. For example, if a manager espoused a research-intensive bottom-up approach to stock selection and we determined that the manager was making sector bets, that would be an area of concern. Our attribution analysis is broken down by sector and industry.

"Some of the items important to us when evaluating managers are

- Block trade reports for the portfolios
- Samples of individual accounts
- Quarterly analysis regime for performance attribution (we can do this on a day-to-day basis, too)
- Periodic visits with managers – once per year in their offices, so we can touch base with all of the key players, and once in our offices to give the entire research group the ability to evaluate the investment manager."

Managers have to undergo complete scrutiny by large numbers of highly trained individuals at the sponsoring firms. The process is similar in most due-diligence cases for most firms. For example, one large wirehouse has a research group of 10 and a due diligence committee of 25 specialists to pay attention to the smallest details. "If we have an interest in a particular manager," says the firm's managing director, "the first step is to have them send in some basic information on the firm in preparation for a formal presentation to the research committee. Our committee will look at such things as the size of the firm, its age, number of portfolio managers and staff, and performance – the customary items. Next, the manager meets members of the due diligence committee. This is an extremely rigorous process that focuses on the infrastructure of the firm." The group then follows up with the manager on his or her turf to substantiate the information they have received.

The firm's ongoing review of managers is a complex process. The monthly analysis includes reviewing the performance of all accounts; assessing dispersion, asset allocation, investment policy breaks and performance of securities. A peer review of each asset class is conducted every two weeks using tools such as Morningstar, PSN and Zephyr. Another common tool that firms use is Mobius (see sample report on page 127). Says the managing director, "The quarterly reviews include the same process, but we add a questionnaire on organizational structure, a review of any changes in the portfolio team, review of the model portfolio, and our accounts versus the manager composite."

A yearly meeting is held in the manager's office where the team reviews Form ADV and then has a round-up of all managers from a sector and asset allocation perspective. They also completely revisit the investment process at the meeting.

What happens when the firm fires a manager? "The termination of managers is not common, but it does happen," says the managing director. "We don't like to terminate a manager just because his or her asset class is out of favor. What may cause us to let a manager go is a combination of the following items: Poor performance relative to the peer group, style drift, process changes, "cap creep," capacity issues and organizational changes. Unfortunately, some financial advisors are too fast in asking us to fire a manager because they just got a beating from a big client. That's a real bad idea. What we may be looking at is just a short-term losing record, so we have to be careful before we consider pulling the plug."

Thoughts on Calculating Performance

It helps to become familiar with industry standards for calculating risk, return, and money manager performance. While you may not do this yourself, you need to understand the process so you can converse with your clients. That's your value.

Don Berryman is national sales director for Phoenix Investment Partners' Private Client Group and a certified investment management analyst. He discusses the technical aspects of common measures of performance evaluation and uses a few lively analogies. Here are his concepts:

Advisor Tip

Hire and Fire

Keats, a successful advisor, confirms the need to use caution in terminating managers. "You fire managers when there is a breakdown in the people and the process," says Keats. "Did key people leave? Why was there a sudden shift in staff? You should rarely fire on performance reasons alone. The biggest mistake is acting too quickly rather than too slowly when it comes to firing managers. Be patient and evaluate before you act. Remember, the client should be the least knowledgeable about the portfolios' investments followed by the consultant and then the investment manager. The power to hire and fire follows the same sequence, meaning the least knowledgeable party (the client) has the most power. The consultant's role, therefore is to educate and help the client to make the best decision by following sound rules of engagement and a disciplined process."

Concept 1: Return on Investment (ROI)

ROI measurement has two aspects – time-weighted measurement and dollar-weighted measurement. Time-weighted measurement is important in measuring manager effectiveness and disregards the effect of the timing of cash contributions or withdrawals from the portfolio. Time-weighted measurement takes into consideration the time value of money over an accumulation, or specified period.

Dollar-weighted measurement focuses more on the client's goals. It uses simple dollars, in and out, without consideration for the time value of money. The timing of cash flows, in or out, does make a difference in dollar-weighted measurement.

Concept 2: Standard Deviation – The Granddaddy of Risk Measurement

Standard deviation is, quite simply, the measurement of how far the price of a market, security or portfolio is expected to deviate from normal. The standard bell curve shows the relationship of this measurement to the normal expected range of the entity. Statistically, approximately 66 percent of all events are within one standard deviation of average. Approximately 95 percent of all events are within two standard deviations of average (see the chart on page 119).

Simple? Let's look at an example.

The San Diego Snowstorm

Let's compare the temperatures in Dallas and San Diego. Assume the average temperature for both cities is 65 degrees, but the standard deviation in Dallas is 20 degrees and the standard deviation in San Diego is 10 degrees. My mom can't tolerate temperatures above 100 degrees or below 40 degrees. Some cities experience extremes, snow in the winter and above 100 degree temperature in the summer, so this parameter would eliminate the cities of Phoenix and Chicago, but which is more likely to please her – Dallas or San Diego? Using our new knowledge of standard deviation we might determine that there is a:

- 66% chance of the temperatures staying between 45 and 85 degrees in Dallas (average of 65 degrees plus or minus 20 degrees standard deviation)
- 66% chance of the temperatures staying between 55 and 75 degrees in San Diego (average of 65 degrees plus or minus 10 degrees standard deviation)
- 95% chance of the temperatures staying between 45 and 85 degrees in San Diego
- 95% chance of temperatures staying between 25 and 105 degrees in Dallas

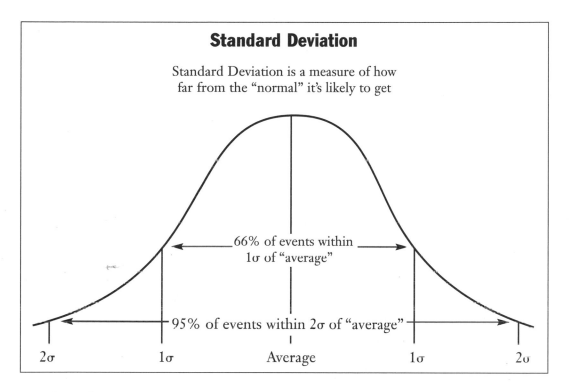

Standard Deviation

Standard Deviation is a measure of how
far from the "normal" it's likely to get

66% of events within
1σ of "average"

95% of events within 2σ of "average"

2σ   1σ   Average   1σ   2σ

So where do I want to send Mom? Take a look at the charts on the next page.

Now let's apply this to the Nasdaq, the S&P, or a money manager:

- Three standard deviations will encompass 99.8 percent of occurrences.
- In 2000-2001, the Nasdaq was more than two standard deviations from normal, which happens less than five percent of the time and is equivalent to a San Diego snowstorm!

Concept 3: Beta and Alpha

Beta: Measuring Volatility

Beta is a measurement of a portfolio's (or security's) volatility relative to a benchmark such as the S&P 500 Index. It tells you how the portfolio is expected to perform given the movements in the benchmark. A beta of 1.0 means that the portfolio should have a return similar to that of the benchmark. If the beta exceeds 1.0, expect more volatility; if it's less than 1.0, expect less.

Let's take an example. If the beta on your client's portfolio is 1.2 and the benchmark gains 10 percent, the portfolio should rise about 12% (1.2 x 10%). If the index falls 8

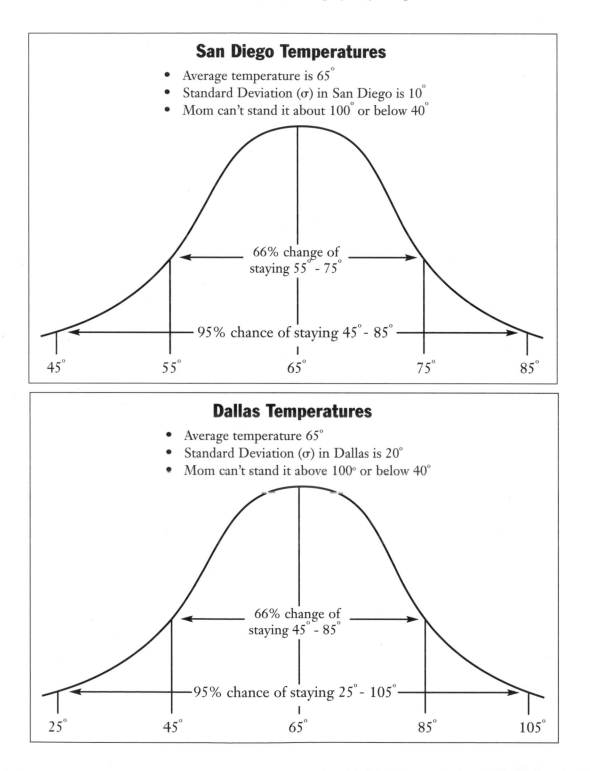

San Diego Temperatures

- Average temperature is 65°
- Standard Deviation (σ) in San Diego is 10°
- Mom can't stand it about 100° or below 40°

66% change of
staying 55° - 75°

95% chance of staying 45° - 85°

45°   55°   65°   75°   85°

Dallas Temperatures

- Average temperature 65°
- Standard Deviation (σ) in Dallas is 20°
- Mom can't stand it above 100° or below 40°

66% change of
staying 45° - 85°

95% chance of staying 25° - 105°

25°   45°   65°   85°   105°

percent, he'll lose about 9.6 percent (1.2 x –8%). A beta that's higher than the benchmark means more volatility in both directions.

Think of two portfolios as sailboats. Given the same wind conditions (the market), the boat with the bigger sail (beta) will move the most.

Alpha: A "Value Added" Measure

Knowing the beta will help you evaluate a portfolio's performance. But there is more to it, especially when returns deviate from the expected beta values. This is where alpha comes in. Alpha is the difference between the return expected, given the beta, and portfolio's actual return. The alpha can be positive or negative.

For example, assume the benchmark returned 12 percent and the beta on your client's portfolio is 1.1. The expected return of the portfolio is 13.2 percent (12 x 1.1). Let's take the two scenarios in the chart below and calculate the alpha.

Portfolio Return	Expected Return	Alpha
15.0%	13.2%	1.8 (15.0 - 3.2 = 1.8)
9.5%	13.2%	-3.7 (9.5 – 13.2 = -3.7)

So, what does the alpha tell you? It's the "value added" (or value subtracted) by the manager. In the first scenario above, the manager's actual return exceeded the expected return by almost 2 percent. In the second case, the portfolio underperformed by 3.7 percent.

Concept 4: R^2 – How Accurate Is Everything Else?

The relevance of all of this depends on how well the data fits the assumption and how closely the portfolio imitates the index – this is R^2. As a simple way to talk about R^2, let's talk about an ice cream salesman and a shoe salesman at the beach. Take a look at the charts on page 128.

If you are at the beach and selling ice cream, temperature affects sales. If you're selling shoes, the temperature has no affect. In other words, the predictability of ice cream sales in relation to temperature is high, while the predictability of shoe sales is low. That, in essence, is R^2. R^2 explains how closely the movement of a portfolio's return relates to it's benchmark. It is a measure of correlation. Over time, if the returns of a portfolio and benchmark behave in a similar manner, they are positively correlated. If they move in opposite directions, they are negatively correlated.

Concept 5: Risk-Adjusted Return

In basic terms, the risk-adjusted return of a portfolio is the measure of how much an investment returned in relation to the amount of risk it took. It compares a high-risk, potentially high-return investment with a low-risk, lower-return investment. Three formulas allow us to compare disparate portfolios on an "apples-to-apples" basis.

Sharpe, Sortino and Treynor Measures

The Sharpe Ratio, named after Dr. William Sharpe, adjusts the return of the portfolio based on the amount of risk taken to achieve it. It indicates how much excess return was achieved per unit of total risk, as measured by standard deviation. Similarly, the Sortino Ratio, named after Dr. Frank Sortino, measures return earned per unit of downside risk, while the Treynor Ratio, named after Jack Treynor, measures return earned per unit of beta, or market risk.[1]

A risk return graph is also a useful tool to illustrate the performance of a portfolio and its risk level as measured by the standard deviation. Also known as a scattergram, the graph is divided into four quadrants, the best being the northwest which reflects returns that exceed the benchmark and have less risk. See the graph on page 123 for an example.

These ratios as well as the other measures we've discussed are useful in evaluating portfolio performance. While no single risk return statistic is a perfect performance measurement tool, together they can offer a relatively clear picture of how well a portfolio performed.[2] Take a look at the chart on page 124 comparing a hypothetical portfolio and its characteristics to the S&P 500 Index.

Additional performance measurement information, including formulas and ratios for concepts reviewed in this section, is provided in Appendix B.

Are Your Clients' Goals Being Met?

Monitoring and supervising the portfolio goes beyond accounting for returns. "You

---

[1] *Performance Measurement and Evaluation*, Investment Management Consultants Association, Denver, 2001.
[2] Ibid

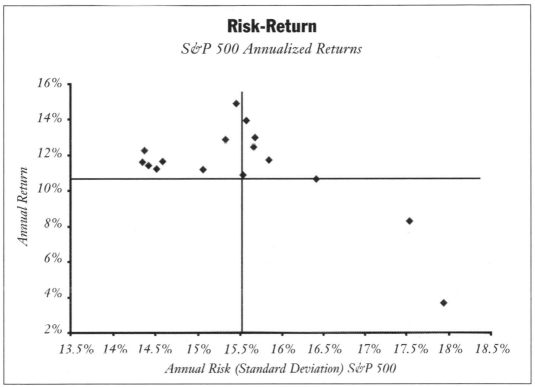

Risk-Return
S&P 500 Annualized Returns

Past performance is not indicative of future results.

also have to determine whether the investment policy statement is meeting its goals," says Don Trone. "Effective monitoring gives the investor sufficient information to evaluate the program's strengths and weaknesses and keeps the program on track." Take a look at the sample investment policy statement (IPS) in Appendix C.

It's important to review costs, too, since expenses can have a significant impact on portfolio returns. This is a key fiduciary responsibility and something you need to be aware of. The four categories of costs are:

- Money manager fees
- Trading costs
- Custodial charges
- Consulting and administrative costs

Now is a good time to establish your process for reviewing client portfolios and issuing reports. Here are some timelines for you to follow:

Performance and Risk Analysis
Hypothetical Equity Portfolio Over 5 years

	Annualized Return	Standard Deviation (Total Risk)	Beta (Market Risk)	R-Squared (Diversification)	Alpha (Risk-adjusted Return)	Deviation ("Bad" Risk)
Portfolio	10%	10.8%	0.9	96.8%	1.6%	6.5%
S&P 500 Index	8.7	11.6	1.0	100.0	0.0	7.0

Portfolio Sharpe Ratio: 0.5%	**Sortino Ratio:** 0.8%	**Treynor Ratio:** 5.5%

Conclusions

- The portfolio earned 1.3% more return than the market index.
- The portfolio took less total risk than the index to achieve that return (10.8% vs. 11.6% standard deviation).
- The portfolio took only 90% of the market risk represented by the index (0.9 vs. 1.0 beta).
- The portfolio was highly correlated, or well-diversified, compared to the market (96.8% R-squared).
- The portfolio earned 1.6% more return (alpha) than expected, based on its market risk.
- On a risk-adjusted basis, the portfolio earned 0.5% (Sharpe ratio) for every unit of total risk taken, 0.8% (Sortino ratio) for every unit of downside risk, and 5.5% (Treynor ratio) for every unit of market risk taken.

Note: Numbers taken from Mobius, M search Database
Source: Performance Measurement and Evaluation ©2001 Investment Management Consultants Association

Monthly: Is the asset allocation in line with your initial guidelines? Are the current holdings consistent within the manager's strategy? Are the costs routine? How does performance compare to market/industry benchmarks?

Quarterly: Are fees in line with your expectations? Is the portfolio still following the investment policy statement? Are there any liquidity requirements for the next quarter? Are any additional assets expected, and how will they be invested? What is the market value of the portfolio? How does the manager's performance compare with other managers' and with industry benchmarks? What is the rate of return overall? By asset class? Style?

Annually: Have there been changes in the manager's organization? Have there been any changes in the manager's brokerage or trading activities? What is the performance of short-term investments and cash?

We believe these components allow you to take the necessary steps to put a comprehensive portfolio-monitoring system in place for your clients.

Important Last Steps

Don Trone offers more strategic help in finalizing your process, including what you need to include in your Request for Proposal (RFP). Don says to operate strictly within the Employee Retirement Income Security Act (ERISA) rules. If you are conducting the manager search yourself and will be choosing your own managers, follow this abbreviated version before making your final decisions.

ERISA Rules

- Have only prudent experts, such as registered investment advisors, make all investment decisions.
- Follow a due-diligence procedure in selecting money managers.
- Provide general investment direction to money managers.
- Ask money managers to acknowledge their fiduciary status in writing or by signing a copy of the IPS.
- Monitor the managers' activities.

Your Request for Proposal

This document should contain a list of specific questions you'll need answered before you make your final selection. Ask also for performance reports that comply with the Association for Investment Management and Research's (AIMR) Level II standards, if possible. Reports should reflect the following:

- Time- and asset-weighted returns
- Actual performance (no model portfolios, unless specifically identified)
- Reported performance net and gross of fees
- Quarterly, annual and cumulative results for three, five and 10 years
- Risk-adjusted returns
- Audits by an independent third party, such as an accounting or investment consulting firm

Last But Not Least – Your Value

When making your final decision in selecting managers, using quantifiable systems such as the ones outlined in this chapter help document that decision. It also helps your clients understand the reasons why you selected their managers. Again, even if you don't engage in the process, it's good to know all the components in a successful search. Plus, when you are ready, your clients will be duly impressed by your knowledge and the care with which you handle their assets through your value-added process of consulting.

Seneca Capital Management LLC
Asset Class: Domestic Equity
Product Name: Growth with Controlled Risk
Return Set: Gross Size

Trailing Returns/Risk Analysis/Scatterplot
Benchmark: Russell 1000 Growth
10 Years Trailing ending 03/31/2002

	Manager	Index
Qtr	-0.529	-2.587
YTD	-0.529	-2.587
1Yr	-1.514	-2.000
2Yr	-15.254	-25.077
3Yr	0.623	-9.027
4Yr	4.735	-0.898
5Yr	12.604	7.589
6Yr	12.499	9.177
7Yr	14.575	12.176
8Yr	14.795	12.842
9Yr	13.514	11.238
10Yr	13.428	11.065

■ Seneca Capital Management LLC   ◆ Russell 1000 Growth

Risk Analysis

Timeframe	Standard Deviation	Sharpe Ratio	R-Squared	Alpha	Beta	Treynor Ratio	Tracking Error	Information Ratio
3Yr	25.066	-0.160	94.185	7.444	0.840	-1.422	7.656	1.158
5Yr	23.994	0.310	94.377	4.751	0.838	12.337	7.288	0.472
10Yr	17.604	0.482	91.404	3.031	0.830	12.134	6.206	0.233

Index: Russell 1000 Growth

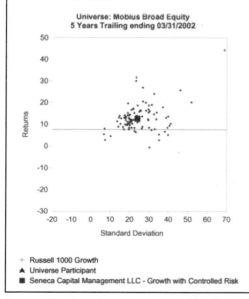

Universe: Mobius Broad Equity
5 Years Trailing ending 03/31/2002

Market Cycle Analysis

Topic	3Yr	5Yr	10Yr
Best Quarter	27.427	27.427	27.427
Worst Quarter	-16.922	-16.922	-16.922
Best 4 Quarters	41.858	50.453	50.453
Worst 4 Quarters	-34.997	-34.997	-34.997
Best Case	41.858	152.078	408.152
Worst Case	-36.309	-36.309	-36.309
Positive Quarters	6.000	13.000	29.000
Negative Quarters	6.000	7.000	11.000
Up-Market Ratio	98.438	95.015	92.911
Down-Market Ratio	68.439	74.602	70.327
Batting Average	75.000	60.000	55.000
Up-Market Return	54.739	51.414	33.375
Down-Market Return	-26.006	-27.783	-18.977

Index: Russell 1000 Growth

+ Russell 1000 Growth
▲ Universe Participant
■ Seneca Capital Management LLC - Growth with Controlled Risk

Source: CheckFree Investment Services' M-Search Investment Manager Database System.
Seneca Capital Management LLC is an investment manager of Phoenix Investment Partners, Ltd.

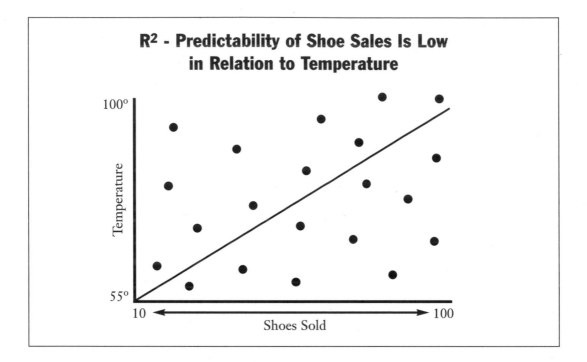

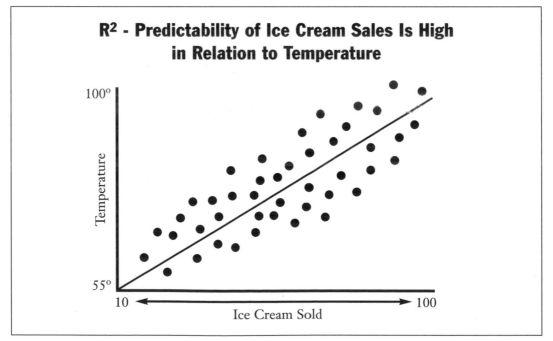

Chapter 7

Developing Your Managed Account Business

Part I: Target Marketing for Managed Accounts

What are the best targets for managed accounts – and why?
Here are the four scenarios most likely to result in managed
account sales.

Significant assets for managed accounts result from four broad scenarios:

1. New clients who have outgrown other advisors – or fired them – and need a new advisor

2. Current clients who have gradually accumulated securities and mutual funds in taxable accounts and could benefit from a higher level of service

3. Events such as the sale of a business, inheritance through life insurance settlements or estates which provide sudden liquidity

4. Rollovers from an employee bonus or profit-sharing plans

Each scenario requires a different marketing approach to maximize your potential success. Events and advisor firings are difficult to target because they occur suddenly. The gradual accumulation areas, as in numbers 2 and 4 above, are the easiest because you track the process and may yourself be helping a client grow the assets.

Scenarios I & II: Helping Your Clients Grow

Successful advisors I know have shown clients the path to growth. They teach their smaller clients the best way to invest in a series of funds or securities and help set the stage for asset accumulation. They discuss the potential of the account and how it will be taken care of as it grows. Eventually, those clients are ready for managed accounts. One of the best opportunities to acquire substantial clients for managed accounts is to capture those whose current advisors have not made the higher level of service available to them.

To illustrate the path to wealth, I use a diagram called "The Wealth Management Lifecycle." This graphic shows the progression of clients as they save and accumulate wealth and have the need for more sophisticated financial planning. It also charts the progression of the advisor's business as he grows his practice to serve those wealth management needs (see page 140).

In 1987 and 1988, clients outgrowing their advisors were ripe pickings for alert consultants. In the aftermath of 1987's double crashes in both stocks and bonds, high-net-worth individuals took matters into their own hands and pulled money away in search of a higher level of service. Don't wait for clients to come to their own conclusions about an advisor. You want to offer a higher level of service using separately managed accounts. Investors are hearing about these services from their friends and business associates.

Imagine this conversation between two investors: One says, "I have a professionally managed account with an array of institutional money managers." And the other investor (perhaps your client) thinks, "Gee, here I sit with my grab bag of securities and mutual funds. I wonder why my advisor hasn't brought this service to my attention?"

Positioning yourself as a resource and making it known to your clients and to centers of influence that you provide this higher level of service is critical to maintaining your clients and capturing more assets.

Scenarios III & IV: Events and Rollovers

There are four basic event-driven markets:

1. Retirement

2. Sale of a business

3. Death and divorce (inheritance, insurance settlements, etc.)

4. Annual cash distributions, such as bonuses or profit-sharing distributions

The retirement event is the most predictable. However, you shouldn't assume your clients will call you as they approach that important date. They may believe you have excellent investment ideas and are great in helping them accumulate assets, but they may not understand your expertise in retirement planning. Retirement planning is an extraordinarily important concept, and one that my life insurance and annuity colleagues know well – it plays a critical role in the client's life and includes many tax-advantaged ways to create an income stream. In addition, many companies provide retirement planning, which can insert a new advisor into the mix.

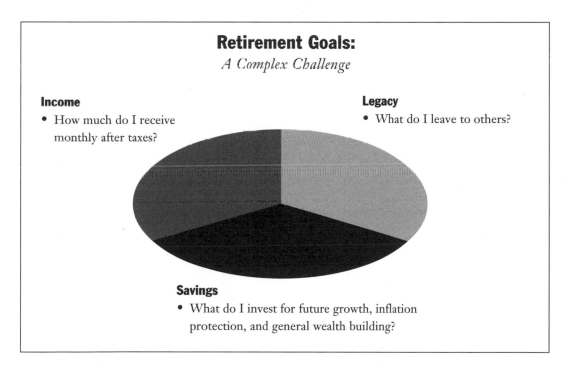

Advisors who include retirement planning in their practice tend to focus on three areas:

1. The client's guaranteed level of income

2. How much discretionary cash they are willing to maintain for growth potential

3. What portion might the client pass on – the legacy

The challenge of working with a client ready for retirement is that she is shifting her focus. Before retirement, she had a singular goal: To obtain the pot of gold at the end of the rainbow. But now, here the client is – at the end of the rainbow, facing retirement. Many retirees don't want to work very much, if at all. But even high-net-worth clients will be challenged to have enough cash and most likely will divide their goals into the three areas just mentioned: guaranteed net income; savings and legacy value.

So retirees move from this singular goal to the three-part goal of dealing with their wealth after retirement. This is the point where many advisors lose clients because the clients aren't ready for this level of complexity.

One veteran advisor I know in Southern California spends most of his time addressing the life insurance needs of clients. He divides the client's assets into the three areas – income, savings and legacy – and uses different financial products to achieve the best overall solution. Rather than taking all of the retirement money and putting it in one vehicle, he solves issues with discrete products. For example, to handle the guaranteed income need, this advisor typically offers an annuity that has a defined income payment. In addition, the annuity can reduce the chance of a client outliving his income, a concern expressed by 30 percent of high-net-worth clients.[1]

For the savings portion of the solution, the advisor employs mutual funds and separately managed accounts. For the legacy or inheritance piece, he uses life insurance. For example, if the client wants to leave $1 million dollars for his children, instead of taking it out of the principal, he buys a life insurance policy of $1 million that dramatically reduces the amount of current cash needed while providing the death benefit.

These strategies are fine for current client planning, but how do you capture that pre-retirement prospect? Connecting with centers of influence such as CPAs or business and estate planning attorneys is a significant way to guide event-driven business your way. To illustrate your process and your value to these powerful reference centers, I recommend you give them in-depth case study solutions. Showing how you solved a client problem gives these referral sources a clearer picture of the target market you

---

[1]2002 Phoenix Wealth Management Survey, conducted in March 2002 by Harris Interactive[SM], © The Phoenix Companies, Inc.

work best with. Give them your ideal client profile and what you can do best for this ideal client. These case studies work better than charts, graphs, or any other way you explain your value to a CPA or attorney – they're real.

The best scenario would be to have a conversation with an accounting professional, for example, and say, "Here's a client situation that we tackled at our firm and here's the solution we provided. If this is something that would be of interest to any of your clients, we'd be happy to work through similar solutions for them." You need to have active, consistent conversations with these centers of influence, because it's too difficult for them to keep track of everybody's processes. You will have an edge if you talk in story or case-study language because we all have a tendency to better remember these situations in story form.

Consider inviting centers of influence to your seminars or client appreciation meetings (more about this follows in the seminar segment later in this chapter). Invite them to meet the portfolio managers you work with and give them copies of client statements (with the client's approval). That way they will feel comfortable knowing that they are in the loop.

The Sale of a Business

The sale of a business is a multi-faceted, complex issue that many advisors get very excited about only to become frustrated by the final result: There may not be a significant amount of cash to be captured. Why? Most businesses in the U.S. are small and many have no end value. The entrepreneur's great dream is to build a successful company they can sell to a giant like Microsoft.

The difficulty is that most small businesses – private practices like those of doctors, lawyers and dentists – may not have sustainable revenues beyond the founder or principal. Even if the business is saleable, most of the transactions are small and, in the majority of cases, many businesses are not sold outright but are transitioned to family members.

For you as an advisor, the potential sale of a closely held business can be lucrative, but you may have to help facilitate the sale. Simply waiting around for the transaction to occur, assuming the client will come to you with the money, is misplaced confidence. Just as investment bankers are valuable rainmakers for their firms, the advisors who facilitate transactions may get the money because they get the first crack at it.

How many of your clients currently own a business that eventually will be sold? A good question to ask yourself is what your role might be in these types of transactions. If your target market is the small business owner, you'll need to be conversant in the process by which they achieve equity. That may include helping them plan in advance of the sale how that equity will be realized. It is unlikely that you will be able to drive the sale of a business without working with other advisors.

You need to know who will help with valuation, who will structure the terms of the sale, and who will fund it. It is possible that a business broker could help you facilitate a small transaction, but on the other hand, it might be too small to warrant a managed account – and not worth your time. The typical small business in the U.S. is sold for between $500,000 and $2 million, so we are not talking about multi-million dollar events.

When the sale does involve a substantial amount of money, you need to be flexible because you want to structure a sound managed account program. You need to be vigilant about how the cash flows will arrive. A systematic investing strategy can be developed and it will make a compelling case for the managed account to the client, especially if you can model their "take" after taxes.

Centers of Influence

One of the best entrees into this small business market is through centers of influence because they know about the business sale long before you will. One of the most successful advisors I know who targets this market spends an enormous amount of time with his CPA firm so they will refer small business clients to him as soon as they begin discussing the sale of the business with a client. The advisor is ready to model a solution on the investment side so the client has a realistic view of what he might receive in a sale.

If you plan to target this market, consider what issues the business owner faces. Be empathetic to their mood and the economic circumstances they are in, because if you are targeting them for additional assets, you need to know whether the assets are available. This is a terrific opportunity to bond with these individuals because what they really need to hear is that someone cares about the situation they are in. There is nothing that a business owner enjoys more than having someone interested and aware of his or her circumstances – and who has helped others.

Insurance, Inheritance, Death Events

We know a financial advisor at a major wirehouse in the Southeast who enjoyed a great relationship with a married couple. Here was the scenario: The husband died at the end of a week, and the following week, the couple's money was transferred away from the advisor to an account at a major trust company. The financial advisor could not believe what was happening because he had a long-term friendship with the couple. He called the widow, who told him the matter was out of her hands and that the money had been earmarked through the husband's will and was to be sent on for placement in the trust. The advisor was perplexed, but when he gave some serious thought to the situation, he realized he had missed the first point of vulnerability. He was a contemporary of theirs – about their same age – and had he been more alert, he would have considered that his own mortality would have entered into the couple's decision. What would they have done if he (the advisor) passed away first?

The important issue to address is what will happen to your relationship with the client if the family founder passes away. According to a study by Prince & Associates, less than 5 percent of advisors are retained by subsequent generations when the key owner dies.[2]

Before you begin thinking opportunistically about the inheritance market, you need to determine the trustee for each of your existing clients. Even though you may have worked with many of your clients for a long time, you can find yourself excluded from the decision-making process. You can deal with this issue in several ways. One is to take the preemptive step of talking with your clients and identifying the trustees. Next, even though you or your firm may or may not have trust powers, you can be appointed the investment manager in their wills.

When managing wealth for your affluent clients, you can gain a great deal by taking a proactive approach and positioning yourself as the central coordinator of their financial affairs. Walt Zultowski, senior vice president, marketing and market research for The Phoenix Companies explains, "One of the things we hear over and over again from high-net-worth people is that they have multiple financial advisors, each typically for a specific product or service. Their major lament, however, is that they can't get these various advisors to talk to one another, much less coordinate their advisory activities. There is a clear opportunity today to position yourself as the

---

[2] "Staying The Apple of Client's Eyes," *Financial Advisor*, June 2001.

client's manager of the stable, rather than just one of the many advisors in the stable. In the context of the "The Wealth Management Lifecycle" (page 140), this is where an advisor moves from being a financial counselor to a trusted counselor and confidant."

To become that valued advisor, you must learn the answers to these questions:

- Who else will your clients be working with?

- In addition to the trust bank, which attorneys will they be using?

- Do these people know who you are and what services you provide?

When a client of an attorney dies, his/her children need advice about investments.

- What is your positioning with the attorney that gives him confidence that you can provide solutions?

- Do you have relationships with the children?

Consider some of the trust banks where they spend a lot of time talking about intergenerational sales. This means they spend a lot of time talking about educating the children about investing. Before a parent dies, they usually suggest that the rest of the family learn more about investments. As part of your practice, you might want to include this concept in your game plan for relating to the client. You should determine:

- Does your client need a plan for the next generation?

- Do you know who the heirs are?

Chip Olson, president and CEO of Phoenix National Trust Company, shares the following perspective, "Taking a consultative sales approach to working with your client is paramount to securing the client relationship for multiple generations. Getting to know the attorney, accountant, insurance specialist and investment advisor(s) is only the first step. As an advisor for the long-term, you will need to get to know your clients' family and the wishes he or she has for them now and in the future. Once you understand your clients wishes, you can create a sound estate and financial plan that provides your client with the confidence in knowing his family will be appropriately provided for."

Chip further suggests, "Getting your client to appoint a corporate trustee to oversee his financial affairs may be just what you need to help secure this relationship from this generation to next. The industry average for the life of a trust account is 22 years. Wouldn't it be comforting to know that you will be working with this client and his heirs for at least that amount of time?"

Here's an important estate-planning fact you should know. Based on the Phoenix Wealth Management Survey 2002 of high-net-worth investors with more than $1 million in investable assets, three out of 10 respondents had no estate plan at all, and another three out of 10 had an estate plan that was over five years old. You need to make sure you can facilitate discussions with clients about estate planning using your available resources and centers of influence, since this is important to establish you as an advisor for the long-term and it is also an easy entry point for your competitors.

Divorce Market

At this writing, early talk is that the divorce between former General Electric Chairman Jack Welch and his wife Jane will catapult her to becoming one of the wealthiest women in America. This much-publicized event should prompt you to think about spouses who capture assets after a divorce, and the guidance they will need to preserve them. Divorce affects more than 50 percent of all married people in this country. It is an event for which you should have a strategy. This is another center-of-influence driven market. Do you have relationships with matrimonial attorneys?

In many cases, one of the two individuals in the divorce equation – male or female alike – may not be entirely familiar with investments and finance. You want to be in the position to show the centers of influence you are conversant with their issues and have sensitivity to people who find themselves in this spot. Understand that no matter what happens in the divorce, if you have a client couple, you will be forced to choose one side or the other.

"It's a highly challenging segment of the market," says Mark McLeland, first vice president of investments for The McLeland Group in Fort Worth, TX. Part of Mark's practice is providing wealth management services for divorced clients. Mark has been an investment advisor for 20 years and has established networks with several matrimonial attorneys. "You have to build a tremendous level of trust with the client, given the emotional intensity of the situation. And it's not easy. In some cases, the client was never a decision-maker in the investment process and suddenly received a substantial amount of liquid assets. With little or no financial background, your client needs a financial advocate, so guidance out of the starting gate is crucial. Some clients are of the mindset that they want to take the cash, buy a new house and move on. The problem is that they don't realize that the $5 million they just received actually reduced their standard of living." Mark's formula for success has been to integrate his expertise with the highest level of trust in what is a niche but growing segment of the affluent market.

Distribution from Bonuses and Business Profits

Few affluent executives or business owners earn their wealth through salary. Most capture the bulk of their compensation from performance bonuses or profit sharing. Typically, these prospects and clients use those big payments to fund their investments. Your primary challenge is to learn when these events will occur. It's also important to determine the formula that your prospect or client uses to pay themselves, if they are the owner of the firm. Many business owners live on their draw, or their salaries from their businesses, then invest their bonuses or their profit-sharing portions from the company. This payout could be an annual one-time event.

If you are prospecting key salespeople or executives within a firm, you need to determine when their bonuses are paid. For the most part, after the books are sorted out at the end of the year, most businesses take a look at their financial situation and distribute bonuses at the first of the year. When do your clients earn their bonuses – or take their distribution?

As we've mentioned elsewhere in this book, the number one competitor for the business owner's assets is the company. Talk to your small-business clients about building wealth outside of their business, as a hedge against their business not having the kind of value they expected when it is eventually sold. At best, it is an alternative strategy to what the client is doing successfully on his or her own anyway. At worst, it is a hedge against their business being worth little or nothing.

A Word About Natural Target Markets

You have a natural connection with some markets. Because of your background, or interests, you naturally gravitate toward these markets. The referral value of individuals within a natural target market is strong enough for your reputation to be established rather quickly on that basis. You may have a lot in common with physicians, college alumni, dry cleaners, or sports figures, and self-promotion within such groups is easy to accomplish. There are too many target markets to effectively cover them here, so please take a look at our resource guide at the end of the book for helpful sources.

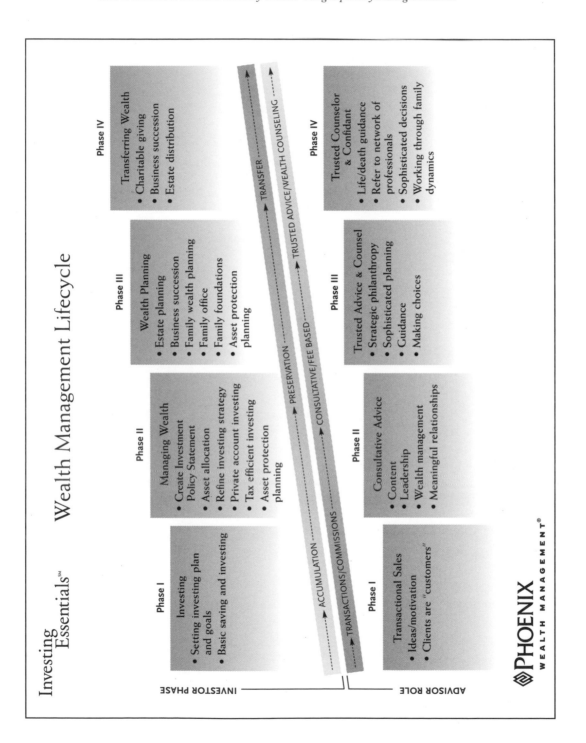

Investing Essentials℠   Wealth Management Lifecycle

INVESTOR PHASE

Phase I — Investing
- Setting investing plan and goals
- Basic saving and investing

Phase II — Managing Wealth
- Create Investment Policy Statement
- Asset allocation
- Refine investing strategy
- Private account investing
- Tax efficient investing
- Asset protection planning

Phase III — Wealth Planning
- Estate planning
- Business succession
- Family wealth planning
- Family office
- Family foundations
- Asset protection planning

Phase IV — Transferring Wealth
- Charitable giving
- Business succession
- Estate distribution

ADVISOR ROLE

Phase I — Transactional Sales
- Ideas/motivation
- Clients are "customers"

Phase II — Consultative Advice
- Content
- Leadership
- Wealth management
- Meaningful relationships

Phase III — Trusted Advice & Counsel
- Strategic philanthropy
- Sophisticated planning
- Guidance
- Making choices

Phase IV — Trusted Counselor & Confidant
- Life/death guidance
- Refer to network of professionals
- Sophisticated decisions
- Working through family dynamics

TRANSACTIONS/COMMISSIONS — ACCUMULATION — CONSULTATIVE/FEE BASED — PRESERVATION — TRUSTED ADVICE/WEALTH COUNSELING — TRANSFER

PHOENIX WEALTH MANAGEMENT®

Part II: Identifying the Best Clients for Managed Accounts

Learn how top advisors determine which prospects are the best potential clients for managed accounts – and how to identify those that are not!

WARNING!

If you have a good feel for the different scenarios and target markets for managed account prospects, let's now consider the *individual* attributes you want in a prospective client. First the warning. As I said earlier, some clients just aren't appropriate prospects for managed accounts. The biggest pitfall that claims many advisors who decide to use managed accounts is their attempt to fit a square client "peg" into a round managed account "hole." Simply, these advisors fail to transition some of their existing clients because they don't realize that some are not right for managed accounts. If you have a good client relationship, you probably shouldn't change it. You might want to do some serious evaluation to determine whether the relationship and the solutions you've provided thus far are working for the client before proposing a different structure.

Too often in the financial services business, clients buy products they don't need or that are inappropriate. The first rule of being a good advisor is to understand the client's goals and needs. You can't take a cookie-cutter approach to your client's financial future. The same principle applies to managed accounts.

Veteran advisor Mike's prospects and clients are all the right fit for managed accounts, otherwise they don't become clients. His typical client is a middle-aged corporate executive. These individuals are interested in taking care of their business, are sophisticated and don't have the interest or time to focus on their finances. Many did not have an investment strategy until they worked with Mike's firm. According to Mike, almost every new relationship must become a managed account, because he doesn't talk about stocks. Each client must have a financial plan that clearly identifies the client's risk tolerance and asset allocation. This plan is attached to and integrated with their managed account program. Many of his clients are affluent and willing to have a professional manage their assets. Says Mike, "One thing we do for all of our clients is to create an organizational chart for their assets. We aren't only interested in the total amount, we want to know how the assets are invested in all the accounts."

Says successful advisor Keats, "For us, the client has to have some degree of financial sophistication and a desire to delegate day-to-day investment management. Assets generally exceed $1 million for separately managed accounts. We will take smaller accounts if we believe there is opportunity to grow the business. For smaller accounts, we will use mutual funds. Mutual funds will be used to mirror what we would construct with separately managed account portfolios. If someone has $400,000, we can create a portfolio with a stable of six managers similar to what someone with $4 million would get. For some clients, we use alternative investments including managed futures, hedge funds and private equity funds. We may use variable annuities for tax-efficiency, living benefits and death benefits. Variable annuities are also used

> ### Who Is Not A Prospect
>
> - **Is your client always involved in decisions about the account?**
>
> - **Will your client be lost not knowing what to do with his free time, now that his account is being managed?**
>
> - **Does your client like to talk about the stock selection and asset allocation?**
>
> - **Does your client like to make his or her own decisions?**
>
> - **Does your client ask for daily reports? Call for quotes?**
>
> - **Does your client call you every day?**
>
> - **Did your client have a bad experience with a money manager?**
>
> **If after applying the questions on this checklist to a specific client or prospect, you find that you're shaking your head "yes" to most of them, then that client is not right for a managed account.**

for tax-deferral with wealthy clients who amassed their wealth through stock options and never had time for deferred plans to accumulate. Our view is to use the most suitable products given the client's needs. We do not subscribe to the argument of process versus product. Both are needed, but process comes first and is the more important of the two in the long-run." Keats has $125 million of assets under management and has been in the industry since 1981.

Based on a recent industry study,[1] approximately 33 percent of all affluent investors were willing to fully delegate the management of their assets to a professional advisor. Think about that – that's only one out of every three affluent individuals. Seventeen percent claimed to be fully discretionary – a role made much easier by the availability

[1]VIP Forum

of so many online tools, like estate planning analyzers and Monte Carlo simulations. The remaining 50 percent want to have some degree of participation in the management process.

Simply put, half of affluent investors are looking for validation but not to assume total control. Therefore, at some level, 83 percent of these individuals wanted a third party helping them manage their money.

Individuals who are very active, with busy careers, family lives, hobbies, or taking part in civic and charitable projects, are all good candidates. Explain to these clients that they will have more time to do what truly interests them, and they will have a more consistent method of financing these activities. These clients want to spend more time with their families and have priorities beyond their money. It doesn't mean they aren't interested in growing their capital; it means they are just as interested, if not more so, in what their money can do for them.

Look for these types of prospects and look for these qualities in your own client base. This type of profile shows they are responsible, grounded people with goals. The more goal-oriented they are, the more likely they will be attracted to the goal-oriented process of a managed account.

I presented some of the benefits of managed accounts in Chapter 6 (see below).

Refer back to the "Benefits of Managed Accounts Prospect Worksheet" that you completed at the end of Chapter 6, Part I. Take the conclusions you drew from that worksheet and use them here to help you decide which clients can best appreciate and utilize managed accounts.

Here are a few good examples of target marketing approaches from successful advisors we know:

"The ideal client for a managed account is a husband and wife team," says advisor Gerry. "The husband is a former corporate executive, has money to invest that represents 30-40 percent of their overall estate." This profile falls below many firms' radar screens, he says.

Steve believes the best targets for managed accounts are the typical clients he has right

> **Benefits of Managed Accounts**
> - **Time Savings**
> - **Access to Expertise**
> - **Consistency of Process**
> - **Finding the Right Manager**
> - **No Conflict of Interest**
> - **Customization**
> - **Prestige**

now: Business owners who didn't inherit the assets. "It's the entrepreneur, in their mid-50s, sophisticated, married with kids," says Steve. "They should be in the high-net-worth category with $1-$10 million to invest." Steve will take any amount if there is promise of capturing more assets later. His business is built strictly on referrals, and he has significant relationships with CPA firms.

Chuck doesn't agree with Steve about referral business. Very little of Chuck's managed account business comes from referrals – by choice. Says Chuck, "That's not to say you can't get good clients from others. Most folks don't think about the potential land mine that they can be. One key issue to worry about with a referral – if the relationship goes south, you can end up with egg on your face, as can the person who referred the prospect. What do you do if you simply don't like the person after you have them as a client? It isn't easy to just fire them!"

Chuck obtains much of his business through his extensive community activities, allowing him routine contact with a large number of wealthy individuals who are suitable for managed accounts. Several years ago, Chuck wanted to develop a community approach to help him establish solid long-term relationships. So, over the course of two years, he read a number of books on community leadership programs because he wanted to interface with high-level business executives who play an active role in community affairs. He quickly developed a database of business leaders and established a local chapter of a national leadership program to give high-level business executives the ability to participate in community affairs. He created several programs that allow business leaders to speak with area colleges on a variety of issues and also holds forums to address concerns faced by many of today's companies. Chuck does not introduce himself as a financial advisor but as the volunteer director of a program whose goal is to improve the quality of the community.

Advisor Tip

WOOFing Down Managed Accounts

The profile of Harry's typical client is 60-75 years old, married, a highly compensated executive or retired executive with a sprinkling of entrepreneurs. He likes to call them "WOOFs," which stands for well-off older folks. Harry says their annual income is $75,000 to $150,000 and their average net worth (excluding home) is $1.25 million. "They like the idea of paying a flat fee for a comprehensive financial plan," he says. "This process includes the following planning modules: investment portfolio with appropriate asset allocation; retirement security analysis; income tax-reduction analysis; risk management (insurance) analysis; survivor/care-giver security analysis; legal document review and family wealth transfer planning."

Most of John's business comes from rollovers. Of his $230 million under management, more than 85 percent is from 401(k) rollovers. John gets a good amount of business from a local company and has captured a number of rollover assets from individuals leaving the firm. Some of their money can't be rolled over immediately after they leave, so he encourages those clients to send him quarterly statements of the assets remaining at the previous employer. He reviews these with the clients on an ongoing basis.

Summary

You may have gleaned some target market ideas from this chapter. Think about your own charities, hobbies, and other activities that could lead to your natural target markets. And armed with a better idea of how your current base of clients fits with managed accounts (or not), and after making that determination, you can proceed to tackle other aspects of the managed account business. In the next segment, I'll give you some thoughts about seminars and client appreciation meetings.

Part III: Attract and Retain Clients Through Successful Seminars and Client Appreciation Meetings

Effective seminars remain an important marketing tactic in the sale of managed accounts. Consider these tips for staging a successful meeting and enhancing your reputation.

When managed accounts were popularized in the late 1980s, many high-net-worth brokers were familiar with using the seminar format to sell tax-sheltered investment products. Many of these brokers also discovered that seminars were a great way to present managed accounts. It was a very attractive venue to showcase the advisor's skills and the relative complexity of the managed account process.

Back then, if you had the acumen and public speaking experience, a seminar was a powerful way to show an audience how knowledgeable you were. To this day, seminars remain the most effective method of promoting managed accounts directly to affluent clients.

There are numerous approaches to organizing an effective seminar. Whether you are prospecting for new clients, attempting to capture additional assets from existing clients, or holding a client appreciation event, the seminar has one purpose: It's a method of getting a face-to-face meeting with a prospect.

Let's start at the beginning and talk about those prospects – your target market. You could begin with people who are prequalified. Consider the individuals you already know: Do they have enough money to invest in a managed account and the interest to use a real process to manage their wealth? It's critical to qualify your audience. In a "basics" seminar, you might simply introduce managed accounts to investors who may not understand the service, or who are currently mutual fund investors. Another audience could be investors who have a higher level of understanding, who may already have managed accounts with you, and from whom you might capture more assets.

Prequalifying Prospects

Regardless of which kind of seminar you hold, top advisors who use seminars understand a few key elements. First, you need a homogeneous audience. Nothing is more difficult to maintain than a seminar where some attendees understand the topic and others have no idea what you are talking about. You will be ineffective at reaching a large percentage of your audience at one end of the spectrum or the other. It's far better to have a smaller audience that has issues in common. Depending on what your topic is, homogeneity of the group is the first key to a successful seminar.

Don't ever be afraid of having too narrow or too specific an audience. One of the first managed account seminar success stories I witnessed in my career was when I worked with preretirees from Procter & Gamble on behalf of advisors Steve and Lew at a wirehouse firm in Cincinnati. The audience was very specific: They worked at the same company, lived in the same town and they had a lot in common, especially retirement. So the questions asked during the seminar were all similar, and it was very easy for them to relate to the topic of managed accounts and retirement planning. It was really like a support group. This was as important to the narrow audience as was the venue. We sat at small tables for dinner, not in a big hotel meeting room.

We've all attended seminars where one or two participants continue to ask basic questions while the rest of the audience – having more knowledge on the subject – become visibly bored and annoyed. You won't be able to speak as personally and specifically to your audience if you have too much variety of attendees.

Size of Audience

This is a hotly debated issue, but successful seminar advisors say the optimal size for a good managed account seminar experience is no more than 20 attendees. Somewhere between eight and 20 individuals is the perfect size, giving consideration to your goal of a homogeneous audience. Nobody sells much at a 300-person seminar. While the numbers sound terrific, you want to use your seminars as part of your sales process to give the investors a sense of who you are and how you work. The more you can personalize your message to them, the more they will feel as though you understand their needs and issues. Remember, your goal is to earn one-on-one appointments with the attendees.

So find the common link among the target markets. Think about how personal you can make your message and about what each potential attendee might have in common with another.

Conducting the Seminar

No matter what the topic or the audience, you are always the seminar host. This is your opportunity to show leadership and your authority on the topic of managed accounts. But should you be the one who delivers the body of the seminar? How complex should it be? If you are presenting your seminar for inexperienced investors, you could have an expert speak on managed accounts. It is absolutely critical that no matter who you choose to fill this role – whether it's you or someone else – this person must show his or her expertise beyond a shadow of a doubt. And not just during the seminar – show it also on paper, in advance of the seminar. Affluent investors are interested in working with people who have defined expertise. If you want to be effective with them, you have to prove your expertise – and that includes your promotion of the seminar to prospective attendees.

Why Should I?

Attempt to prove your expertise on paper beforehand, either with a biography or with a published article or other credentials such as a Certified Investment Management Analyst (CIMA) or Certified Investment Management Consultant (CIMC), and increase your chances of drawing a qualified audience. Why would someone attend your program? They would attend if they knew they would be hearing someone who was an expert on the subject. Don't hesitate to list the specific topics to be addressed and the key questions that will be answered.

Some of the most successful managed account seminar programs present the entire investment process. These meetings show attendees what it would be like to have their money managed using separately managed accounts. You can demonstrate the value of having an investment policy statement, the value of diversification of managers by asset class and investment style. Illustrate the historical interplay between value and growth styles and the efficient frontier among different portfolio choices. By showing the benefits, you are pointing out that managed accounts are the vehicle of choice by other affluent individuals and major institutions.

If you are new to managed accounts, you might want your firm's managed accounts coordinator for the region to give the presentation, or perhaps a representative or wholesaler from a managed accounts firm. For a historic perspective, this is how EF Hutton did most of its training and promotion of managed accounts. Hutton's regional coordinators worked around the national branch system and gave client presentations for the brokers and advisors.

Seminar Location

Give considerable thought about where you'd like to have your seminar, keeping in mind the professional nature and the exclusivity of the managed account solution for your audience. Remember, the typical affluent investor with a managed account has a net worth of more than $1 million. If you work in a major city and seek to represent yourself to an upscale clientele, an exclusive club or restaurant would quickly set the stage for a serious message. Think about the impression you are making in advance when you send your invitation to your prospects. Where would they *expect* an upscale meeting to be held in your community?

Food for Thought

Are you wondering whether or not you should serve your attendees a meal? It really depends on your style, how long you want your audience to stay, and how much you want to invest. I've seen greater success with an upscale location rather than the fact the audience is getting a free meal.

Time of day or night is important, too. I've seen advisors who have tried to hold dinner seminars only to fail because many on their invitation list had trains to catch after work and the restaurant did not serve the meals on time. Yet others in the same city have been successful with breakfast meetings because many individuals are willing to come in early but are not willing to stay late. I've seen advisors in the suburbs have successful dinner seminars because their prospects drive home and it's more convenient than mornings, when many people drop children at school.

The general rule of thumb is to make sure you are making the most efficient use of the attendees' time.

Know Your Market

Before you set the date and time of your seminar, watch the newspapers for a few weeks to learn when other organizations are having their programs. If the local chamber of commerce is an important organization in your area and it typically holds its meetings in the morning, take your cue from that fact. That organization picked that time for a reason.

What you really want is for your audience to be relaxed and not under a lot of pressure to leave. Roger, a successful advisor and branch manager in Buffalo, built his business with the breakfast seminar. He says people are very focused in the morning and he reports fewer cancellations. Because they have the greatest control over their day at the beginning, people tend to schedule the seminar first. When he began holding seminars on a frequent basis, his prospects and clients began bringing their friends and colleagues. They got to know the location and frequency of his weekly sessions.

Another advisor I know was targeting the executives of a major corporation and determined that the best location for his seminar was at a nice hotel right around the corner from the company. It was incredibly easy for the attendees to walk over and not worry about driving and parking again.

Home or Away?

Some advisors question whether or not to have a seminar in their office. While we have seen advisors use the office, it tends not to work as well for the newer audience because they are still in an educational mode, not ready to commit, and may not feel comfortable arriving at your branch. You may need the perception of objectivity gained from an unrelated location, like a club.

You want to make the most efficient use of your prospects' time, as well as that of you and your speaker. It's better to have three programs in one day with audiences segmented according to their levels of interest and understanding rather than miss an opportunity and jam mismatched people into a single meeting. Many top advisors recommend multiple locations and multiple times for the same topic. This is particularly important when you are soliciting attendance at the seminar.

When you get to the invitation follow-up, it's always better in a sales situation to give your prospects the choice of locations and times. For example, say, "Which meeting would you like to attend?" rather than, "Are you going to be there?"

Think creatively about locations. One of the most successful seminars I've ever seen was held in the press box of an empty college football stadium. The advisor holding the seminar was an alumnus of the college; it was unique and everyone had a good time – and it was free!

Exclusive country clubs are a great location, too, because you have the added benefit of promoting your seminar to the members of the club by posting a notice, even if you're not a member.

Restaurants can be very expensive because of the cost of food, of course, and then you need to consider adding wine to the food bill and whether you should serve cocktails in advance. This is the most expensive way of working with your prospects, however you may find it necessary because your competition serves food and drinks. Meals add complexity and potential disappointment to your plan, though. Why take a chance with finicky eaters, or folks who can't hold their booze?

Give a lot of thought to securing a location that captures people's attention. This is the first indication to them of your style, how you operate, and what you are like. Just remember the keys: Easy location, easy to find, easy to get in and out, good time of day, and prestige. And for gosh sakes, pay for the parking if necessary!

The Invitation: You Are Cordially Invited To Learn Something Important

Give considerable thought to the physical appearance of your invitation. Ask yourself, if you received this invitation in the mail, would you be intrigued? The look and feel need to speak directly to the target audience.

Do you entice a prospect with the way an invitation looks? When people receive mail, either they open it or they don't. They open the mail that looks professional. Sticking a mailing label on an envelope does not look personalized. These days, every printer in every office has the capability to print an original address on an envelope. Do it.

While it might seem sophomoric, generic mailings from brokerage firms have the postage meter stamps. A coach I know advocates using a first-class stamp on all mailings, but I believe it's far more important to have the envelope look professional and be directed specifically to the prospect. It goes without saying that the person's name, company, and address should be spelled correctly.

Successful seminar-givers report that it is not a bad idea to send a copy of the invitation to the prospect's home, as well. Sometimes you never know who actually opens the mail. There is also an added benefit for just the cost of another envelope and stamp: You get two chances to get the prospect's attention.

In the body of the invitation, explain precisely what the seminar is about, who will be presenting (their biographies and credentials) and what seminar attendees will learn. Be sure the benefits are spelled out clearly in the very beginning.

Be Specific

You don't want to be as generic about your topic as, "Outlook for 2002." You think you might want to use that headline because one of your speakers will be talking about what's happening in the marketplace, however, it's critical to be more specific.

It's not an exclusive topic and it probably won't be a good draw. For example, if your seminar topic is about the benefits of investing in separately managed accounts, your headline could be as straightforward as, "Professionally Managed Accounts: A Personal Strategy for Your Hard-Earned Money."

A savvy advisor we know lists all of the questions that would be answered at the seminar on his invitation to pique the interest of prospective attendees and help make it easy for them to determine the value of attending. You have nothing here to lose – if the prospects don't see anything on your list that interests them, they aren't good prospects!

Managed Account Seminar
Sample Topics and Questions

- What is a professionally managed individual account?
- What is the minimum investment?
- What is an investment policy statement?
- What is asset allocation?
- How do you select a professional investment manager?
- How do you monitor the managers?
- What should be the benchmark of performance?
- Do I need more than one manager?
- What are the fees involved? Are they negotiable?
- How do I know how I'm doing?
- What are the tax benefits to me?

The invitation might include some text that is similar to this:

> *Separately managed accounts are the investment vehicle of choice for affluent individuals and wealthy families, as well as public and private pension funds. These accounts are also available to individual clients of [add your firm name] for amounts as low as $100,000. If you'd like to learn more about the advantages of separately managed accounts, and if you are an investor in mutual funds and securities and you're ready for a comprehensive solution to your investment needs, we welcome your participation. This educational opportunity is being presented at the following locations [add dates and at least two locations].*

See Appendix D for more helpful seminar ideas, including sample invitations and a seminar checklist.

After the delivery of your program, at which you can impart information that individuals can take with them, you need to make it very clear how they can take the next step if they are interested in your services. Give them something personalized. If they have their own meeting agenda, notes, questionnaire, and a name tag you can clip to the seminar package, it shows you have taken the time to customize something for them. One successful advisor we know always includes a nice folder with pockets for information and a letter inside describing the advisor's initial new client process – the first meeting with the client, how long it normally takes, financial information needed and so on.

I Do and I Understand...

It's a good idea to ask attendees to fill out the questionnaire you've included in the packet. It allows them to get involved, and they move from being passive to being active in the discussion, and it becomes real. Much of the data they write on the questionnaire you've provided can be used for the investment policy statement. But the important thing is to allow them to take part in the meeting.

Confucius understood the importance of activity in the learning process: "I hear and I forget; I see and I remember; I do and I understand."

Repeat After Thee

Repetition is the key to success in using seminars for prospecting. For example, a repetitive seminar program is a great way to introduce current clients to new investment managers. The seminar is presented on an ongoing basis, and it becomes a way to effectively "drip" on prospects. Drip marketing is a consistent form of messaging done on a frequent basis to help brand your name and your services.

Again, the goal of the seminar is to introduce yourself and to showcase your skills in order to get a one-on-one meeting. The key to success becomes making the event an ongoing process – a part of your overall marketing strategy. If a prospect can't attend, but a colleague does and reports back to the original prospect about what a great seminar it was, it would be a shame if there was no repeat opportunity. Be sure to tell all of the attendees at the close of the meeting that you provide these seminars regularly, and that it's an educational service you offer. Also give each attendee an invitation for a future program to pass on to a colleague or a friend.

The easiest referral to obtain is from someone who attended your seminar and told others about it. One of the most successful seminar programs I ever participated in myself was when I was with Systematic Financial Management in the early '90s. It was run by a financial advisor in the Tyson's Corner, Virginia, office of a wirehouse. He held a dinner program once a month at a restaurant within the same complex as his office. The key to his success was familiarity – it was always at the same location, the same day and same time. He used the same four investment managers, rotating them in teams of two every other month. New attendees would greet us, "I came here to hear you two – my friend Jim said you both were great!"

Added Benefit for You

Mailing seminar announcements to your prospect list is the least expensive advertising you can utilize. Treat each announcement as an advertisement for your services, so include your biography and other credentials. The recipient may not want to attend the seminar, but might need your services.

Other Types of Seminars

The Investment Manager Seminar

Another type of event you may wish to hold is for either existing clients or other individuals who are new to the managed account process. In this type of event you can expose these people to one or two of your managers who are particularly strong in articulating both the investment process and the benefits of managed accounts, as well as the state of the markets (for more information on working with managers and other allies, see Chapter 8).

In the investment manager seminar, you follow all the seminar rules previously mentioned, only now you want to emphasize the underlying style and process of the specific investment managers. It is not appropriate to share performance records in these meetings at this time because you are working with multi-manager solutions not based on performance, but on the process. Otherwise, you will have individuals trying to second-guess the manager's performance and miss the educational aspects.

One Lump or Two?

One of the most common issues about manager seminars is whether or not to have multiple managers in a single seminar program. Two managers can work well to reinforce issues around process so that you do not get lost in talking about performance records, which is strictly prohibited by compliance departments at some firms.

Regardless of how closely the managers are aligned – that is, if they are complementary managers in style – they will always reinforce the issues of process because they know that getting part of an overall solution is better than getting 100 percent of a client's assets and having that individual overconcentrated in a particular style. All of the management styles you are likely to come across have already been through the experience of having too much concentration, and none of them wants to repeat that situation.

Make sure the manager or managers who speak at your event – based on your early knowledge of your attendee demographics – are potential hires by anyone in the audience. For example, what could be more of a misfit than presenting an aggressive growth manager to a group of retirees? Don't risk disenfranchising the audience by inappropriate manager selection.

Regardless of whether or not your attendees are new to managed accounts, you need to establish your value early in the program. As the host, you must be crisp and articulate on the topic of manager selection and how they have performed for you in the past. Provide a recap of the current market environment and the investment management consulting process so that attendees are very clear about what your added value is and will continue to be. Your goal is to convey confidence to your audience that you know what you're doing and that you would be a valuable advocate for them.

Client Appreciation Meetings

The goal of seminars is to schedule one-on-one meetings with new qualified prospects. However, a terrific way to use the leverage of multiple clients already working with you is to bring them together on a common topic and show the group your appreciation for their business.

There are many varieties of client appreciation meetings. Some are focused entirely on business, while others are pure fun. It all depends on your style. One of the biggest and most successful advisor teams produces more than $7 million in revenue each year. The group was seeking a way to bring clients together more often. They tried a client appreciation event with a city museum. It is now an annual event.

Group client meetings show clients you care. Since most of them have multiple needs, you also get the opportunity to educate them in a group setting, taking advantage of the leverage that's created by the availability of an individual expert. They also get to meet other people like themselves.

Create A Community

Client appreciation meetings are usually categorized in three ways: educational workshops, manager or market reviews, and pure appreciation social functions. To begin, let's talk about the social function. We know a very successful multi-million dollar advisor team in Connecticut that organizes a barbeque every year for about 1,500 clients. The advisors take photographs and send the custom photos back to the clients with a thank-you note for their business. They maintain a yearbook of the event with pictures of all attendees at each yearly barbeque, and they keep the books in their office for prospective clients to flip through while they are waiting for their appointment. In other words, they try to create a family-type setting for their clients – a sense of community.

For manager and market events, some of the most successful investment management firms we know, such as Kayne Anderson Rudnick and Chase Investment Counsel, hold annual client meetings that feature not only the chief investment officer of the firm holding forth on the market, but also top Wall Street analysts interspersed throughout the weekend, opportunities to play golf and tennis at the local country club and a special dinner on Friday night.

My colleague, money manager Roger Engemann, has maintained close ties with financial advisors and high-net-worth clients by hosting an annual client gathering at the Ritz Carlton in Pasadena. Consistent with the firm's personality and style, the Engemann meeting is intended to show clients they are part of a family.

Sometimes advisors ask whether it's appropriate to bring clients together at one big event. On the basis of having fun or learning, it's always appropriate. Some have said that they fear clients will not like the lack of confidentiality, but you can always invite them and they may choose not to attend. And that's ok, too.

Share the Wealth

Appreciation gatherings can serve to educate your clients, keep the lines of communication open and as an important retention tool. For the most part, most wealthy people who come to you for advice have generated their wealth through other means outside of investing. While your client may be relatively new to investing, he or she may also be new to being wealthy. These clients need to understand their overall wealth management, and if they become more acquainted with the topics and information in this area, the more comfortable they become with you. Consequently, the easier it will be to discuss investment matters with them. It is extremely powerful for wealth management advisors to be in front of their clients to say, "We feel it's important for you to learn more about these particular areas of wealth management." The practical reality is: If you don't teach them, another advisor will.

I estimate that more than half of all affluent individuals want to learn the best ways to manage their money. Very few clients have the enthusiasm to take on more than one investment topic at a time, though. Advisors Richard and Jock stage topics they feel are important for their clients to understand and hold educational events throughout the year, year after year. Keeping clients on a continual educational track keeps them moving up the wealth management lifecycle and learning curve.

Time to Get Started

If you're ready to add seminars and client appreciation nights into your business strategy, you can begin by examining the seminar invitations and checklist in Appendix D. Use them as a model, adding your own personal touch and creativity. Remember to include these events in your business plan and to review the level of their success when you revisit your plan.

Advisor Tip

The Art of Advice

Appreciation meetings don't have to be about investments. You might discover a topic that some of your affluent clients want to know more about. For example, Gary in Toledo knows many of his clients are interested in art and antiques. He found that by working with Sotheby's, a major east coast auction house, he was able to work with key experts there, who were happy to come to Toledo and converse with his affluent clients over lunch about the art markets, or over cocktails in the evening about valuable wines.

Gary also recognizes the charitable interests of wealthy individuals. What he has tapped into over the years is that his clients want to know more – and do more – in the area of family foundations. Gary will have wine and cheese gatherings at his home to talk about charitable giving and the opportunities for his clients.

Part IV: Managed Accounts as Part of an Overall Wealth Management Strategy

Affluent clients increasingly require a financial gameplan to help them tackle their complex financial needs. What are their most important concerns and how can you use wealth management to earn more managed account assets?

Many brokerage firms and financial advisory businesses are struggling with the challenge of wealth management – the multiple financial needs of a client beyond investments. The Phoenix Companies, Inc., based in Hartford, Connecticut, has branded itself as the wealth management company by developing solutions to these varied financial needs and helping financial advisors apply those solutions. But what does "wealth management" really mean?

"In its purest form, wealth management means guiding individuals through the financial risks and opportunities they encounter at each stage of their life," says Dona Young, president and chief operating officer of The Phoenix Companies. "More broadly, it means helping the affluent and high net worth do three essential things: accumulate wealth, preserve it and then transfer it. In my opinion, unless a company or firm can do all three, they cannot say they are truly in the wealth management business. At Phoenix, our strong position in the market is based on our ability to manufacture a broad range of products and services – from investments to insurance – that help advisors deliver wealth management solutions to their clients."

Wealth Is Just a Phase

Clients progress in the financial planning and investment management areas as they grow in stature as affluent investors. As they become more wealthy, they pass through four phases:

- In the *Investing Phase*, they begin to take money out of their business, or salary, and invest and build wealth.

- In the *Management Phase*, their collection of investments should be organized with an investment policy statement. Here, they focus on risk and return in conjunction with an overall game plan to achieve the risk-adjusted results they seek.

- In the *Planning Phase*, clients realize the need to plan for the ultimate disposition of their assets and minimize taxes.

- In the *Transfer Phase*, clients consider various ways to take care of the next generation, e.g., charitable giving, family foundations and business succession.

"The Wealth Management Lifecyle" chart on page 165 offers a visual depiction of these phases.

One of the challenges to financial advisors is staying relevant to your clients as they progress through the four phases. Wealth management means you, as the advisor, need to maintain your value to clients as they become more wealthy. Many advisors have helped with their client's initial savings or investments, only to be fired later because they didn't share the client's interest in moving to the planning stages and eventual transfer of the assets.

Fear of Wealth

Some advisors are intimidated talking about wealth management. Not so for seasoned advisor Diane. When discussing the use of managed accounts to form a wealth management program for her clients, Diane asks her prospect a series of emotionally challenging questions: "What will you do if you become disabled? What will your spouse and children do? Suppose you suddenly died? Would your family be secure financially?" The purpose of these questions is to get clients to open up and address situations that most people refuse to even think about. "Sure, they're upsetting issues, but how can you expect to develop a formal plan if you don't understand what the client wants to do in the midst of a devastating event?" asks Diane. These questions also help her discover whether the client has other assets with multiple advisors. "The last thing you want to have is the domino effect when a life event occurs," Diane explains. "That is why you must have all the pieces of the puzzle to be of value to your clients."

Ted has no problem talking about wealth management to his prospects and small business clients, either. Ted tells his clients that, as business people, they need to focus on running their companies, and let his team manage the finances. Says Ted, "The client must have the mentality of 'I have other things to do and can't focus on managing my assets, too.'"

More Than Just Money

Some advisors don't want to get involved in all of the complexities of the client's financial future – they prefer to handle only the investments. The challenge for that role is that now the industry is being driven by a younger baby boomer clientele that needs help with more financial services like disability and estate planning.

Since the baby boomers are now dominating the financial services industry, it is crucial to have a solutions-based approach to the wealth of a client. The boomers need guidance with more issues (such as elder care and business succession, for example) and as a result, advisors who sell only investments lose these prospects and clients because they don't have an orientation to (or an interest in) the challenges presented by their clients.

One of the most successful wirehouse advisor teams I know was invited by the senior executive team of a major company to present their financial solutions. It was one of the great opportunities of all time. Unfortunately, the team failed to close the deal because their presentation focused almost exclusively on investments – an area the executives of the financial institution felt they already understood.

The team was so excited about their investment solutions they didn't present anything else. The CEO of the prospective client firm said his group needed help with the financial issues, not the investment issues, and was very disappointed. He needed to hear about succession plans, charitable giving and estate planning. The team fell flat on its face because they not only didn't understand the prospect's needs, and consequently did not have solutions, but they also didn't realize the importance of those issues. Being a smart and resourceful advisor, the wirehouse team leader saw the experience as a wake-up call for his practice and has made aggressive moves to refocus his team's skills and direction.

Changing Priorities

For many advisors, the 1980s and '90s bull market masked the need to focus on wealth management. The former head of the managed account and retirement plan area for a major wirehouse called me one day and asked for a referral to a financial advisor for a wealthy friend of his who made his fortune in the oil business. I said, "Why are you asking me? You were in charge of this major division for years and you know thousands of advisors." He said, "I only know *investment* advisors, not financial advisors." That was a sad commentary. But, he is right – there is a significant difference between the two roles.

Consider your role with clients – are you solely an investment advisor, or are you quarterbacking their total wealth picture? Look at the wealth management lifecycle chart again (page 165) and note where your best clients fit right now. Are you helping them move to the next level? If you're not, is someone else?

Watch Your Wealth Management "Doors"

Wealth management encompasses a wide variety of needs – each of which represents a potential door of access to your clients. Consider "The Wealth Management Picture" which we discussed in Chapter 6, Parts II and IV. Each one of the boxes in the diagram represent a wealth planning need of the affluent client. Savvy competitors who have learned to target overlooked needs will exploit those opportunities.

One example is estate planning. The 2002 Phoenix Wealth Management Survey reports that three of 10 affluent clients have no estate plan and another 30 percent have a plan that is over five years old. With two-thirds of affluent clients in need of a current estate plan, any advisor could pursue that topic alone and have excellent chances of success. Why? If a client has any concern about the welfare of his or her family, an updated estate plan represents protection – and shouldn't the family be protected? And bringing up these concerns are not entirely for the benefit of the financial advisor. Consider an experienced life agent and advisor I met recently. Telling the story of his career, which spans an incredible 50 years, he relates his greatest accomplishments not in terms of personal earnings, but in the satisfaction of helping his client families. One particularly moving story was about a young man, 29 years old, who had a very successful business and four young children. At the advisor's insistence, this entrepreneur completed a comprehensive estate plan with several million dollars in life insurance. The timing was propitious. Shortly after completing the estate process, the young man died in a water-skiing accident. While the story is a horrible tragedy, explained the advisor – still moved to tears many years later – the situation would have been doubly tragic without the benefit of that estate plan.

Minimize Risk

Smart advisors know how to relate risks to clients – and much of wealth management is protection from risk. Risk is also a timeless sale. It is not dependent on stock market conditions. One of the difficulties for wealth managers in the heady days of the 1990s bull market was trying to get clients to focus on wealth management needs rather than buying tech stocks. Who wants to focus on risk when you're making money?

But these risks give savvy competitors access to your clients. Consider the estate planning vulnerability and ask yourself whether you have brought up that topic with your best clients. How easy would it be for a competitor to challenge them about whether they had protection for their families? What if an advisor – like the one I described above – was talking to your client and related that story? How would they respond? Would they wonder why you hadn't called them about the same topic?

Trust banks use the estate planning issue to access clients. Northern Trust and similar institutions have leveraged their custody and banking relationships with affluent clients by offering estate and trust services. Since most clients have no estate plan, in part because of their perception of the plans' cost and complexity, Northern makes the process easy. The services are turnkey and often entirely within the bank itself. The goal is to solve the problem for the client, but also to be named trustee for the estate – thus ensuring a multi-generational relationship with the family. Investment management services are an ancillary sale – the real goal is control of the client.

Banks are becoming increasingly aggressive with affluent marketing plans. Every business owner needs a bank, and the potential to leverage that relationship with other products is very compelling. Consider the mega-mergers in the financial services industry. Most of the biggest deals involve banks – First Union's acquisitions of Kemper and Wheat First, Citigroup/Smith Barney, UBS and PaineWebber. E*Trade made an important change in its business plan through the purchase of a bank, which allowed the firm to offer FDIC-insured CDs and money funds at higher rates than most competitors.

Several years ago, First Union searched for ways in which it could be more valuable to its clients and identified nonqualified retirement plans. First Union did not have the in-house expertise to provide such plans, so it created a business alliance with Management Compensation Group Southeast (MCG) in Atlanta. MCG had built nonqualified plans for Coca-Cola, Bell South and Home Depot. Offering the plans through a joint venture proved to be a great strategy for providing much-needed services to the First Union clients, and for capturing more assets to manage.

Watch for this banking battle to heat up – the stakes are high and spoils great in the battle for affluent clients.

Other "boxes" warrant your attention. Consider John Hancock, traditionally regarded as a successful insurance company, but also with good results from selling mutual funds to affluent investors. Recently, Hancock has been capturing affluent investors by offering long-term care (LTC) insurance. LTC insurance is a financial need of affluent investors seeking relief from the sky-rocketing costs of health care in retirement and is also a protective measure for baby boomers seeking financial protection from having to underwrite the long-term health care of their parents. By first capturing affluent individuals with LTC insurance, John Hancock agents earn the opportunity to talk about other solutions, including the investments, where their higher-level agents have offered – surprise – a managed account!

Intimidated by the complexity of wealth management? Don't be. No one expects you to be an expert in so many areas. "You must be *conversationally proficient* in the needs of the affluent to have credibility and do business with them," says affluent investor guru Russ Prince of Prince & Associates. This conversational proficiency means having the ability to query clients about their financial needs. It also means challenging your clients to address those needs – most of which provide no short-term satisfaction. After all, who really wants to do estate planning – or pay for it?

The bottom line is most of the challenges faced by affluent business owners are not those of how and where to invest. The real-world issues are those we discussed above, such as minimizing health care costs and having a good estate plan.

Market Share Warfare

There is a sense of urgency about the wealth management concept that is sending brokerage houses scrambling for ways to get their advisors to focus on this target market. The urgency is compounded by so many nontraditional competitors, such as John Hancock and Northern Trust, accessing affluent clients through financial doors like estate planning and long-term care, and then using that access to cross-sell investment management.

So, you might be thinking, "But I don't have the time, or the expertise, to be a wealth manager. How on earth can I do that?" That is, in fact, why the investment management solution is such a good one. No one person can meet all of the client's needs. It's important to understand the context in which the affluent have achieved their wealth, as well as the financial challenges they face. You need to be able to talk about these topics. No one really expects you to handle all of the issues alone. Delegating investment management to professional advisory firms gives you the time to have these financial conversations with you clients and prospects.

Investors who are happy with their advisors say their advisors prompt them to think about the important issues. Many financial advisors who are simply reactive to the needs of the client miss out on the opportunity to distinguish themselves by challenging their clients. By farming out the management of your clients' assets to investment managers, you free up time to work more with your clients on the big picture of wealth management.

Team Approach

To tackle wealth management, many advisors are teaming up with other specialists to fully address their clients' needs. In addition to the traditional partners like CPAs, some advisors also work with estate planning attorneys, insurance professionals, business consultants, and even lifestyle advisors such as psychologists and career counselors. Most of these arrangements are informal, but we see a trend toward advisors hiring technical analysts, technology specialists, marketing experts and others who may be important to the client and a complement to the advisor's day-to-day business and skill sets.

The Bottom Line

While wealth management seeks to address all of the client's financial needs, the primary revenue source for most wealth management advisory practices is the assets under management for a fee. Other products and services offer one-time commissions or fees, but the managed account typically offers the greatest overall return because of the long-term annuity income stream and the leverage of using the market's growth to increase that income over time. Managed accounts also leverage your time as an overall wealth advisor by freeing you from the daily chore of investment management. By subcontracting the investment duties to professional portfolio managers, you are able to invest that additional time in working with clients and prospecting for new business.

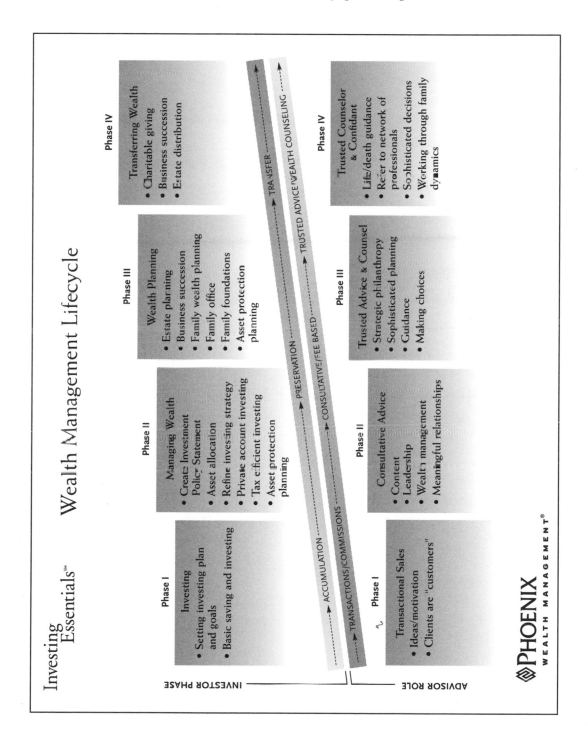

Investing Essentials℠

Wealth Management Lifecycle

INVESTOR PHASE

Phase I

Investing
- Setting investing plan and goals
- Basic saving and investing

Phase II

Managing Wealth
- Create Investment Policy Statement
- Asset allocation
- Refine investing strategy
- Private account investing
- Tax efficient investing
- Asset protection planning

Phase III

Wealth Planning
- Estate planning
- Business succession
- Family wealth planning
- Family office
- Family foundations
- Asset protection planning

Phase IV

Transferring Wealth
- Charitable giving
- Business succession
- Estate distribution

ADVISOR ROLE

Phase I

Transactional Sales
- Ideas/motivation
- Clients are "customers"

Phase II

Consultative Advice
- Content
- Leadership
- Wealth management
- Meaningful relationships

Phase III

Trusted Advice & Counsel
- Strategic philanthropy
- Sophisticated planning
- Guidance
- Making choices

Phase IV

Trusted Counselor & Confidant
- Life/death guidance
- Refer to network of professionals
- Sophisticated decisions
- Working through family dynamics

TRANSACTIONS/COMMISSIONS

CONSULTATIVE/FEE BASED

TRUSTED ADVICE/WEALTH COUNSELING

ACCUMULATION

PRESERVATION

TRANSFER

PHOENIX
WEALTH MANAGEMENT®

Part V: Attracting Additional Assets for Managed Accounts

There are five strategies for capturing additional assets from your managed account clients.

Y ou can capture more assets from your current clients in five ways:

1. Aggregation of information

2. Higher account minimums

3. Exposure to new asset classes

4. Rebalancing

5. Offering additional services

Let's explore each of these areas in detail.

Asset Capture 1: Aggregation of Information

Knowing the location of your clients' assets is the first step in capturing more assets for your new managed account business. Here are a few questions you might want to consider: Do you have the lion's share of your clients' assets? How do you know? Have you asked them? Are they the type of individuals who would be forthcoming with that information? Is there any incentive for them to reveal assets?

Savvy advisors know their clients keep assets elsewhere. The typical $1 million client has 3-4 advisors. These advisors are increasingly asking for – and getting – account statements from their best clients, revealing the assets held with other firms. A managed account creates a great incentive for individuals to consolidate their assets in one place. This is particularly important as clients are growing their wealth. If you are truly serious about bringing in more assets, you should attempt an "asset-capture" strategy.

Asset Capture

Account and performance reporting has developed into an asset-capture opportunity. Clients will volunteer additional assets they want considered in a report because they like to see the entire picture of their holdings. Seldom would a bank or brokerage firm be willing to provide such a report if they didn't hold all the assets, yet many advisors use this as a strategy. They say, "If we knew about your other holdings, we could put them on your statement – wouldn't that be convenient?" Large clients at brokerage firms today can, in fact, receive this benefit that is a highly sought-after service requested by the affluent. This service is also provided by many successful independent advisors.

Many online investment firms have been very successful in attracting affluent investors because they can hold multiple securities in a single account. These firms have also offered comprehensive accounts that give clients the ability to "scrape" account data from different custodians and report it in a single place. Get ready – you'll see more of this technology in the near future as information aggregation becomes the standard.

A Capture Process

Advisor Carroll says, "Most of our clients have all of their assets invested with us. We follow a six-step process which includes:

1. Understand the client's life goals

2. Structure the investments

3. Structure the allocation

4. Define how the client wants the money managed

5. Begin making the investments

6. Ongoing service/process

The very first step in our process mandates that we know everything about our clients, including where they have their assets. If they don't tell us, we're unable to give an appropriate allocation strategy. Clients are almost always cooperative and provide us with other advisor statements, copies of trusts, wills, tax returns, etc. This information also helps us to identify important issues such as a capital loss carry-forward or whether clients are subject to the alternative minimum tax. We do recognize that once we get into the $20+ million range, it is more likely investors will have multiple relationships with advisors. Still, you must know the details. We have one client who uses a bank, in addition to our group, to manage his assets. Every year we accompany the client to the bank to conduct a meeting with the manager there and review the entire portfolio. Because of the process that we followed, this client became dissatisfied with the bank and recently moved the remainder of his assets to us."

When I talk to advisors across the country, I always query how many ask their clients for statements from other advisors. In my travels, 25 to 50 percent of good advisors ask their clients and do receive statements. For most advisors it's most important to know where the assets are and to have a good enough relationship with each client so that she is willing to disclose the location of her assets.

The Quarterback Needs to Know the Team

Gerry's approach is to just "go for it." Says Gerry, "We want to know where everything is, but try not to be in a horse race to capture assets. We also track out-of-custody assets, but push the client to consolidate. It is important to be the quarterback. We try to get the client in front of our estate planning professionals whenever possible to help capture assets, and only focus on serious money. If the individual wants a trading account, they can go somewhere else. We don't want any 'funny money.' We don't say this stuff to be lofty, but we want to be held accountable."

Too Many Cooks Dilute the Soup

The asset-capture process involves determining why your clients might be motivated to give you additional assets. In many cases, the managed account process removes the barrier to the client giving you additional assets. The concept of working with multiple managers, multiple asset classes and multiple styles – whether in a mutual fund managed account or separately managed account, or both – is that it is better to have all the assets in one place so you can develop a coherent investment solution for each client.

You can explain to your client that it's important not to duplicate the efforts of other advisors or managers because it tends to reduce the value of the investment solution.

You might want to say something like this to your clients. "If you go to another firm that offers separately managed accounts and they also create an investment policy statement, putting you with multiple managers, multiple asset classes and styles, you may be deadening your overall potential return. If you have too many similar managers and styles, you'll end up with something resembling an index fund, and that will defeat the purpose of your investment goals. The goal, through your investment policy statement and the managed account process, is to create diversification for a better risk-adjusted return. In reality, you might be over-diversifying by placing your assets with various advisors and managers."

In many cases, clients are predisposed to over-diversify. The good news about diversification is that your clients listened to you. But the bad news is also that they now have too many accounts. Use these behaviors as an opportunity to educate your clients.

Asset Capture 2: Higher Account Minimums

Some of the early success stories for capturing assets with managed accounts employed a simple feature – account minimums. Some advisors said to clients, "I know you have a number of mutual funds and securities, and that's a great strategy for the beginning investor and the initial stages of building wealth, but for me to better manage your wealth, at a certain point, you earn the right to have a more customized portfolio. And this is possible when we have assets of $_____." (You fill in the blank here.) Eager to avail themselves of the higher level of service, some clients would produce assets enough to make the minimum. This phenomenon is reminiscent of the pre-money fund days when investors would scrape together enough cash to buy a $10,000 T-bill. The exclusivity implied by a minimum is often a lure to affluent investors. A top advisor team we know has had a minimum account size for many years. Originally $1 million back in 1980, the minimum was so widely publicized that it became a status symbol to be a client of the group. When you told a friend that you were a client, the friend now knew you were a millionaire!

Asset Capture 3: Exposure to New Asset Classes

Another asset-capture strategy is adding exposure to new asset classes. The goal of every advisor should be to create a solution that achieves the highest risk-adjusted return appropriate for every client. This tactic of extending the reach of the client is achieved successfully by firms that offer international investments. The diagram of the efficient frontier showing how an investment in international would improve the risk-adjusted return of the portfolio illustrates this well (see page 170).

More recently, the use of alternative investments, such as hedge funds, as a new asset class has been effective strategy for affluent investors looking for something more than traditional asset classes or styles.

Other examples of capturing additional assets using a different investment style or improvement to the risk-adjusted return would be non-correlating or low-correlating assets like real estate investment trusts, which worked well at the end of 2000 and early 2001, timberland trusts and other natural resources such as gold.

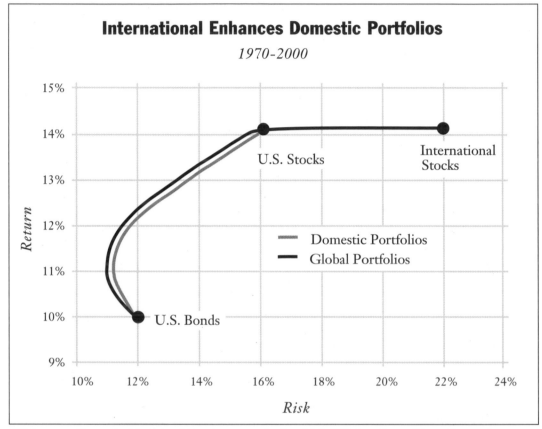

Risk is measured by standard deviation. Risk and return are based on 1970-2000 data. Source: Ibbotson Presentation Materials, © 2002 Ibbotson Associates, Inc. All rights reserved. Used with permission. This chart is for illustrative purposes only and does not represent the performance of any investment. Past performance is not indicative of future results.

Successful advisor Ted explains how he uses new asset classes to capture more assets. "I call my clients up and say, 'we are going to help you more than we already do.' We generally know what they own and who has it, and we don't hesitate to ask for more of it. For example, if we have 10 to 20 percent of a client's assets, we'll ask the client to show us what else he owns to balance the allocation. If you are lucky, the guy on the other side is asleep at the wheel and you can capture those assets."

Tools to use in the process of promoting new asset classes include the *Elements of Diversification* chart (see Chapter 6, Part III, pages 96 and 97) and portfolio modeling analyses such as the *Complementary Investment Analysis*^{SM} (see in Chapter 6, Part III, pages 98 and 99).

Asset Capture 4: Rebalancing

Perhaps the greatest challenge for advisors and consultants who create comprehensive solutions for clients using complementary asset classes and manager styles is that at any point in time, one manager, class or style will perform better than the rest. Since performance of each sector is unpredictable, the only way to take advantage of these unpredictable events is to expose the clients to different asset classes and styles so that when one of them takes off, clients will already be in place to benefit. Generations of investors still try to hopscotch ahead of the next asset class, only to find themselves buying last year's winner.

Again, use the *Elements of Diversification* chart that shows the leadership of different market sectors, asset classes and styles. Discuss this concept with your clients. To help your clients avoid chasing the "hot dot," it is imperative for you to show how market leadership changes based on the various manager styles and asset classes.

Talk to clients about the opportunity to put additional assets to work and the concept of placing them with managers who are performing at different rates of speed. Rebalancing is a great way to take advantage of shifting market leadership and is also proof of your active management of client portfolios. For example, if the initial managed account solution of 25 percent in large cap growth, 25 percent in large cap value, 25 percent in small- to mid-cap core and 25 percent in small cap core was involved in the move in the market (like in 2000 and 2001) and the large cap growth manager was knocked down, you now have an opportunity to put money to work with the large cap growth manager and bring up the percentage so that all allocations are equal again. In other words, the performance of the value manager and the relative bad performance of the growth manager may have ended up with the account looking like 35 percent value, 15 percent large cap growth, and in correcting the imbalance, there is potential to get new money from your client to shore up that imbalance. See an example of an un-rebalanced portfolio on the next page.

Market changes, rebalancing, and shifting leadership style create the sense of opportunity so you can go back to your client and say, "We could take away from the more successful managers who are doing better by comparison, or we can shore up your account with extra cash."

Rebalancing is not always a function of market activity alone. Steve, a seasoned advisor in the Northeast, asks at every meeting whether the client's objectives have changed. Says Steve, "We want to be sure no personal event is overlooked because it could require portfolio rebalancing." He captures more assets from clients simply by asking.

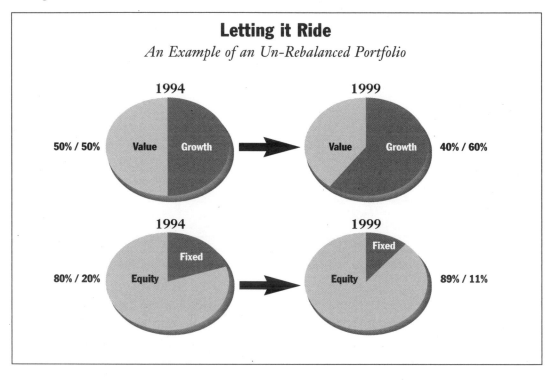

Letting it Ride

An Example of an Un-Rebalanced Portfolio

Many top advisors prepare their clients in advance for rebalancing opportunities, knowing that getting those clients to act in the moment can be difficult. Before the markets took a nosedive in 2000 and 2001, gung-ho investors were throwing their money at the Dow at 11,000. At 8,000 those same investors were reluctant to commit more money. That's just human nature. But as professional advisors, we need to help our clients act more like institutions and move when the values are there.

Take an educational approach and teach your clients why this is a good time to put money to work. Here are some points you might want to pass on to them:

• At the start of every normal recession, few investors believe we're in a recession.

• There's a point late in the recession when most investors acknowledge we are in a recession.

- Profits decline, stocks decline, unemployment increases, consumer confidence declines, consumer spending slows.

- Observers start to believe that the recession will be deeper and longer than any similar period before.

- Every "normal" recession has some particularly dangerous features, for example, the 1970 stagflation, 1974 oil embargo, 1982 oil collapse, 1990 banking crisis.

- In the last three months of a recession, the pace of Fed easing accelerates.

- In the last three months of a recession, the stock market rallies.

- At the end of every "normal" recession, few believe it's the end of the recession.

At the same time, discuss with your clients a few of the principles for disciplined investing in an undisciplined market:

- Performance chasing can be hazardous to their wealth!

- Take the emotion of out of investing.

- Have an investment policy statement.

- Re-balance your portfolio opportunistically.

- Stick to your plan even when your emotions are telling you to do the opposite.

Take a look at the series of bear market charts on pages 175, 176 and 177 for some additional perspective.

The bottom line is that you find many investors "zig when the markets zag." In the aftermath of the tragedy of September 11, 2001, when the markets plunged, the institutional investing community moved its cash to stocks, while individual investors ran to money funds and intermediate term bonds. Institutions were moving with opportunity, while individuals reacted to their emotions.

Business Owner's Investing Dilemma

Most affluent investors made their own wealth – about 80 percent are business people in some form. The challenge of obtaining additional assets from these clients at the right time is that their businesses are tied to the economy – and many business owners will not be comfortable investing when the economy is not doing well.

The number one competitor you have in gathering more assets from affluent business owners is their business or practice. They don't want to take money out of their business when they think they might need it in a sagging economy. Human nature and events conspire against the business owner-investor. The business owner might be reluctant to take money out of the business during a recession, but ask your client whether he feels the market is a leading or lagging indicator.

Of course, it's a leading indicator. When you look at the history of modern markets, whenever there has been a recession, the investors who waited until the end of the recession missed about half of the gain in the market, since it begins to rise right at the depth of the recession. So investors have missed the opportunity.

Don't forget, capturing more assets for your managed accounts is a market-share battle. At this stage in our industry – with the development of countless investment products and financial advice available everywhere – it is unlikely that affluent investors don't know where they can go to get good investments. Be aware that if you don't lead your clients, offering ideas of where to go next, they will soon wonder why they work with you.

Asset Capture 5: Offering Additional Services

The more you work with affluent clients, the more you realize the importance of not just the investments, but how the investments should be held by your clients. For example, a wealthy business owner may place assets in a trust or life insurance contract for tax benefits. This kind of strategy can become a way to capture more managed account assets.

Gary in Toledo uses the concept of family foundations to free up assets from affluent clients. Other advisors have become more active in suggesting to clients they consider ways to own assets to take advantage of lower taxes and other benefits.

Conclusion: If You Don't Ask, You Don't Get

In the AIM/Gresham Wealth Management Survey 2000 of advisors earning over $300,000 per year, 15 of 18 who asked their top 50 clients for additional assets got them. Now is the time to take action!

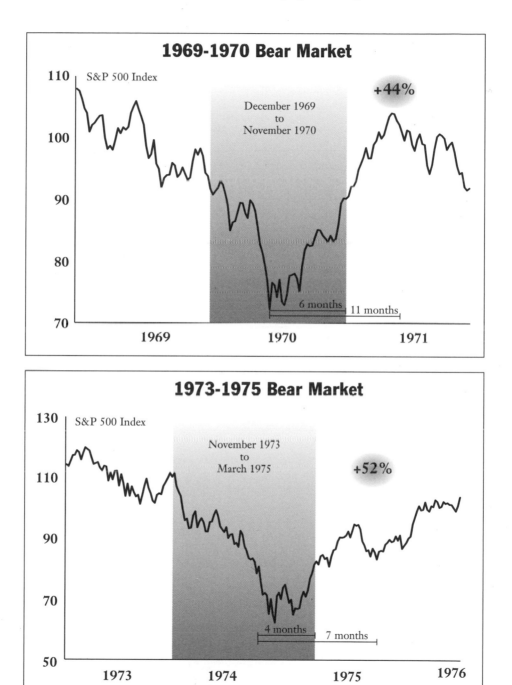

Past performance is not indicative of future results.

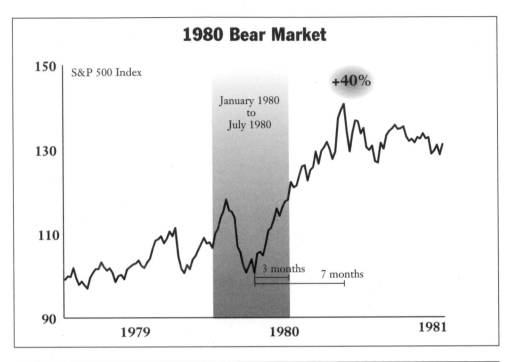

1980 Bear Market

S&P 500 Index

January 1980 to July 1980

+40%

3 months   7 months

1979   1980   1981

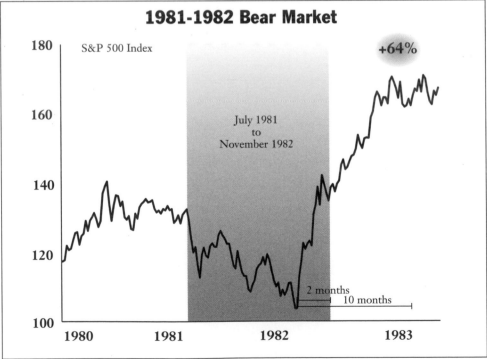

1981-1982 Bear Market

S&P 500 Index

July 1981 to November 1982

+64%

2 months   10 months

1980   1981   1982   1983

Past performance is not indicative of future results.

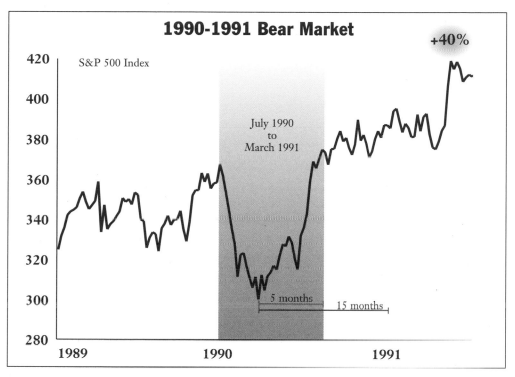

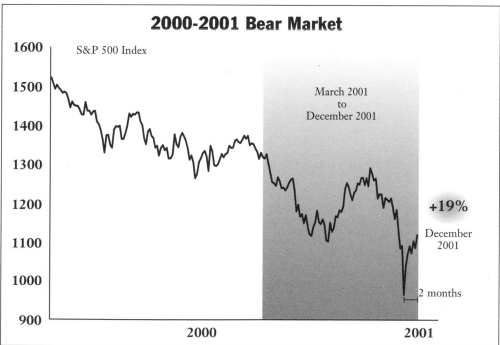

Past performance is not indicative of future results.

Chapter

Teaming Up with Allies

Help is available to grow your business. Investment companies and other professionals can contribute to your success if you know how to use their skills.

So far in this book I have discussed the various components of the managed account process, along with marketing and sales ideas. Together, we have covered a lot of topics – the sheer volume of which can be a little daunting. Now we'll consider how to get help for your managed account practice in the form of supportive vendors, other professionals like attorneys and potential additions to your practice in the form of partners.

Wholesale Advice

Investment managers and fund companies compete for your attention and they can be great allies to help you build your business. One of the most critical factors in presenting a new product or process, such as a managed account, is the ability of a firm to promote it through advisors. This means training the advisors in the specifics of the product itself as well as helping them portray the product to the prospective client. You can benefit from these efforts.

Consultants to affluent investors should search for helpful and suitable partners in the process of reaching their market. A wholesaler can help you with more than just personalized delivery of marketing materials. A good wholesaler can be a true business development partner who can help you open a marketplace in your local area.

Keats, a seasoned advisor, considers the wholesalers he works with his allies, not just product-delivery people. "A wholesaler should provide value in terms of helping me grow my business through target marketing, for example, and assisting me with relationship management."

Ground Rules

When you begin your search for managers, think of it as searching for a strategic alliance partner. You will need managers who can provide investment solutions for your clients. For example, large cap value and large cap growth managers are the most pervasive managers in the separately managed account world. And they are the important components of most asset allocation solutions. Although you are not limited to these categories, it's a good place to start.

When you find the right managers you need to create an incentive for a firm and its wholesaler to work with you. You may not be the largest managed account advisor or consultant in the area, but you may work in the same office with other advisors who also are interested in the same managers and need help, too. You may want to consider aligning with those advisors to leverage the wholesaler's time when visiting your office, especially if you are in the process of transitioning your business.

If you are a more experienced advisor, you may be interested in financial support for ongoing client appreciation meetings, for which the manager's economic support is helpful and also justified by the business you've done with the firm. Partnering with wholesalers for business development assistance is the highest and best use of their time. They see all of the best practices and marketing strategies being used by the most successful advisors. The best wholesalers are walking libraries of information for you.

Competition helps your case. While managers strive to create better product solutions, products are not enough. Advisors are often not interested in more product; they are interested in more support. "Research confirms," Russ Prince and I wrote in *Financial Planning* magazine, "that independent advisors would much rather have fewer, but better, selling arrangements and are starting to urge financial product firms to provide a rich menu of value-added services, especially training in marketing and practice management." [1]

---

[1] "Value Added Wholesaling," Financial Planning, June 1998

Skilled wholesalers put a tremendous amount of energy into helping advisors build their businesses. Because a good wholesaler has an incentive to keep your business growing, this person can also act as a coach if you have shared your business plan with him or her.

Performance Still Rules

All of this value-added help notwithstanding, I am not suggesting that you should select a manager and wholesaler based solely on their business development programs. First, and foremost, you need the talent and capability of the investment manager. All things being equal, though, why wouldn't you opt for the individuals who can give you the most assistance in capturing more assets?

The ideal arrangement for your practice would be to build an array of managers to cover the style boxes and asset classes that you need the most and at the same time, be able to extract additional value from each of the managers – whether education, financial support, or expertise – and recognize the professional quid pro quo of working with the management firms and benefiting from their tools.

Take Advantage of Wholesalers' Expertise

Make wholesalers your strategic partners. They can help you with marketing, business building, and servicing your clients. They can assist you in making one-on-one presentations and conference calls and act as a speaker at one of your seminars or client appreciation meetings (see the segment on seminars in Chapter 7 for more information on this topic).

The Best Don't Hide

We interviewed a number of financial advisors and asked about their relationships with wholesalers and what they expect from them. Carroll says, "The best partnership with wholesalers can be achieved when they:

- Provide outstanding service, communicate good *and* bad news, don't hide when the manager's style is out of favor, tell us what is happening without yes-ing us.

- Agree to participate in client appreciation meetings when we need them.

- Provide other communications to the team on what is going on with the manager. We need more due diligence on how the manager is performing in addition to our firm's due-diligence process.

- Visit with us two to four times per year."

The two basic categories of help and support are: 1) business development and marketing and 2) product information. Wholesalers can assist you in obtaining new clients, as well as provide better information about portfolios, access to portfolio managers, and training for new products.

Category: Business Development and Marketing

"When selecting managers and working with wholesalers, one of the biggest issues is service support," says advisor Paul. "We make it a point to conduct business with people who help support ours. We let our firm do the initial screening because they are very good at it, and then we decide who is best to work with. Seminar support is critical for us."

Keats has valuable insight on how he feels wholesalers can help him build his business. Says Keats, "The wholesaling industry sometimes can be out of step with the times. Some wholesalers are still moving products off the shelf. Successful wholesalers have learned that this business is not about moving product off the shelf. It is about helping financial advisors build strong relationships with clients and add real value to their client's lives through comprehensive wealth management. In our practice, we don't want to have multiple meetings with outside wholesalers. In fact, I limited myself to two meetings with wholesalers in my office all of last year. Even though I sometimes get six to eight calls a day from wholesalers, there is simply no time to meet. The really successful wholesaler has to talk about something that I don't know – things like client and asset retention practices, value propositions and other unique business development tools. What can we do that is better than our competition? That is the question we want answered."

Adding Value By Adding Business

Keats continues by saying, "The right way to get out there (for the wholesaler) is to find out who the top 25 producers are at each firm. Tell them how they can grow their business strategically. Give them an architectural plan. Tell them how they can set up a quality review with a client. Go to these top people and tell them you are providing tools to grow a business. Don't confuse activity with productivity. Help us paint a vision of what it's like to be a client of ours. We call every client once per month and have a formal quarterly review. If a client calls with an administrative issue, we get back to them the same day. Here is the reality: people share two kinds of experiences, really good and really bad. If you see a lousy movie or a great movie, you tell others about it. You generally don't share average experiences like a so-so movie or an o.k. financial advisor. It's the same with referrals, if you want positive referrals then create a great client experience for your existing clients. The same concept applies to the wholesaler working with the financial advisor. If you create a great experience (wholesaler with advisor or financial advisor with client), people will share the experience."

Problem Solvers

Advisor Mike says, "The great ideas we get from wholesalers are those that help us to find solutions for those clients with problems. These could be investment problems or retirement problems with suggestions or guidance that can be provided to the client. New business or prospecting ideas to get us through the tough times in the market are great types of communications."

Speak Up

On the wholesaling side, David Wadley, senior vice president, investment consultant, and one of the most sought-after speakers from Phoenix's Private Client Group, says, "The stellar wholesaler is a great public speaker. The financial advisor can use the wholesaler's speaking skills in seminars with clients to provide the educational bent. It's not a product sale; it's a learning process. Nine out of 10 investors don't even know what a managed account is. It's not that the advisor can't explain it, but a good wholesaler adds credibility and can be a part of the team. We need to help advisors grow their business. We can do one-on-one meetings with their clients or sit in on team meetings and comment on how they are managing their business. We give them a resource to carry their business to the next level because we are visible."

Jim Miklas, senior vice president, investment consultant, and his internal partner, Darren Morgan, internal investment consultant, both with Phoenix's Private Client Group, have this to say about working with advisors. "We usually tell advisors, 'The reason we are here is to help you ask yourself

> **Create A Personal Advisory Board**
>
> If you want to improve your practice, ask your best clients how to do it. Forming an "advisory board" can help. Use the worksheet on page 190 to create your own personal advisory board.

some basic questions about your practice. Give us the three critical objectives of your practice.' For example, one advisor said, 'Maintain our current client base, annuitize and get new accounts, and capture new money.' We send the advisor one great idea per week to help him with his business. We like to think of the Ford Motor Company Quality One program as what we do: great products; great marketing and engineering; and a long-term partnership to help grow business revenue."

Both Jim and Darren are discerning to whom they deliver their value-added service. "Who do we, as wholesalers, want to do business with? We try to avoid the performance-fixated advisors and ideally, want to do business with advisors who like us as much as we like them."

The Managed Account Role

Mary Kralis-Hoppe, senior vice president, investment consultant for Phoenix's Private Client Group, tries to understand how managed accounts fit in to the advisor's practice. Says Mary, "The key is understanding how the wholesaler can help the advisor develop a better practice. It doesn't matter if it is an established financial advisor or a rookie. The role of the wholesaler is changing. Before, we would tell advisors the story of *why* they should use managed accounts. The more important question is *how* they are used. You can't get traction with an advisor when you only discuss "why" [taxes, control issues, etc.]. Focus on the "how." I recommend that advisors use the product to balance their business. And keep in mind, it is more challenging to integrate this approach into the practice when we are in a down market, like now [mid-2002]. The client may say 'I'm paying 2 percent for this?' The fee business is a comfortable one when you are in a bull market, but hit the doldrums and watch out ... you need to focus on client retention."

A Story, Not A Product

Mary continues, "We also like to talk to the advisor about how the market has performed historically so the information can be used more effectively with clients. One advisor was very discouraged because of the recent market downturn. His business was good – he was bringing in new clients and wasn't losing accounts. Unfortunately, because his asset level was down in this unfriendly market, he slipped from being number one in the country to number five. Under these conditions, we like to work with the advisor to keep the focus on retention, service and the long-term picture. My overall goal is to help the advisor do the following:

- Examine his/her existing practice. What changes can be made? How can the practice be enhanced? What are the risks? What are the weaknesses?

- Help educate the financial advisor's clients on the managed account process. Move away from the transaction mentality.

- Retention-Retention-Retention – Bring assets in the door and keep them. Focus on the clients you already have and maintain a superior relationship. Give them a story, not a product."

Category: Product Information

Advisor Paul tells us, "The wholesalers we work best with also understand their niche – their bucket, as we call it. Don't try to give us a bunch of products just to boost the assets we have with your company."

Crisis Communications

Dan, an advisor who's been in the business for over 10 years, explains how to partner effectively with wholesalers. "Not only do wholesalers have to provide us with new ideas when things are good, but they have to be available to do so when the markets are in bad shape too. Communicate when there is a crisis! Give us advice on how to conduct better client meetings in challenging times and bring a manager to the meeting who has a great story. What does he or she do that is unique and what are the steps in his or her process? Tell us more than 'we buy great companies that have the best products.' The best wholesalers I've seen are not out-of-sight, out-of-mind when the markets reverse course."

Advisor Mike also tells us, "We look forward to learning about new products. For example, a recent presentation I heard discussed a market-neutral fund. This product may fit into some of our clients' portfolios."

"The best support we can receive from our wholesaler relationships," says advisor John, "is to give us the inside track about the portfolio. In other words, provide us a solid knowledge level about weightings on stocks and other key data changes about the portfolio. We also need to be kept up-to-speed about manager changes. We look for tools to use in client seminars and for assistance in helping to write client proposals. As an advisor, I'm not a research analyst; I'm a relationship manager. Sure, we can do the evaluation ourselves, however, it takes a significant amount of time and is quite difficult to do. If our wholesaling partner can look at a client's entire portfolio, evaluate it using Morningstar and other tools and suggest the best fit with their company's products, we would have the golden goose egg."

Jim Miklas discusses the literature and materials provided by many firms, "Some firms have excellent material for advisors, while others either have none or information that is poorly presented. Advisors get inundated with right-brain stuff from their firms. Focus on the left brain. My partner, Darren and I provide concepts and value. What value means to us is giving support to advisors to help them make an impact on their practice. One concept piece we use a lot is the *Elements of Diversification* [see Chapter 6, Part III, pages 96 and 97], which shows changing market leadership among investment styles and the benefit of diversification in lowering portfolio volatility."

Working Together for the Client

Wholesalers and other managed accounts support people also have a lot to say in terms of how you can best work with them, and what they bring to the table. It's all about developing trust and rapport with each other and surrounding that with education and support. Here are a few more important words of wisdom from the experts:

Jim and Darren also help advisors with the investment process. Says Jim, "We help advisors with the firing component of manager evaluation. We help them set their boundaries with *their* investment policy program with managers: For example, three years underperformance to the benchmark and the fund manager is gone. Or, advise the manager that he is under probation for the next year and if things don't improve, he's gone. We try to build expectations into the advisor's business. Here's another example – get advisors to think about the concept of attribution. We can help them evaluate why the portfolio is underperforming – is one stock driving 80 percent of the underperformance?"

Mary Kralis-Hoppe believes that advisors who take a holistic approach to the business are the most successful ones. She wants to establish relationships with advisors who present a host of global wealth management solutions to clients – in other words, she avoids the product pusher.

Advisor Mike also tells us, "Physical presence is important, too. We have 5,000 things in the hopper at one time, and we can't always communicate with our wholesalers in the most effective manner by phone. They need to be there."

Team Up with Colleagues Who Complement Your Expertise

In addition to working with wholesalers, you can build a virtual team with centers of influence, e.g., CPAs, estate-planning attorneys, and business consultants. Consider doing this with your client's circle of professionals so you have a better picture of where that client's additional assets are.

Harry works with a certified elder law attorney who focuses on long-term care planning. Elder law is the legal practice of counseling older persons about the legal aspects of health and long-term care planning, public benefits, surrogate decision-making, and the conservation, disposition and administration of their estates. It also includes implementation of their decisions in these matters, the tax consequences and the need for more sophisticated tax expertise. Having this expertise on board, Harry has the capabilities to specialize in this market.

Ron Weiner of RDM Financial Group, Inc. in Fairfield, Connecticut, depends on skilled partners and associates. He says, "Our business requires expertise in sales, trusts, taxes, investments, and operations. It is very difficult for a one-, two- or even three-person practice to have excellent command of all of these different skill sets. The larger the scale and the more experts you have in house – Ron has a staff of 12 – the more effective you will be in helping a client to achieve his or her total financial goals. By being both detailed financial planners, as well as discretionary money managers, we not only design solutions that fit clients' needs, but we have the ability to act more efficiently when allocating or rebalancing portfolios. Having this kind of scale adds tremendous value to your practice."

In addition to partnering with other professionals, don't overlook teaming up with your fellow advisors. Teams are growing in importance and many are specializing in wealth management. For example: You capture the assets; your partner does the asset allocation, monitoring and performance reviews. Other members of your team can be adjunct specialists like analysts, computer experts, and marketing strategists.

Ted and his partners have determined that they can manage about 75-100 relationships to be effective. Beyond that, the capability of being a point person diminishes significantly. Ted developed a model team with his partners to operate the business horizontally, rather than vertically. This way, each partner knows the other's clients. Each partner's specialty or segment also can be presented to the client to focus on total wealth management services. The three general areas he and his partners focus on are public relations/marketing, investment management (manager selection and asset allocation), and financial planning.

A team approach in capturing and managing the existing business results in multiple levels of expertise. This frees up John's time to focus on assets, client service and generating profits. Currently, John partners with three advisors and employs four full-time associates. John's focus is on insurance and estate planning, in addition to money management. A second partner focuses on 401(k)s, and the third has expertise in debt and credit issues. "It's not a good use of our time for all three associates to know the details of all of the clients," says John. "Our philosophy is to have a primary relationship manager (usually the person who landed the account). This person knows the intimate details of the client's financial situation. In some instances, personality attributes don't mesh, so we change the partner's relationship to someone else."

Mentoring

Other successful advisors and consultants may be willing to be a mentor until you have transitioned, or at least to give you professional support along the way. If you are interested in this approach, try to locate someone who is inside your branch or someone outside your office. Lately, more firms are developing formal and informal mentoring programs for their advisors and are encouraging the veterans to lend a hand to rookies.

Gerry has a very successful wirehouse practice in Hartford, Connecticut, and is a fan of teaming up veterans with rookies. "For the new kids on the block, Wall Street can partner trainees with advisors who have been in the business for a while," he says. "You have to give the new consultant time to build relationships, given the competitive nature of this business."

Dan and his partner act as mentors for financial consultants just entering the business. "New guys will need tremendous strength for the next two to three years in this market," says Dan. "The key to success is to have a detailed strategy and develop a game plan with specific goals at specific times." Steve in Boston agrees and attends sales meetings with younger brokers to help them with the sales process.

Advisor Gary concurs with both Steve and Dan about mentoring. He is emphatic about mentoring new advisors who are transitioning into the managed account business. "For those trying to build a plan, I say, 'get yourself into a mentoring program. Have a senior advisor serve as your mentor,'" says Gary. "It is incumbent upon the firm to help the new advisor, too. Many training programs fail – this is why turnover is so high in some firms."

Sometimes a Little Coaching Helps You Stay in the Game

Don't overlook the advantages of hiring an industry coach or trainer if your firm does not support the training effort or if you want to take your business to a higher level. Or hire a coach if you need someone to help keep you on track with a strict, disciplined approach. At the very least, think about retaining someone to help keep you accountable and motivated. It is an investment in your own future. Fees for coaches and trainers depend on the amount of time spent on each session, depth of coaching, in-person or telephone coaching, and how long you retain the coach.

No Stone Unturned

All in all, possibilities to ally and partner with other professionals and colleagues who will take a keen interest in your business are myriad. Investigate the choices we've outlined in this chapter, and you might be surprised to discover a few ways to not only boost your business but to develop friendships and strong professional relationships along the way.

Feedback Loop

Create A Personal Advisory Board

How are you doing? What are your resources?

Personal Advisory Board Members

Client Name: _____   *Profession/Expertise:* _____

Client Name: _____   *Profession/Expertise:* _____

Client Name: _____   *Profession/Expertise:* _____

Client Name: _____   *Profession/Expertise:* _____

Questions:

What do you like about our practice?

_____
_____
_____

How can we improve our services?

_____
_____
_____

What other companies or advisors have you spoken with/worked with recently?

_____
_____
_____

What do you like about those firms/advisors? Their services/products?

_____
_____
_____

If you could change one aspect of our practice, what would it be?

_____
_____
_____

Source: Attract and Retain the Affluent Investor, Dearborn Trade, 2001

Chapter 9

The Future of Managed Accounts

Where do we go from here? Competition, fees, account minimums and new product developments are all on the horizon. Industry leaders present their vision.

The managed account industry is at a critical crossroads. The separate account business is growing so rapidly that industry opinions on what the future holds are quite varied. In this chapter, we'll explore the evolving industry fronts and present the opinions of industry veterans and experts. It is thought-provoking to see the areas in which these opinions concur, noteworthy to hear new slants on old ideas as well as innovative new thinking that is emerging.

We have now come full circle in the financial advice industry. In the pre-May Day environment of 1975, competition was intense because of the similarities of products and costs, and differentiation among advisors was based on the service they provided. Today, financial information, products and services are ubiquitous, overwhelming many investors. The ability of an advisor to articulate his unique value and to demonstrate the quality of service he provides are the deciding factors of future business success.

Opportunities abound for the value-driven advisor. Keys to success are the ability to accurately identify the competition and to develop high-quality service and levels of trust with clients. These factors will create loyalty and longevity in client relationships. As clients have difficulty differentiating among various investment professionals, your in-depth competitive research, savvy marketing, and introspective examination of your unique value to clients become critical to your success.

The Future: Proving Your Value Beyond Investments

With this perceived lack of differentiation in the client's mind, how is today's financial advisor able to compete? Adding value is the simple answer. We hear it all the time, but what exactly does that mean? And how does that translate into ever-increasing profits (value) for client and advisor? How do you truly differentiate yourself in the crowded marketplace, now and in the future?

One of the first steps in positioning yourself is identifying your natural market. This part of the process allows you to build on your success already in place. The products and services you offer have created your success up to this point and can now be shifted into the next phase: Adding *unique* value to the client. You can add unique value through ease of use. Make overall wealth management easier for your clients.

Since investors have access to the same products at numerous firms, making the solutions easier is a way you can help your clients save time. Saving time for those who don't have enough of it is a very valuable service. Investors don't have time to research asset classes and styles. And they certainly don't have time to research the universe of money managers available, much less monitor their performance after they've been chosen. This is the entire package of solutions you can provide for your clients and prospects.

Reduced price sensitivity is the prize for giving your clients more time and more convenience. This ease-of-use principle is exactly the reason people continue to buy products at Amazon.com. It's not the least expensive way to buy books and music online, but Amazon is certainly the easiest and most reliable. We are going to see a lot more of this ease-of-use concept in the future.

Fees and Profitability

Clients tend to link fees to performance. In the past, performance was defined solely in terms of the returns clients experienced in their portfolios. The meaning of performance in today's world, especially considering the majority of clients' market experiences beginning in 2000, may have more to do with an advisor's level and quality of service to the client than with actual portfolio performance.

This is not to say that portfolio performance is unimportant. It *is* to say that in a time of less-than-stellar portfolio performance, a client may experience so much confidence and peace of mind as a result of the well-founded, trusted relationship with the advisor that he or she is willing to tolerate a little less return in exchange. This is why it is increasingly important to model returns and manage expectations from the client's investment policy statement.

No matter how complex we try to make financial planning, clients look at their personal situations in terms of how much available cash they need monthly or annually. Outlining what you can do for clients overall has become the new definition of performance. For some clients, consistency of return and your ability to provide it are far more attractive than volatile ups and downs that have to be annualized to show benefit.

Competing on price alone will be a loser's game. Other financial providers will be willing to live with profit margins less than those currently expected by many financial advisors. If banks provide multiple investment managers in a single program with an investment policy statement, asset allocation, manager selection and monitoring, and deliver that program through an online solution for their salaried employees, their cost of distribution is less. They don't have to pay their employees as much as a wirehouse brokerage firm, for example, and this creates a price disparity.

Account Minimums

Since the early days of the managed account industry, minimum account sizes have been all over the map. Institutional-level managers required minimums of $10 million, which decreased over the years to $1 million, then $500,000, all the way down to $100,000 with the development of new technology, and this relieved money managers from such duties as portfolio accounting and reporting and back-office duties. These functions were taken over by the sponsors, freeing the money manager to do what he or she does best: manage money.

In the current environment, account minimums continue to decrease, which causes many of us to question the asset level at which managed accounts are no longer feasible for the client. Technology and the advent of multiple discipline portfolios make it possible for a client to achieve diversification at almost any asset level.

There is a point where a client may better be served by mutual funds, exchange-traded funds or index products. Exactly where that level may be is likely to be debated for some time. General consensus seems to be heading toward the $100,000 to $250,000 range for separate accounts, with minimums increasing when multiple disciplines are added. Undoubtedly, future technological developments will have a great influence on minimum account levels, but many in our industry believe that the needs of the client and best practices in the industry will be the eventual determinant.

Product vs. Process

With minimums ever-decreasing and the increasing availability of new products such as multiple discipline portfolios, many feel the days of managed accounts being thought of as a process are numbered. Contrary to established industry opinion, the migration of separately managed accounts from process to product status is not necessarily a bad thing. "Managed accounts are a service, a process, and not a product" is the oldest mantra in the business. But remember, technology allows us to make simple what, at one time, was complicated and to build in best practices in the process. Technology also creates efficiency and allows the level of service to increase without limit.

Len Reinhart, chairman of Lockwood Financial Advisors, Inc., agrees. "Like it or not, the IMA (individual managed account) is a product. It is no better or worse than a mutual fund or an annuity. It simply has different features that make it more attractive to certain investor-types. The only way the industry will break out of the cottage stage and move on is to view IMAs this way. Many will consider this statement sacrilegious. But the process must go beyond a one-product solution.

"For 25 years, the process has ended in one or multiple IMAs being recommended. When mutual fund wraps came out in the '90s, they used a very similar process, but also had a one-product solution – mutual funds. This single-product solution will have to disappear. The process is broadening to include all products in the solution set, and IMAs must be recognized as one of the product options, not be mislabeled as a process.

"You can see this trend developing at the major wirehouses. The consulting process that traditionally has been promoted from the managed account is now being embraced at the firm level. Over the next few years, the firms will take control of the process, including financial and estate planning, and the IMA will become one of the many possible product solutions the firms offer.

"If you were to ask a client what is the highest level of service you could provide them, it would probably not be building a portfolio. Their service standard is higher. What is most important is the creation, preservation and transfer of their wealth. Essentially, one major ramification of competition in the future is that the service bar is raised higher. The packaging of investments becomes more and more focused on best practices, so that the packages themselves solve the funding problems.

"The very fact that the service bar has been raised says that whomever is working on the product area is less valuable. If you are meeting the higher service standards, you will still be able to extract a competitive fee from your client. Advisors who want to maintain their profit margin based on the old level of service, which is very easy to duplicate, will be unable to continue maintaining the same profit margin."[1]

Strength in Numbers

The realization that the higher level of service is basically a wealth management model is one reason for the rapid increase in the number of advisor teams. More advisors will be creating strategic alliances and partnerships within firms and with other firms to glean better efficiency from the existing clientele of both entities. For example, at an organizational level, Northwestern Mutual Life is teaming up with Northern Trust to provide trust services to its clients doing estate planning. This type of partnering will increase as the industry evolves and firms buy and merge with other firms.

The growing interest of large insurance companies in the managed account arena, as well as CPAs, attorneys and other professionals, will foster pricing of the products and services of these entities on a wholesale basis, allowing those products and services to be included in a fee-based structure. This will make it easier for firms to offer complementary services, just as teams within large wirehouses offer an assortment of expertise to fulfill a client's every need.

What the Industry Thinks

I thought it would provide interesting insight if, in this chapter, I shared with you the viewpoints of both industry pioneers and innovators. You will find a variety of beliefs about technology, profitability, what it will take to remain competitive, and various topics we have mentioned so far. We are poised at an inflection point for industry growth. Exactly how things will evolve remains to be seen, but here are some expert opinions on the possibilities.

Russ Prince, president, Prince & Associates

Russ Prince, noted industry consultant and author of 20 books on the affluent, including his most recent, *Advanced Planning With The Ultra Affluent*, says, "According to our research, there's still a very small portion of the brokerage

---

[1] *2010: A Managed Account Odyssey. Projections on the Future of the Managed Accounts Industry.* Leonard A. Reinhart and Jay N. Whipple III, Lockwood Financial Services, Inc.

community and an even smaller portion of the independent financial community making managed accounts the core of investment services. However, there's tremendous interest in both of those worlds to *make* managed accounts a much more significant component of that business. So there's clearly demand for the product. To this we add that the managed account platform is just that – a platform that's in the process of metamorphosing. There's a good chance that with this evolution of the product, we're going to have people move in this direction increasingly."

Adding Value

"Those who identify as consultants and are selling through the process are basically tapping into the needs and preferences of the more affluent clients. The people who are selling managed accounts as a product will come and go – it's the equivalent of a passing ticket, so to speak, as opposed to someone who is making this a core part of their investment offering. Making it that core element and doing it as a consulting process helps solidify the relationship with the client. Affluent clients like the approach and many of the advisors doing it are seeing really positive reaction overall. The more astute advisors inside the brokerages understand the value that the managed account model brings to the table."

Product versus Process

"What managed accounts will look like, as we see it, is basically a pricing structure and a technological platform providing a client with a portfolio comprised of money managers to mutual funds to individual securities. Technology is making all of that possible. In the short term, the multi-discipline account is what's really driving the interest. The affluent client is going to be the primary source – it's what appeals to them. As you approach the ultra-high-net-worth client, managed accounts are not going to be enough anymore. We're going to find that managed accounts will become one component of a larger process of wealth management."

Jay Whipple, co-founder of Security APL and Chairman, Osprey Partners

Technology and Industry Development

Jay Whipple, founder of Security APL, the most commonly used operational platform for separately managed accounts, says, "The technology in the industry now can be a tremendous frustration for advisors. Setting up an account is not an easy process right now. It can take anywhere from less than a week to more than four weeks depending on the transfer account process, where the assets are, whether they've set up a temporary account – there are a host of complexities implicit in today's systems.

"But the momentum that's really going to drive change here is going to be the mutual funds. Fund companies are going to realize that if they don't support the managed account solutions, they're going to have their business taken away. They are the ones concerned with the issue of cannibalizing a profitable business for a less profitable one. The problem is they're going to lose the business anyway, and they're looking for a simple solution for managing their back office. They're very familiar with the process in the mutual fund world and they're looking for that same process in the separately managed account world. But they can't believe the absurd complexities that exist in the separately managed account world.

"Also, industry utilities are going to have to be consolidated for managed accounts to continue to grow and be successful. You have to have all these pieces to make the separately managed account world work. You have to have custody and you have to have tax lot accounting. You also need to have brokerage to do the clearing and settling of trades – all those elements are required in some way, shape or form. And there is no one system that provides all of that right now.

"The development has to be moved on quickly and the game is changing very dramatically."

Christopher L. Davis, executive director, Money Management Institute (MMI)

"I've often said to reporters who ask about the growth of managed accounts that it's a demand-side pull and a supply-side push. Producers are migrating toward managed accounts because managed accounts are the platform upon which the consulting relationship is delivered. They also facilitate the alignment of the firm's and the advisor's interests with those of the client.

"Clients want something better than a broker calling with periodic stock tips or mutual fund recommendations. No one's approached anymore at the cocktail party talking about the sixth mutual fund he just bought. All of that is pushing toward the more consultative relationship between client and trusted advisor, and managed accounts will ride that wave beautifully."

Compensation

"Former SEC Chairman Arthur Levitt asked Dan Tully, the former chairman of Merrill Lynch, to chair a blue ribbon panel that looked at compensation systems for financial advisors. The 1995 Tully Commission report concluded that if a compensation system was designed from scratch, they hardly would have developed what has been in place for years – the transaction-oriented commission. They would much rather have preferred to have developed some sort of fee-based advisory relationship that saw the advisor compensation grow as the portfolio grew. So the stars and planets seem to be aligning with the consultative relationship and managed accounts are the momentum behind that continuing growth."

Multiple Discipline Portfolios

"Having what Len Reinhart calls a 'control account' at the core of the trusted advisor relationship is going to present all kinds of opportunities for the advisor to better serve the client. A multiple discipline portfolio is probably the 'autopilot' of the relationship, but it has to be carefully established. It's a pretty sophisticated autopilot because it's taking into consideration all of the concerns of the client. But the managed account, because of its inherent customization and tax sensitivity, can be tuned to developments in and outside the portfolio. The control account will be the second booster stage of the consulting relationship rocketship."

Technology

"Part of Paul Hatch's [COO Salomon Smith Barney] presentation at the MMI conference this year [2002] really wowed the audience. He said that technology had enabled the managed accounts industry to develop and expand aggressively, but that technology and operations today are no longer the solution, they are now the problem. We are at a critical point in the growth of the industry's capability to handle asset growth. And I think a lot of execs in the industry who had postponed a hard look at the infrastructure are now willing to look at it and acknowledge that the infrastructure is not adequate to handle the expected rapid run-up in assets."

Minimums

"I think minimums are probably going to be a quarter of a million because it's tough to get good portfolio diversification in smaller amounts and mutual funds will do a magnificent job for clients with smaller portfolios."

Product vs. Process

"A process takes a long time to explain. A product simply has a brand developed and we're not there yet. The differentiation in the levels of services within the managed account sector will probably complicate it, but it will happen some day when everyone at the party has one. Either they, or the advisors, or the media will start to use some kind of descriptive or, as Len has predicted, some huge behemoth will come in, an insurance company, a bank, and brand it with a descriptor and everyone will grab on to it. Perhaps The Money Management Institute's repetitive use of 'separately managed accounts' will win out and become the accepted name."

Competitive Advantage

"Trusted advisors will have to demonstrate value added to maintain and expand their relationships. If you're aware of the client's total portfolio and objectives, you can periodically bring to the client interesting investment opportunities within the managed account. The client doesn't have to invest in them, but he will simply be appreciative and aware that the advisor is demonstrating value to the relationship by bringing, say, a venture capital opportunity that the client knows the advisor has researched within the client's investment objectives and brought to their attention."

Crossing the Lines

"One of the interesting developments at the MMI meeting was the very careful surveillance and participation in the meetings by two enormous insurance companies. So they're asking questions and they're looking at this sector from the sidelines, trying to figure out what's going on here."

Russell Smith, director of sales and marketing, Managed Assets Group, Merrill Lynch

"Today's clients have access to more information on investments than they have ever had. Television, books and magazines flood investors with financial news and updates. This has had both a positive and negative effect. The positive is that clients have become more sophisticated and have a greater understanding of a broader range of investments that ever before. The negative is that clients are more confused on how best to implement a sound investment strategy utilizing the breadth of choices now available. The acceptance of the separately managed account is largely due to clients' increased knowledge and understanding of these offerings coupled with the need for expert consulting advise on the best way to build appropriate risk-adjusted portfolios customized to their needs."

Product vs. Process

"The real winners in the industry are those who focus on addressing client needs rather than a product push. The true consultant is one who is passionate about understanding a client's individual needs and getting the client to their goal, but who is indifferent about the products that are used to achieve that goal. A holistic approach translates into success. Separate accounts are one of the many arrows a financial advisor has in his quiver to solve these problems. There is a natural win-win relationship established between the client and the financial advisor as long and the advisor stays aligned with the goals of the client and not a product. This is much easier said than done – and becomes the real challenge for the advisor."

Adding Value

"The wholesaler talent pool that the advisor draws from must be superior. We are seeing extreme segmentation of advice-givers. High-net-worth clients use sophisticated products in a big way. Today, effective wholesalers build relationships with advisors who, in turn, build relationships with clients. The wholesaler must have substantial knowledge and experience and must be able to explain complicated concepts and sophisticated ideas to asset holders. The bottom line is that the future wholesaler will become more of an 'advisor-to-the-advisor' with a very high knowledge level on a broad range of financial issues not just focused on their product."

Jack Sharry, president, Private Client Group, Phoenix Investment Partners

In seven years of leading Phoenix's managed account distribution effort, Jack Sharry attests that, "One of the biggest advantages of managed accounts is the ability to provide customized solutions. While the benefits of the investment process are the key appeal to investors, the right distribution formula in support of advisors and their clients is also vital. To be successful, a manager needs highly trained, skilled wholesalers and marketers who know and understand the consulting process and can work with the advisor in support of the consulting they provide the client. With an appropriately constructed and diversified managed account offering, performance is important but second to process.

"Today more than ever, clients want customized investment solutions – but without taking on too much risk. Since the technology bubble burst, there's a greater recognition of the importance of personal attention. Essentially, it's the baby boom mantra – we want it all."

Adding Value

"At Phoenix, our wholesalers support advisors in three basic ways; we take the approach of what we call: 'Know, Guide and Invest.' By 'Know,' we assist the advisor with understanding the issues, fears, concerns – the mindset – of the client and then assist the advisor in the development, growth and expansion of their managed account business. 'Guide' is the variety of practical, client-useable tools and presentations we provide to inform, educate and clarify the managed account process to the client. And 'Invest' is providing information about our products, how they correlate with other products, as well as a high level of context and perspective relative to changing markets. Our focus is giving the advisor everything they need to help their client buy quality, diversify properly and fit these decisions into a larger financial plan. While products are the ultimate solution, how you get there with your client is critical."

Multiple Discipline Portfolios

"The evolution of the multiple discipline portfolio is an interesting development and one that will clearly broaden the market to involve more advisors and reach more investors who want the advantages of managed accounts. The appeal is the diversification already in place within the investment vehicle itself; and by virtue of the automatic re-balancing feature, the account will re-balance at a pre-set time, thus removing for the investor the emotional decision-making process of whether to make changes or not. These features also enable the advisor to focus more on asset-gathering. From the wholesaler *and* advisor perspectives, public seminars are a terrific venue for gathering assets for this product."

Frank Campanale, president and CEO, Salomon Smith Barney Consulting Group

"There has been a confluence of events – the development of technology and the extended correction in the capital markets that really has not occurred, if you think about it, since the early '80s. It has presented an opportunity for the industry that hasn't existed to this degree since the middle '70s. Even in the early '80s when we had a recession that bordered on a depression, there was still an escape route for clients. They could go to fixed income and get a high rate of return. Even in money market funds, they could get a 13 1/2 percent to 14 percent rate of return. So today [2002], we have an extended correction in the capital markets and now our clients are looking for specific advice."

Product vs. Process

"The investment strategy is what's important and it's the trusted advisor who has the competency to develop the investment strategy – that's really the product – it's not the mutual fund, it's not the separately managed account, it's not stocks and bonds, it's not variable annuities. It's the combination of all of those built into an investment strategy."

Teams

"We foster the development of teams by assisting in the training of analysts and other professionals the individual teams may hire. These analysts' sole function is to generate reports for the client. We have fostered the development of a unique environment at Salomon Smith Barney where an advisor can come into his or her office each day and focus completely on the entrepreneurial opportunities available. We lift many of the responsibilities of a regular entrepreneur from the advisor's shoulders. They have their own business within the firm. They can walk into their office and get right to work on executing their business plan. They've created their own team and, in addition, we have created a supplementary team to be at their disposal, assuring that the client will be served in a value-added manner."

Technology

"Technology is providing leverage for people to be able to handle more clients with more money for less fees than ever before, which means if a client comes to us with $350,000, theoretically we can use seven different money managers with seven different styles in a well-allocated, properly balanced and weighted portfolio for that client. You're doing a better job for the client, whereas before, the only way you could do that was by using mutual funds, which was fine, but not as good as a separately managed account.

"That same technology is going to allow us, in the not too distant future, to run accounts with even smaller minimum account sizes, maybe $20,000. So if someone comes in with $125,000, you may be able to use four or five different managers. You may be able to use a small cap growth, large cap growth, small cap value, large cap value, and an international portfolio and have it be separately managed because technology is allowing that to happen. So when I talk about that in the future, that's the very near future, almost today [2002]. It's just the trend and nature of human beings to slice and dice things into atoms, and we have to be careful because we can almost overdo it. We begin to lose the basic fundamentals of what we're trying to do for the client."

Profitability

"This business is not only the best thing for the client, but it also creates a predictable revenue stream so you, the advisor, can do real business planning predicated on what you think next year's business is going to be. When it was truly a transaction business, we were nothing but a bunch of merchants. We were out there just selling something for the commission."

A. Peter Cieszko, Jr., managing director, Citigroup Asset Management

Peter Cieszko, head of U.S. retail and high-net-worth asset management for Citigroup Asset Management[2] says, "The managed account business will change the scope of the investment management industry for the high-net-worth client. We look at separately managed accounts as the most liquid and customizable segment of the business. It's where the serious money needs to be. The goal is to take the investment management expertise, make it acceptable to the needs of financial advisors and let them use their process for a menu of investment vehicles with a pricing menu that matches the needs of the client."

Multiple Discipline Accounts (MDAs) and Alternatives

"The Multiple Discipline Account®[3] is style diversification in its simplest format, the core centerpiece of an individual's investment management program. The MDA will be the centerpiece product for the advisor and other investments will be built around that. The MDA is both liquid and customizable. We won't limit the way we package this product. It's an attractive strategy for the investor because you can pull down what you need.

"Firms will merge and strategic relationships will be formed to create MDAs. What do you do if you need a value manager? Will you buy one? How will you play on the MDA field? Organizations will need an all-encompassing solution for the client – firms will make acquisitions, form joint ventures and form strategic alliances to achieve this goal. Alternative investments will also be injected into the equation because they offer noncorrelation. Other specialized asset classes will also develop – all taking different pricing forms."

Minimums

"Some accounts will require a higher minimum than $100,000. If you are creating a mix of large cap, small cap, fixed income and international, the complexities require a higher cost structure and the minimum might be closer to $500,000. Fee structure – going forward – will accommodate a range of investors, but minimums will not get really low. On the opposite end of the spectrum, once an investor hits the $5 million mark, it will be considered 'serious money.'

"Individuals will continue to gravitate toward advice. For the serious investor, taxable

---

[2]Citigroup Asset Management is a Citigroup business unit comprised of Smith Barney Asset Management, a division of Salomon Smith Barney Inc., Salomon Brothers Asset Management, Citibank Global Asset Management and other affiliated advisory entities.
[3]Multiple Discipline Account is a registered service mark of Salomon Smith Barney Inc.

money will continue to move in the direction of managed accounts. Investors need help with taxes, defining their time horizon and determining how much money they will need to live on. The educated business professional doesn't have the time to manage money. Besides, did anyone really think that the stock market autopilot would work forever?"

Advice for Advisors

"Financial advisors need experienced, qualified, degreed people who may have managed money in the past representing the money management firms they work with. Someone who has worked on the trust side or investment side of the business would be better in the field and have a better perspective. You simply can't take a mutual fund wholesaler and convert him/her into a managed account wholesaler overnight."

Michael Dieschbourg, former national director, Salomon Smith Barney Consulting Group and current principal, Silver Creek SV (Hedge Fund of Funds)

"The separately managed account has been beneficial for everyone. Technology is now allowing us to provide multiple investment styles with multiple managers within a single account. This is the next generation of multidiscipline accounts. High-net-worth clients want customization and tax efficiency; it's a major market that has emerged and is growing.

"From my experience, I believe that the $100,000 minimum is a very good minimum and when you start adding multiple styles and managers, you may see this minimum go up. Technology enables us do multiple styles with $100,000 successfully. But if you reduce the minimum to $50,000, you could end up with over 100 individual securities, and that dilutes the investment results. What clients really want are separately managed accounts versus a mutual fund. These accounts should be actively managed for net after-tax investment returns and for their personal risk tolerance, reducing the emotional element of investing."

Adding Value

"The biggest opportunity for consultants is going to be developing portfolios for the client's total asset allocation, but also being able to reach across, from a tax management standpoint, all of the client's assets. What is happening is an evolution – a consultant providing not only advice on a specific pool of assets, but also creating an asset allocation strategy for the client's total wealth."

Technology

"With technology, advisors are going to be able to look not only at their own client's account, but they will also be able to aggregate all of the client's accounts at different custodians. The investment consultant will take all accounts into consideration and make decisions based on how assets should be allocated for overall wealth and tax management.

"Clients need someone who can provide an open architecture, who can be objective, and who wants to be on the same side of the table with them. An asset-based fee becomes the equalizer, unlike a transaction fee, which drives the client to question every decision made."

Multiple Discipline Portfolios

"I view multiple discipline portfolios as another tool in the toolbox; another efficient way to implement portfolio decisions. It's all about the consulting process. If you go back to a product sale, you end up with the same thing that happened to mutual funds, real estate limited partnerships and oil and gas limited partnerships – you're reverting back to a transaction business. Clients are telling us they don't want us in the transaction business! They want us in the advice business and if we're going to be in the advice business, we need to charge for advice but also maintain our objectivity."

Alternative Investments

"Alternative investments are another area that will provide more opportunity for value-added consultative advice. Alternatives are becoming a larger segment of portfolios. Investment consultants must increase their knowledge and expertise because clients are demanding it. It's another great tool to help solve clients' wealth management issues. The consultants will have to be able to understand different alternative strategies, understand the potential use of leverage and its impact on portfolios, and realize that the traditional manager research process must be rebuilt for the alternative investment arena. Manager style boxes do not work, manager due diligence is different than manager research, relationships are critical to the process and capacity and access has to be valued."

Teams

"Teams are a major growth area of the investment industry because in order to manage the client's total wealth you need people with experience in tax, investments, estate planning, alternatives, liabilities, and insurance in order to take advantage of the opportunities available such as charitable trusts, philanthropic issues, balance sheet and generational wealth transfer.

"Firms are creating platforms, so if a consultant doesn't want to create their own team, they can pull in a team of experts and have a virtual team. The term 'team' doesn't always mean people in your own company, but can include virtual support. There are firms that have hired CPAs and attorneys so they can cover all aspects of the process. I'm seeing more team sales versus individual sales.

"The investment consultant needs to become the client's architect, bringing together all the experts to aid the client in achieving their lifelong wealth management goals. This is a critical role that will keep clients on track to reach all their goals over time and minimize the impact of market volatility."

Richard Schilffarth, senior vice president, B.C. Ziegler

In 1975, Richard (Dick) Schilffarth created the "wrap fee account" and in 1976, started the investment management division, Hutton Investment Management. In 1979, he introduced Hutton Capital Management to the brokers of EF Hutton; in 1980, created Hutton Portfolio Management; in 1981, created the Hutton Trust Company in Wilmington, Delaware; in 1982, introduced Hutton's cash management account, the Asset Management Account; and in 1983, secured the legal and government charter for Hutton Bank.

Dick says of the industry, "We're just starting to see the tip of the iceberg of interest in separate account programs. The percentage of growth in mutual funds is declining and the percentage of growth in managed accounts is just getting started. I was quoted as saying in an article in *Business Week* about a decade ago that by the year 2012, the separate account world would be at $2 trillion in assets. That certainly wasn't rocket science!"

The "Donut Hole" Investment Model

"The investment consulting model is going to expand into a wealth management model. You're going to see investment consulting grow to include financial planning, estate planning, retirement planning and gift planning – the whole circle of events, including investment planning – as the advisor tries to control every need of the high-net-worth and ultra-high-net-worth individual.

"I talk about the 'donut hole' as the center of a circle called investment management. Investment consulting takes care of the hole in the middle. Right now, the investment consultant is only taking the investable assets out of that business, but there are a lot of other investment products he could have in that program."

Third-Party Providers

"I believe the third-party wrap account provider may be in serious trouble. When I started doing it, there were four of us in the business – my company, Portfolio Consulting Services, Portfolio Management Consultants, Brinker and Lockwood Financial. Now there are over 39 providers. Today, I could go out as an experienced consultant, go to my IMCA manager forum meeting, walk around that exhibition hall of 60 some-odd managers and I could get 50 of them to handle my accounts for 50 basis points whether or not I have a wrap program."

Product vs. Process

"Product pushers will fall by the wayside. The successful advisors will get away from product pushing, and the unsuccessful ones will drop out of the business. Also, as money management becomes more web-oriented, money managers will have to develop a brand identity. They must have multiple styles because having only one style means they'll be out of phase with the market too many times to effectively market themselves."

Jeffrey Cusack, senior vice president of separate accounts, Charles Schwab & Co., Inc.

"The growth in the managed accounts industry is driven primarily by the growth in the affluent market, as it is the affluent who can benefit the most from the features of managed accounts. Some researchers expect the affluent market to grow 33 percent over the next 10 years and that is a very positive indicator for managed accounts. However, it is important to note that I believe it is not the "managed account" that adds the value for the client. In fact, the only way a client will truly enjoy all the benefits of a managed account is with the aid of a skilled practitioner. You must understand the client's entire financial life – real estate, wills, trusts, taxes, etc. The flexibility of managed accounts combined with a skilled practitioner who has a global view and uses sophisticated tools will provide a better chance for reaching investment goals."

Fees

"The managed account market is not price-driven – you don't see firms advertising the lowest managed account fees in town. What is driving investment decisions today is not claims of the lowest price or the hottest performance. That approach frankly, has not worked well for clients. I think investors are more concerned with investment process now than investment product. Asset allocation, prudent selection of investment vehicles and monitoring are the key components of a consultative approach."

Adding Value

"Managed accounts and mutual funds are both methods of outsourcing asset management. Advisors often use them in combination. The key is to not engage in a debate about which one is better, but rather to understand the strengths and weaknesses of each and when and how a client may benefit. Managed accounts are not a business approach, outsourcing is, and managed accounts provide the flexibility to help manage complex client relationships. Advisors play the role of quarterback and relationship manager, not portfolio manager.

"One of the main distinctions between these roles is the fact that the typical mutual fund wholesaler seldom meets with the client. Managed account wholesalers, on the other hand, are often expected to. Advisors require that manager representatives be able to make effective presentations to the advisor's largest or most important high-net-worth clients, or make committee presentations to foundations or endowments as an example."

Bob Padgette, founder of Mobius

Technology

Said Bob Padgette, "I think we have a wonderful opportunity with technology to serve the 401(k) markets. The growth is going to be very large. Clients who now have $500,000 locked up in their 401(k) really don't have many options. But as those people start retiring, they've got to start the planning process. I believe some of the next technology will be integration of the entire planning process along with the asset management. What happened with Enron really opened people's eyes. Now people are beginning to see the importance of protection of assets. Technology will allow us to take the next step in integrating portfolios in various locations – financial planners have done this for a long time, but they've done it manually – and some of the larger firms are going to start looking at ways to do it, and it's not easy. The Internet is going to make that possible because you can move data around and get data from different sources. Interconnectivity issues are getting better and better. When we first did an interface – with M Watch – to download information directly from the back office, that was a big deal. Nowadays, if you're not doing that, you're not in business. And that was only a few years ago. One of the reasons the growth is going to be so large is because as we drop the minimum asset level, that pyramid is going to get a lot bigger at the base. We're trying to get down to what *The Wall Street Journal* called the 'mass affluent.'"

Fees

"As for the direction of fees, it's a very broad question. In most industries, as the competition increases, the price generally goes down. In financial services, the products offered on a fee basis continues to increase, so the average fee may continue to decrease. However, I don't feel there will be as dramatic a drop in the future as there has been over the past 10 years. At a certain fee level, some suppliers will stop production, and the remaining suppliers will be able to keep a relatively constant fee level.

"The one exception, I feel, is for highly specialized services. These will always command a premium fee, because they will create a premium value, generally for very high net worth investors. But, premium services only apply to a small segment of the total marketplace. So the short answer to what will happen to fees – yes, they will go up, down, and stay the same – would seem sarcastic, but only depending on the service/product being offered, and that really is the answer."

Epilogue: A Call to Action

As we wrap up production of this book in the fall of 2002, the financial advice industry has taken a pounding. The miserable double-down of 2000-2001 left investors bloodied and their advisors battered. Advisors face the greatest crisis of confidence I've witnessed in my 22 years of industry experience. Client retention is a battle, and many advisors lack the energy to talk with new prospects. As one longtime friend and advisor laments, "The clients don't even open their statements anymore." My careful reading of one wirehouse firm's annual report indicates that it lost over $32 billion in client assets in 2001 – a time in which the baby boom demographics alone should be propelling business to all-time highs. Is the party truly over?

Longtime advisors will tell you they've seen this movie before. While the plunge in stock prices is tragic, a correction is the periodic cleansing that occurs naturally in any overheated market and is a valuable education for investors that diversification and long-term investing are lessons for a lifetime of investing. And though it is regrettable that many advisors will not retain the clients gathered during the bull market, it is also a natural evolution that the industry filters out advisors who cannot help those clients. The job of a financial advisor is first to help clients protect their wealth – then grow it commensurate with their tolerance for risk. Many advisors have failed in that job.

What grows from the scorched earth of the advisory landscape is a different kind of affluent clientele. Humbled by their experience with technology stocks, many of these investors will now focus on more prudent strategies for building wealth. They now understand better the need for overall wealth management – estate planning, business succession, long-term care – and will embrace financial planning instead of buying lottery tickets on the Nasdaq. Affluent clients are seeking advisors who will challenge their ideas and protect them from unknown risks. With virtually all of the affluent population having become affluent during the bull market, they need help in coping with their financial issues, not just investments. They need your help.

The dawn of this new era in financial advice also shines on the good financial advisor. If you can rise to the challenge of wealth management, you can enjoy success beyond what you achieved in the best days of the bull market. Advisors whose shortcomings were masked by rising stock prices are on their way out, leaving behind the best advisors to step in and take over the abandoned clients. It is the nature of competition that survival is for the fittest.

If you have taken the time to read this book, I believe you will be one of the success stories. You have taken your valuable time to learn more about your industry, and that interest in learning will help you move to greater heights. If you want to put theory into practice, I suggest you do the following right now:

Personal Positioning — Get Your Story in Order

How will you respond when you have the chance to serve a new affluent client? How will you represent your added value? What is it like to be a client of your practice? Why should the client work with you instead of another advisor? What advantages and services do you provide to your clients? The exercises throughout this book will help you answer those critical questions and prepare you to capture your share of new affluent clients.

Implement Best Practices in Your Practice

The tactics in this book were sourced from some of the best advisors in the business who generously gave their time to share those ideas with you. Find your natural markets (Chapter 7, Part I). Consider the best target markets for new clients and additional assets for your managed accounts (Chapter 7, Parts I and V). Determine your most appropriate sales and marketing approach (Chapters 7 and 8). Develop an effective transition strategy (Chapter 5). Create a compelling client appreciation meeting or seminar (Chapter 7, Part III). Discuss the wealth management needs of your clients (Chapter 6, Parts II and IV; Chapter 7, Part IV). Find partners who can help you grow your business (Chapter 8).

Make a Plan — and Measure Your Progress

Create a written business plan that includes specific tactics and activities you believe will lead to more assets and more clients. Add to that plan solid numerical targets and track those benchmarks as you implement your plan. You can't manage what you can't measure, and you will quickly become aware of those activities that lead to results. Review your business plan with some of your top clients and seek their counsel.

On behalf of my colleagues at Phoenix Investment Partners, I thank you for the opportunity to share ideas about the managed account and wealth management business, and I look forward to working with you.

Resource Guide

Here's a listing of organizations and individuals who can help with your marketing plan, business development activities and training objectives. We've obtained the names of some popular services and products from advisors around the country. Take advantage of these resources to enhance your practice.

Industry Organizations

It's vital to join industry associations such as the Investment Management Consultants Association (IMCA – newly merged with ICIMC), National Association of Personal Financial Advisors (NAPFA), Financial Planning Association (FPA) or others that provide educational courseware, continuing education credits and conferences for networking and learning. These organizations also offer marketing help and sponsor professional designations (such as CFA, CFP, CIMC and CIMA) to give you a higher level of knowledge, credibility and professionalism. Becoming an active member of these types of organizations and obtaining professional designations will differentiate you from the crowd. Here is a partial listing:

Investment Management Consultants Association (IMCA), 9101 E. Kenyon Avenue, Suite 3000, Denver, CO 80237, telephone: 303-770-3377, web: www.imca.org

Financial Planning Association (FPA), 5775 Glenridge Drive, Suite B300, Atlanta, GA 30238, telephone: 800-322-4237, 404-845-0011, web: www.fpanet.org

The College for Financial Planning, 6161 S. Syracuse Way, Greenwood Village, CO 80111-4707, telephone: 800-237-9990, web: www.fp.edu.

The American College, 270 S. Bryn Mawr Avenue, Bryn Mawr, PA 19010-2196, telephone: 888-263-7265, web: www.amercoll.edu

National Association of Insurance and Financial Advisors (NAIFA), 2901 Telestar Court, P.O. Box 12012, Falls Church, VA 22042-1205, telephone: 703-770-8100, web: www.naifa.org

National Association of Investment Professionals (NAIP), 12664 Emmer Place, Suite 201, St. Paul, MN 55124, telephone: 952-322-6247, web: www.naip.com

National Association of Philanthropic Planners, 176 W. Logan Street, #434, Noblesville, IN 46060, telephone: 800-342-6215, web: www.napp.net

Center for Fiduciary Studies, 2004 E. Carson Street, Pittsburgh, PA 15203, telephone: 412-390-5080, web: www.cfstudies.com

Industry Periodicals

Industry trade publications are additional resources to help you learn more about managed accounts and the investment process. Most are free to the trade.

Financial Advisor – www.financialadvisormagazine.com

Investment Advisor – www.investmentadvisor.com

Journal of Financial Planning – www.journalfp.net

On Wall Street – www.onwallstreet.com

Pensions & Investments – www.pionline.com

Plan Sponsor – www.plansponsor.com

Registered Representative – www.registeredrep.com

Research – www.researchmag.com

Senior Consultant News Journal – www.srconsultant.com

Books

Advanced Planning With The Ultra Affluent, by Russ Alan Prince and Richard L. Harris

Against the Gods: The Remarkable Story of Risk, by Peter Bernstein

Attract and Retain the Affluent Investor: Winning Tactics for Today's Financial Advisor, by Stephen D. Gresham and Evan Cooper

Be Your Own Brand, by David McNally and Karl D. Speak

Best Practices for Financial Advisors, by Mary Rowland

The Brand Called You, by Peter Montoya and Tim Vandehey

Character Counts, by John Bogle

Deena Katz on Practice Management, by Deena B. Katz

The E-Myth Revisited, by Michael E. Gerber

Effort-Less Marketing for Financial Advisors: 5 Steps to a Super-Profitable Business and Wonderful Life, by Steve Moeller

Gray Dawn, by Peter G. Peterson

High Impact Philanthropy: How Donors, Boards, and Nonprofit Organizations Can Transform Communities, by Kay Sprinkel and Alan Wendroff

High Net Worth Psychology, by Russ Alan Prince and Karen Maru File

History of Managed Accounts, by Sydney LeBlanc, Money Management Institute

How to Acquire Clients: Powerful Techniques for the Successful Practitioner, by Alan Weiss

The Intelligent Investor, by Benjamin Graham and David Dodd

The Marketing Imagination, by Theodore Levitt

Marketing to the Affluent, by Dr. Thomas J. Stanley

Mirror Mirror On The Wall Am I The Most Valued Of Them All?, by Leo J. Pusateri

Networking with the Affluent, by Dr. Thomas J. Stanley

New Strategies for College Funding: An Advisor's Guide, by Raymond D. Loewe

Positioning: The Battle for Your Mind, by Al Ries and Jack Trout

Procedural Prudence, by Donald B. Trone

The Psychology of Money, by Jim Ward

The 7 Habits of Highly Effective People, by Stephen R. Covey

Simple Asset Allocation Strategies, by Roger C. Gibson

True Wealth: An expert guide for high-net-worth individuals (and their advisors), by Thane Stenner

Books

The Trusted Advisor, by Bill Bachrach

Understanding ERISA: A Compact Guide to the Landmark Act, by Ken Ziesenheim

Unlimited Referrals, by Bill Cates

Values-Based Financial Planning: The Art of Creating an Inspiring Financial Strategy, by Bill Bachrach

Values-Based Selling: The Art of Building High-Trust Client Relationships, by Bill Bachrach

Wealth Management Index, by Ross Levin

The Winner's Circle: How 30 Financial Advisors Became the Best in the Business, by Robert L. Shook

Online Marketing and Training Solutions

A number of excellent online resources are also available. Some are free, some are subscriber based. Among the most popular are:

www.horsesmouth.com   www.morningstaradvisor.com

www.stockbrokerpro.com   www.brokerville.com

www.theprogresscenter.com   www.pbstraining.com

Contact Management Tools

Allied Financial Software, Inc.
www.software4advisors.com

NASI North American Software, Inc.
www.nasoftware.com

AS&A brokersoft
www.brokersoft.com

Fugent, Inc.
www.fugent.com

E-Z Data, Inc.
www.ez-data.com

Broker's Ally
www.brokersally.com

Financial Planning Consultants, Inc.
www.financialsoftware.com

Springwater Software
www.springwatersoftware.com

National Datamax, Inc.
www.nationaldatamax.com

Mailing Lists

Harris InfoSource
www.harrisinfo.com

W.S. Ponton, Inc.
www.wsponton.com

D&B Small Business Solutions
www.dnb.com

D&B Sales & Marketing Solutions
www.zapdata.com

infoUSA.com, Inc.
www.infousa.com

DMG
www.leaddogs.com

Judy Diamond Associates, Inc.
www.judydiamond.com

Trainers and Coaches

Steve Moeller, American Business Visions, LLC
www.businessvisions.com

Bill Bachrach, AM Enterprises
www.amehigh.com

Leo Pusateri, Pusateri Consulting and Training, LLC
www.pusatericonsulting.com

Steve Saenz, Paragon Resources, Inc.
www.paragonresources.com

Bill Good Marketing, Inc.
www.billgood.com

Industry Consultants

Don Trone, *i*nvest^mgt.
www.investmgt.com

Bob Dunwoody, R.C. Dunwoody & Associates, Inc.
www.bobdunwoody.com

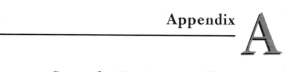

Appendix A

Sample Business Plan

Sample Business Plan

Name: _____   Date: _____

I. MISSION STATEMENT

My mission is to help high-net-worth individuals feel confident about the handling of their financial assets and estates. I do this by providing comprehensive wealth management for individuals and families with assets over $1M. I counsel people on how to grow, protect, tax shelter, and transition their wealth using the extensive resources of (your firm). I offer personal attention, management, and coordination of a wide range of high quality products and services. Consolidating my clients' assets is an important part of what I do for them.

II. BUSINESS GOALS

1. Open 9 new $1M accounts and 3 new $2M accounts for $15M in new assets by the end of 2003. Ideally these will all be fee-based relationships.

2. Gross production should be at least 2% of fee-based assets under management, $350K+ GP from $18M in assets should yield $100K+ gross income.

3. Focus on niche marketing

4. Begin the process to become a Certified Financial Planner (CFP)

5. Establish a working partnership along with administrative support

III. PERSONAL GOALS

1. Get involved in a charity

2. Continue to participate in community activities

3. Take the family to Holland

4. Buy a new home

IV. MARKETING PLAN

50+ divorced or professional, high-net-worth women

Needs
Plan for adequate income, preservation of capital, growth of capital, plan with attention to tax considerations, estate planning, mortgages and/or home equity loans, consolidation of financial assets.

Reprinted with the permission of Joseph J. Lukacs, *Founder*, International Performance Group, LLC

Rationale
This group has the financial resources at the level I seek. I can help in terms of obtaining steady income, tax planning, asset growth, referrals to tax and legal advisors.

Approach
Referrals, Seminars, Strategic Alliances, Cold-calling, Door-knocking, Community service, Directory listings (online and offline)

V. MONTHLY GOALS

1. Business Goals

Open 9 new $1M accounts and 3 new $2M accounts for $15M in assets by the end of 2003. Ideally these will be fee-based relationships.

Why: This is the level of asset acquisition I need to maintain to reach my performance and income goals

By: the end of 2003

How: By working within my networks for new clients, seeking referrals from high-net-worth individuals, participating in carefully chosen affinity groups, and working with estate planning lawyers and CPAs.

Reward: If I can pull this off by the end of Dec 2003, I'll take the kids for a week of skiing.

Month	Goal, New Assets	Cumulative Assets	Actual, New Assets
Oct 2002		$6M	
Nov		$7M	
Dec	$1M	$8M	800K
Jan 2003	$1M	$9M	
Feb	$1M	$10M	
Mar	$1M	$11M	
Apr	$1M	$12M	
May	$2M	$14M	
Jun	$1M	$15M	
Jul	$1M	$16M	
Aug	$2M	$18M	
Sep	$1M	$19M	
Oct	$1M	$20M	
Nov	$2M	$22M	
Dec	$1M	$23M	

Reprinted with the permission of Joseph J. Lukacs, *Founder*, International Performance Group, LLC

2. Personal Goals

Take the family to Holland

Why: I'd like the kids to have the experience of seeing Europe and Holland in particular with their mother/father. They would benefit in the future from understanding more about their own and their mother's/father's background. I'd like them to be comfortable with international travel.

By: December 2004, latest.

How: Need one or two weeks and around $8K or so to do it. The time is more of an issue than the money. We have to factor in spouse's work as well as mine. I would like to do this before our first child completes college.

Reward: This is the reward for my business starting to take shape.

VI. DAILY GAME PLAN

- My highest energy time of day is early morning.

- I will be in the office by 7:30 a.m.

- Check appropriate information first thing every morning.

- I need to work in an office environment in which I feel comfortable, safe, empowered, and supported. Flowers, artwork, personal items make my office space a location where I can work for long periods of time and still feel energized. It also gives my clients a particular impression of me.

- My daily reading is the morning research reports, news flashes, other materials, depending on availability and time. I'll review the *Wall Street Journal* or *Boston Business Journal* over lunch. Most important weekly reading is the global economic view according to (your firm).

- I will exercise for 30 to 45 minutes in the evening.

- I will plan my day first thing each morning.

Reprinted with the permission of Joseph J. Lukacs, *Founder*, International Performance Group, LLC

Appendix **B**

Manager Evaluation Formulas and Ratios

Standard Deviation Formula

Measures the volatility of the manager's return relative to the average return

$$\sigma = \sqrt{\sigma^2} = \sqrt{\frac{\sum_{i=1}^{n}(x_i - \bar{x})^2}{n}}$$

σ = Standard deviation

Σ = Summation graphic

χ_i = Sample return

$\overline{\chi}$ = Sample average return

n = number of observations

Beta Formula

Risk relative to a market index

$$\beta_I = \frac{COV_{i,\,market}\,\sigma_i\,\sigma_{market}}{\sigma_{market}\,\sigma_{market}} =$$

$$\frac{\rho_{i,market}\,\sigma_i}{\sigma_{market}}$$

COV_i = Covariance of asset i to the market

σ_i = Standard deviation of asset i

σ_{market} = Standard deviation of the market

P_i = Covariance of asset i to the market

Market index always = 1.0

Alpha Formula

Measures a portfolio's return in excess of the market return adjusted for risk

$$Alpha = Excess\ Return - [Beta \times (Benchmark - Treasury)]$$

R² Formula

Measures how closely a portfolio's return tracks a given index

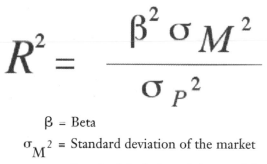

$$R^2 = \frac{\beta^2 \sigma_M{}^2}{\sigma_P{}^2}$$

β = Beta

$\sigma_M{}^2$ = Standard deviation of the market

$\sigma_p{}^2$ = Standard deviation of the portfolio

Sharpe Ratio

*Ratio of portfolio excess return relative to standard deviation;
one measure of risk-adjusted returns*

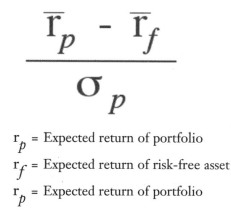

$$\frac{\overline{r}_p - \overline{r}_f}{\sigma_p}$$

r_p = Expected return of portfolio

r_f = Expected return of risk-free asset

r_p = Expected return of portfolio

Sortino Ratio

*Measures downside variability in relation to the minimal acceptable return;
one measure of risk-adjusted returns*

Minimal Acceptable Return (MAR)

$$\sqrt{\int_{\infty}^{m}(m - r_A)^2 \; f(r_A) \; dr_A}$$

m = Return on index

r_A = Return on asset A

$f(r_A)$ = Probability distribution function of returns on asset A

dr_A = Downside risk of asset A

Treynor Ratio

*Ratio of portfolio excess return to beta;
one measure of risk-adjusted returns*

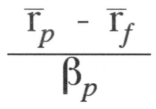

$$\frac{\overline{r}_p - \overline{r}_f}{\beta_p}$$

r_p = Expected return of portfolio

r_f = Expected return of risk-free asset

β_p = Expected return of portfolio

Appendix C

Sample Investment Policy Statement

SAMPLE

INVESTMENT POLICY STATEMENT

For

Family Wealth

(Client)

Approved on July 1, 2001

It is intended that this investment policy statement be reviewed and updated at least annually. Any change to this policy should be communicated in writing on a timely basis to all interested parties.

This Investment Policy Statement (IPS) has been prepared by invest^mgt. It is intended to serve as an example of the type of information that would be included in a comprehensive IPS. Clients are advised to have legal counsel review their IPS before it is approved.

Copyright ©2001, invest^mgt. Version: July 2001

Courtesy of Donald B. Trone, *CEO*, of invest^mgt. Used with permission.

EXECUTIVE SUMMARY

Type of Client:	Taxable, Individual
Current Assets:	$650,000
Time Horizon:	Greater than 5 years
Modeled Return:	8.0% (5.0% over CPI)
Modeled Risk Level:	Modeled loss at - 8.4% for a single year (Statistical confidence level of 90%)

Asset Allocation:	Lower Limit	Strategic Allocation	Upper Limit
Domestic Large Cap Equities			
Value	5%	10%	15%
Blend	5%	10%	15%
Growth	5%	10%	15%
Mid Cap	5%	10%	15%
Small Cap	5%	10%	15%
International Equities	5%	10%	15%
Intermediate-Term Fixed Income	30%	35%	40%
Cash Equivalents	0%	5%	10%

Copyright ©2001, *invest*^mgt. Used with permission. Version: July 2001

BACKGROUND and PURPOSE

This Investment Policy Statement (IPS) has been prepared for John and Mary HNW Client (Client), a taxable entity. The assets covered by this IPS currently total approximately $650,000 in market value, but the Client's net worth is estimated to be $1,225,000. Assets not covered by this IPS include: (1) corporate sponsored defined contribution programs where both the husband and wife participate (combined, valued at $350,000); and (2) a vacation condo valued at $225,000.

Key Information:

SSN: _____

Investment Advisor: _____

Custodian: _____

Accountant: _____, CPA

Attorney: _____, Esq.

The purpose of this IPS is to assist the Client and Investment Advisor (Advisor) in effectively supervising, monitoring and evaluating the management of the Client's Portfolio (Portfolio). The Client's investment program is defined in the various sections of this IPS by:

1. Stating in a written document the Client's attitudes, expectations, objectives and guidelines in the management of their assets.

2. Setting forth an investment structure for managing the Client's Portfolio. This structure includes various asset classes, investment management styles, asset allocation and acceptable ranges that, in total, are expected to produce an appropriate level of overall diversification and total investment return over the investment time horizon.

3. Encouraging effective communications between the Client and the Advisor.

4. Establishing formal criteria to select, monitor, evaluate and compare the performance of money managers on a regular basis.

Copyright ©2001, *invest*^mgt. Used with permission. Version: July 2001

STATEMENT of OBJECTIVES

This IPS describes the prudent investment process the Advisor deems appropriate for the Client's situation. The Client desires to maximize returns within prudent levels of risk and to meet the following stated investment objectives:

> [**Advisor lists investment objectives – retire with sufficient assets to support a lifestyle of _____. Provide college tuition to grand children, etc.**]

Risk Tolerances

The Client recognizes and acknowledges some risk must be assumed in order to achieve long-term investment objectives, and there are uncertainties and complexities associated with contemporary investment markets.

In establishing the risk tolerances for this IPS, the Client's ability to withstand short and intermediate term variability was considered. The Client's prospects for the future, current financial condition, and several other factors suggest collectively some interim fluctuations in market value and rates of return may be tolerated in order to achieve the longer-term objectives.

Time Horizon

The investment guidelines are based upon an investment horizon of greater than five years; therefore interim fluctuations should be viewed with appropriate perspective. Short-term liquidity requirements are anticipated to be minimal.

Expected Return

In general, the Client would like the assets to earn at least a targeted return of 8.0%. It is understood an average return of 8.0% will require superior manager performance to: (1) retain principal value; and, (2) purchasing power. Furthermore, the objective is to earn a long-term rate of return at least 5.0% greater than the rate of inflation as measured by the Consumer Price Index (CPI).

Asset Class Preferences

The Client understands long-term investment performance, in large part, is primarily a function of asset class mix. The Client has reviewed the long-term performance characteristics of the broad asset classes, focusing on balancing the risks and rewards.

History shows while interest-generating investments, such as bond portfolios, have the advantage of relative stability of principal value, they provide little opportunity for real

Copyright ©2001, *invest*^{mgt.} Used with permission. Version: July 2001 long-term capital growth due to their susceptibility to inflation. On the other hand, equity investments, such as common stocks, clearly have a significantly higher expected return but have the disadvantage of much greater year-by-year variability of return. From an investment decision-making point of view, this year-by-year variability may be worth accepting, provided the time horizon for the equity portion of the portfolio is sufficiently long (five years or greater).

The following eight asset classes were selected and ranked in ascending order of "risk" (least to most).

> Money Market (MM)
> Intermediate Bond (IB)
> Large Cap Value (LCV)
> Large Cap Blend (LCB)
> Large Cap Growth (LCG)
> Mid Cap Blend (MCB)
> Small Cap Blend (SCB)
> International Equity (IE)

Rebalancing of Strategic Allocation

The percentage allocation to each asset class may vary as much as plus or minus 5% depending upon market conditions. When necessary and/or available, cash inflows/outflows will be deployed in a manner consistent with the strategic asset allocation of the Portfolio. If there are no cash flows, the allocation of the Portfolio will be reviewed quarterly.

If the Advisor judges cash flows to be insufficient to bring the Portfolio within the strategic allocation ranges, the Client shall decide whether to effect transactions to bring the strategic allocation within the threshold ranges (**Strategic Allocation**).

DUTIES and RESPONSIBILITIES

Investment Advisor

The Client has retained an objective, third-party Advisor to assist in managing the investments. The Advisor will be responsible for guiding the Client through a disciplined and rigorous investment process. As a fiduciary to the Client, the primary responsibilities of the Advisor are:

1. Prepare and maintain this investment policy statement (IPS).

2. Provide sufficient asset classes with different and distinct risk/return profiles so the Client can prudently diversify the Portfolio.

Copyright ©2001, *invest*^mgt. Used with permission. Version: July 2001

3. Prudently select investment options.

4. Control and account for all investment expenses.

5. Monitor and supervise all service vendors and investment options.

6. Avoid prohibited transactions and conflicts of interest.

Investment Managers

As distinguished from the Advisor, who is responsible for <u>managing</u> the investment process, investment managers are co-fiduciaries responsible for <u>making</u> investment decisions (security selection and price decisions). The specific duties and responsibilities of each investment manager are:

1. Manage the assets under their supervision in accordance with the guidelines and objectives outlined in their respective Prospectus or Trust Agreement.

2. Exercise full investment discretion with regards to buying, managing, and selling assets held in the portfolios.

3. If managing a separate account (as opposed to a mutual fund or a commingled account), to seek approval from the Client prior to purchasing and/or implementing the following securities and transactions:

   ◆ Letter stock and other unregistered securities; commodities or other commodity contracts; and short sales or margin transactions.

   ◆ Securities lending; pledging or hypothecating securities.

   ◆ Investments in the equity securities of any company with a record of less than three years' continuous operation, including the operation of any predecessor.

   ◆ Investments for the purpose of exercising control of management.

4. Vote promptly all proxies and related actions in a manner consistent with the long-term interest and objectives of the Portfolio as described in this IPS. Each investment manager shall keep detailed records of the voting of proxies and related actions and will comply with all applicable regulatory obligations.

5. Communicate with the Client all significant changes pertaining to the fund it manages or the firm itself. Changes in ownership, organizational structure, financial condition, and professional staff are examples of changes to the firm in which the Client is interested.

Copyright ©2001, *invest*^mgt. Used with permission. Version: July 2001

6. Effect all transactions for the Portfolio subject "to best price and execution."
   If a manager utilizes brokerage from the Portfolio assets to effect "soft dollar"
   transactions, detailed records will be kept and communicated to the client.

7. Use the same care, skill, prudence, and due diligence under the circumstances then
   prevailing that experienced investment professionals acting in a like capacity and
   fully familiar with such matters would use in like activities for like Portfolios with
   like aims in accordance and compliance with Uniform Prudent Investment Act and
   all applicable laws, rules, and regulations.

Custodian

Custodians are responsible for the safekeeping of the Portfolio's assets. The specific
duties and responsibilities of the custodian are:

1. Maintain accounts by legal registration.

2. Value the holdings.

3. Collect all income and dividends owed to the Portfolio.

4. Settle all transactions (buy-sell orders) initiated by the Investment Manager.

5. Provide monthly reports that detail transactions, cash flows, securities held and
   their current value, and change in value of each security and the overall portfolio
   since the previous report.

INVESTMENT MANAGER SELECTION

The Advisor will apply the following due diligence criteria in selecting each individual
investment option.

1. *Regulatory oversight:* Each investment manager should be a regulated bank, an
   insurance company, a mutual fund organization, or a registered investment adviser.

2. *Correlation to style or peer group:* The product should be highly correlated to the
   asset class of the investment option. This is one of the most critical parts of the
   analysis since most of the remaining due diligence involves comparisons of the
   manager to the appropriate peer group.

3. *Performance relative to a peer group:* The product's performance should be
   evaluated against the peer group's median manager return, for 1-, 3- and 5-year
   cumulative periods.

Copyright ©2001, *invest*^mgt. Used with permission. Version: July 2001

4. *Performance relative to assumed risk:* The product's risk-adjusted performance (Alpha and/or Sharpe Ratio) should be evaluated against the peer group's median manager's risk-adjusted performance.

5. *Minimum track record:* The product's inception date should be greater than three years.

6. *Assets under management:* The product should have at least $75 million under management.

7. *Holdings consistent with style:* The screened product should have no more than 20% of the portfolio invested in "unrelated" asset class securities. For example, a Large Cap Growth product should not hold more than 20% in cash, fixed income and/or international securities.

8. *Expense ratios/fees:* The product's fees should not be in the bottom quartile (most expensive) of their peer group.

9. *Stability of the organization:* There should be no perceived organizational problems – the same portfolio management team should be in place for at least two years.

CONTROL PROCEDURES

Performance Objectives

The Client acknowledges fluctuating rates of return characterize the securities markets, particularly during short-term time periods. Recognizing short-term fluctuations may cause variations in performance, the Advisor intends to evaluate manager performance from a long-term perspective.

The Client is aware the ongoing review and analysis of the investment managers is just as important as the due diligence implemented during the manager selection process. The performance of the investment managers will be monitored on an ongoing basis and it is at the Client's discretion to take corrective action by replacing a manager if they deem it appropriate at any time.

On a timely basis, but not less than quarterly, the Advisor will meet with the Client to review whether each manager continues to conform to the search criteria outlined in the previous section; specifically:

1. The manager's adherence to the Portfolio's investment guidelines;

2. Material changes in the manager's organization, investment philosophy and/or personnel; and,

Copyright ©2001, *invest*^mgt. Used with permission. Version: July 2001

3. Any legal, SEC and/or other regulatory agency proceedings affecting the manager.

The Advisor has determined it is in the best interest of the Client that performance objectives be established for each investment manager. Manager performance will be evaluated in terms of an appropriate market index (e.g. the S&P 500 stock index for large cap domestic equity manager) and the relevant peer group (e.g. the large cap growth mutual fund universe for a large cap growth mutual fund).

Asset Class/Peer Group	Index	Peer Group Universe
Large Cap Equity		
Large Cap Value	S&P 500	Large Cap Value
Large Cap Blend	S&P 500	Large Cap Blend
Large Cap Growth	S&P 500	Large Cap Growth
Mid Cap Equities	S&P 400	Mid Cap Blend
Small Cap Equities	Russell 2000	Small Cap Blend
International Equity	MSCI EAFE	Foreign Stock
Fixed Income		
Intermediate Bond	Salomon 3-7 Year Treas.	Intermediate-Term Bond
Money Market	90 day T-Bills	Money Market Database

A manager may be placed on a <u>Watchlist</u> and a thorough <u>review</u> and <u>analysis</u> of the investment manager may be conducted, when:

1. A manager performs below median for their peer group over a 1-, 3- and/or 5-year cumulative period.

2. A manager's 3-year risk adjusted return (Alpha and/or Sharpe) falls below the peer group's median risk adjusted return.

3. There is a change in the professionals managing the portfolio.

4. There is a significant decrease in the product's assets.

5. There is an indication the manager is deviating from his/her stated style and/or strategy.

6. There is an increase in the product's fees and expenses.

7. Any extraordinary event occurs that may interfere with the manager's ability to fulfill their role in the future.

Copyright ©2001, *invest*^{mgt.} Used with permission. Version: July 2001

A manager evaluation may include the following steps:

1. A letter to the manager asking for an analysis of their underperformance.

2. An analysis of recent transactions, holdings and portfolio characteristics to determine the cause for underperformance or to check for a change in style.

3. A meeting with the manager, which may be conducted on-site, to gain insight into organizational changes and any changes in strategy or discipline.

Ultimately the decision to retain or terminate a manager cannot be made by a formula. It is the Client's confidence in the manager's ability to perform in the future that ultimately determines the retention of a manager.

Measuring Costs

The Advisor will review with the Client at least annually all costs associated with the management of the Portfolio's investment program, including:

1. Expense ratios of each investment option against the appropriate peer group.

2. Custody fees: The holding of the assets, collection of the income and disbursement of payments.

3. Whether the manager is demonstrating attention to "best execution" in trading securities.

The Advisor will review this IPS with the Client at least annually to determine whether stated investment objectives are still relevant and the continued feasibility of achieving the same. It is not expected that the IPS will change frequently. In particular, short-term changes in the financial markets should not require adjustments to the IPS.

Prepared: *Approved:*

July 1, 2001   July 1, 2001

Advisor   Client

Copyright ©2001, *invest*^mgt. Used with permission. Version: July 2001

Appendix **D**

Sample Seminar Invitations and Checklist

Sample: Client Seminar Invitation

XYZ Financial Group
cordially invites you...

to attend an investment seminar

The Benefits of Managed Money

Hosted by:

Larry Smith

Senior Vice President
XYZ Financial Group

Guest Speaker:

Mike Adams

Financial Advisor
Smith, Jones & Wilson

Tuesday, September 24, 2002
6:00 p.m.

Location:

Four Seasons Hotel

100 Main Street
New York, NY
(555) 555-1234

*Your guests with reservations are welcome. Seating is limited.
For reservations please call Mary at (555) 555-0000 before September 10, 2002.*

Sample: Client Seminar Invitation/Multiple Hosts & Speakers

XYZ Financial Group
cordially invites you...

to attend an investment seminar

The Benefits of Managed Money

Hosted by:

Larry Smith	**Chris Brown**
Senior Vice President	Senior Vice President
XYZ Financial Group	XYZ Financial Group

Guest Speakers:

Mike Adams	**Sara Peterson**
Financial Advisor	Portfolio Manager
Smith, Jones & Wilson	Acme Investment Management

Tuesday, September 24, 2002
6:00 p.m.

Location:

The Ritz Carlton
100 Main Street
New York, NY
(555) 555-1234

Your guests with reservations are welcome. Seating is limited.
For reservations please call Mary at (555) 555-0000 before September 10, 2002.

Sample: Client Seminar Invitation Wording

"Are you one of the best money managers in the country?"

Neither Am I —

Come see
Sara Peterson, *Portfolio Manager*
and why using professional managers
could benefit you.

The Benefits of Managed Money

Hosted by:
John Morris

September 24, 2002
6:00 p.m.

Location:
The Manhattan Club
100 Main Street
New York, NY
(555) 555-1234

Sample: Client Appreciation Meeting

XYZ Financial Group
cordially invites you...

to their Client Appreciation Dinner

Featuring Guest Speakers:

Michael Adams
Financial Advisor
Smith, Jones & Wilson

Tuesday, September 24, 2002
6:00 p.m.

Location:

Morton's
100 Main Street
New York, NY
(555) 555-1234

Your guests with reservations are welcome. Seating is limited.
For reservations please call Mary at (555) 555-0000 before September 10, 2002.

Sample: Client Appreciation Meeting

*Mr. William Donovan, Jr.
requests the honor of your presence for a
Black Tie evening of Client Appreciation*

*featuring a piano performance
by Elise Taylor*

*Saturday, the fifth of October
Two thousand and two
at seven o'clock*

*La Chinoiseue
Windsor Court Hotel
Twenty-third Floor
Westport, Connecticut*

Music by Myrage

*Please RSVP by calling Pamela Jones at
(860) 555-1234 by September 16, 2002*

Client Seminar Checklist

The following seminar checklist can help you plan for your seminar and serve as a guide in organizing your client seminars and client appreciation meetings. Since everyone prefers to do things a little differently, you can change or supplement this list to make it appropriate to your individualized events.

Before Your Seminar

3 Months Prior

- ❏ Choose date and reserve location
- ❏ Reserve speakers and determine topics
- ❏ Draft seminar invitation (see samples provided on previous pages) and agenda
- ❏ Submit agenda and invitation to compliance for approval
- ❏ Compile list of invitees
- ❏ Hold a staff meeting to discuss the seminar, prepare a checklist and assign responsibilities

2 Months Prior

- ❏ Mail seminar invitations

1 Month Prior

- ❏ Touch base with speakers or special guests to finalize topics, materials and equipment
- ❏ Order any special materials for your seminar
- ❏ Select menu and convey delivery/serving instructions
- ❏ Arrange for any special equipment in room for speakers and you
- ❏ Draft your presentation, accompanying materials and host remarks
- ❏ Submit presentation and materials to compliance for approval
- ❏ Confirm status of RSVPs and place follow up calls/send reminder notes

1-2 Weeks Prior

❏ Finalize agenda and confirm speakers

❏ Finalize all presentations and written materials/handouts

❏ Final follow up calls/notes to invitees who have not yet responded

3 Days Prior

❏ Reconfirm location, equipment, menu and provide final head counts

❏ Draft seminar follow-up letter and submit to compliance

1 Day Prior

❏ Reminder phone calls to attendees with reservations (if desired)

❏ Assemble all material for distribution to attendees

❏ Make name tags and place cards (if desired)

During Your Seminar

❏ Arrive at least 45 minutes early to coordinate final details, test equipment and greet speakers

❏ Assign a staff member to greet people, direct guests to the right room and be on hand for general assistance

❏ Set out materials and handouts for attendees

❏ Schedule appointments with seminar attendees at the end of your seminar — be sure to bring your calendar!

After Your Seminar

❏ Send follow up letters to attendees to thank them for their participation and reinforce seminar concepts and action steps. Include any educational pieces that are appropriate and your business card.

Other Helpful Seminar Hints

Seminar Location

Accessibility: Select a location that is suitable for the type of event you will host. Find a place that will be convenient for your guests to travel to.

Directions:	Be sure to have written directions to your location.
Parking:	Make sure that there is adequate parking and that the area is well-lighted if the seminar is held at night.
Room:	Pick a room that is private so that your group will not be distracted by others who are not part of your event. Select a room and table set up that is appropriate to the size of your event and creates the atmosphere that you want for the seminar.
Contact Person:	Establish an on-site contact person to help with details (room set up, menu selections, audio visual arrangements, etc.) before and during your seminar.

Selecting a Date/Time

Plan Ahead:	Pick a date three months ahead to give you ample time to prepare, schedule speakers, send invitations and give your invitees time to reserve the date on their calendars.
Check the Date:	Check the calendar for potential conflicts such as national or religious holidays, school vacations and busy times for certain business owner clients.
Convenience:	Consider your clients' work and family schedules when setting the time of day. Try to select the most convenient time for your invitees to maximize attendance.
Timing:	When planning the length of your event, design your seminar agenda to allow for guests to arrive, food to be served and speakers to present. Leave time for questions when speakers are finished and time for you to close out the event (thank guests for coming, recap the topics covered and suggest action steps).
Speakers:	Be sure speakers arrive early for their portion of the meeting. Reinforce their time frame and the format that you would like them to follow.

A Final Note

Seminars can be a very effective way to educate, retain and build lasting relationships with existing clients, as well as introduce prospective clients to new ideas and show them how they can benefit by working with you.

Index